MY UNEXPECTED LIFE

an international memoir of
two pandemics, HIV and COVID-19

martina clark

NORTHAMPTON HOUSE PRESS

Jacket and interior design by Naia Poyer. Jacket photos: world map by Yuri_B/132 images/Pixabay.com; passport and visa stamps courtesy of author

First Northampton House Press edition, 2021, ISBN: 978-1-950668-11-3

Library of Congress Control Number: 2021908580

To my siblings and my niblings, blood and chosen;
thank you for perpetually indulging my whims, woes, and words.

*"If you think you are too small to make a difference,
try sleeping with a mosquito."*

—Dalai Lama XIV

*"If you can't find somethin' to live for,
you best find somethin' to die for."*

—Afeni Shakur

INTRODUCTION

converging pandemics

Hey HIV, Hold My Beer...

The People's Republic of Brooklyn, NY
Population: 2.6 million

When I began this memoir about the HIV pandemic, I never imagined I'd be doing the final edits during a new one: COVID-19. No one could. From New York City, *the* initial epicenter in the United States, no less. In fact, in the fall of 2019, immediately prior to the first known cases, I was working in the neighborhood hardest hit in the country: Corona, Queens.

In the mid-1980's I lived on Castro Street in the fabulously gay hub of San Francisco. At the time, *it* was an epicenter of a mysterious new disease: Human Immunodeficiency Virus (HIV), the pathogen that leads to AIDS.

In San Francisco, all those decades ago, when I heard an ambulance in the Castro, I assumed that inside was a patient with a grim prognosis. People—gay men in particular—were dying from an invisible virus.

Now, in Brooklyn, sirens are a regular soundtrack to my life. I can distinguish the honks of a fire truck from the woot-woot of a squad car from the more traditional wail of an ambulance.

As we were living under stay-at-home rules in the first weeks of spring 2020, however, the sirens entered my psyche in a different way. Those thirty-five-year-old warnings haunted me, day and night.

With the relative quiet of the city on lockdown, each ambulance that passed sent me back to those early days on Castro Street. Unnerved by my memories of the men who died in those years—neighbors who left for the hospital and never returned, the relentless funerals—I found myself reliving the grief of decades past. History was repeating itself. Again, far too many did not heed the warnings.

The greatest difference, of course, is that HIV is not as easily transmitted as COVID. HIV has dealt an irreversible blow to humankind, but it started slowly and spread—and continues to—over decades. This newest plague, in contrast, is like a supersonic bullet train, reaching all ends of the globe in months.

Please dear reader, trust the warnings. COVID is not "somebody else's" disease. A virus knows no borders and does not discriminate. This is real and people are dying.

Each of us must do our part to protect one another. For the love of humanity, wear a mask, damnit. And, knowing that variant strains multiply and pose greater threats, make sure those are N95/KN95 or three-ply surgical-quality. Vaccines work. But the global rollout is slow and stopping this pandemic will take time.

Don't wait until you know someone dying to take this seriously. It is here and we are all in the crosshairs.

As I write this, I have now lived more than half of my fifty-seven years with HIV. I do not intend to be taken down by COVID-19. Wear a mask (or two). Wash your hands. Maintain social distancing. Stay safe. Protect yourself *and* others. Please.

CHAPTER 1

navigating a new path with HIV

Blue Marlin

San Francisco, California

United States of America: North America
Population: 334.9 million
Capital: Washington, DC
Capital of My World: San Francisco, California

I t was one of those rare hot days in San Francisco. That worked out well, since I was basically naked. A makeup artist from the San Francisco Ballet was taking a break from his regular duties and was painting my twenty-nine-year-old body blue. The brush tickled; it felt like a tiny dog had been licking me for hours. At least it wasn't the rough tongue of a cat.

I was in an artist's loft-cum-studio somewhere south of Market Street, preparing for a photo shoot with Annie Leibovitz. A dozen of us were being painted, all in varying stages of nakedness, all of us women living with HIV. Leibovitz was in town to shoot the second phase of an outreach campaign for the San Francisco AIDS Foundation titled *Be Here for the*

Cure, conceived of by then campaign development coordinator, Bill Hayes. My favorite image from the campaign was, and remains, from the initial phase that featured the campaign slogan *Be Here for the Cure* superimposed on a picture of planet Earth taken from space. Being alive for that day—for the cure—was a goal I intended to work toward. Ms. Leibovitz's images were intended to complement that message with images of healthy, happy HIV-positive people, to counter the ravaged faces we'd seen so often, for so long.

We'd first heard about the campaign—'we' being the women I knew living with HIV in the San Francisco Bay area—through a local group called WORLD (Women Organized to Respond to Life-Threatening Disease), where many of us worked, volunteered, or participated in support groups. This was not long after Demi Moore had appeared on that iconic cover of *Vanity Fair,* pregnant and naked. A year later, she was on it again, in a trompe l'oeil painting by artist Joanne Gair depicting her in a men's black pin-striped suit, a red tie, white shirt, and plaid vest. Both cover images, taken by Annie Leibovitz, had rocked the field of photography.

A few of us decided it would make a powerful statement if we depicted ourselves the way we saw the virus in our bodies. The world of HIV was a small one (still is) so word of our idea reached the San Francisco AIDS Foundation and Ms. Leibovitz. I was chosen to be a part of the shoot, to balance out a group of about a dozen women of varying ages and ethnicities.

Some chose to be painted to resemble their medications. Some, like wild animals: one with a snake and one with her hands covering a chest making the shape of a heart. My design probably resembled the shimmery scales of a mermaid, but in fact I was trying to be a blue marlin.

"Are you sure about the worms?" the artist asked, pausing. He held a three-inch length of brownish-red yarn in one hand. "You look so gorgeous just as a fish. I mean, the blues make your eyes look like sapphires!"

"I'm sure. The worms stay." I nodded. "Remember the story?"

"Okay. It's your story, so here come your worms." He brought out eyelash glue to stick them to my belly, then painted a simulated gash around them.

2

The story referred to both my distant and more recent pasts. The day it was confirmed that I had HIV, in May 1992, I'd had a flashback to sailing through the South Pacific some ten years prior, when I was in my late teens and crewing on sailboats.

Somewhere between Hawaii and Tahiti, we'd been trolling a line, as usual. When it tightened, we struggled to pull our catch on board. The fish turned out to be a six-foot marlin, the kind people stuff and hang on a wall. I'd never seen such a beautiful living thing up close. The massive fish shimmered like a slice of South Pacific Sea, glistening in the setting sun. It flipped its tail in protest. Being a hospitable crew, we got the fish drunk by pouring a shot or two of rum in its mouth before delivering a swift, fatal blow to the head.

We were stunned that such a magnificent fish had taken our bait. When my crewmate sliced into the marlin's belly, however, we quickly understood why. What should've been vibrant white or pink flesh was dull and graying. Inch-long worms were chewing through its innards, like children playing in a maze; up and down and back and forth, hiding and reappearing as they ate their way through this dying creature's core.

When I received the diagnosis I was HIV-positive, the haunting image of that infested fish and those hungry worms flooded my brain. It'd been so beautiful, yet was being eaten alive from within. That was how I felt. I knew I must look perfectly normal and healthy to everyone else, but I suddenly saw HIV like an evil Pac-Man, devouring my essential parts. So when I met with my artist, in preparation for the shoot, I'd shared that experience. We'd agreed it would make a powerful image.

And soon there I was, transformed into the marlin. Beautiful and blue and iridescent, yet with worms spilling out of my belly. Inside, an incurable virus really was eating away at me. At that moment, by chance, k.d. lang's dulcet voice wafted from a radio while the worms were being glued to my belly.

Even through the darkest phase...here, beneath my skin...

What struck me as even more peculiar than being naked and painted and about to be photographed by one of our greatest living photographers was that I was still alive. And, at least in that moment, in great spirits.

By then I could barely remember what my life had been like before

3

HIV. The virus might not have consumed my entire immune system yet, but it had taken over my existence. One year post-diagnosis, I was only twenty-nine, and wondered if I'd see thirty. I'd aged decades emotionally in the preceding twelve months.

The day I'd first heard the news that would forever alter my life still recurred, like an old record I had to reset the needle on over and over so I could hear the rest of the song. It took a conscious effort to not stay stuck in that scratched groove in my story. To remember I was alive. Without warning, a feeling or a word could send me back in time, yet again, to replay the moment I learned of my death sentence.

Standing barefoot on the smooth terracotta-tiled kitchen floor where I was housesitting—a place I called The Garden House—I returned a call from my doctor's office. It was a Tuesday in May, and I was gazing out over the landscaped yard of the Zen oasis the owners had created up on a hill, overlooking San Francisco.

Within a few moments, my doctor came on the line. Never chatty, he jumped right in.

"So, Martina. I have your results." I could hear him shuffling papers, then taking a sip of something and clearing his throat. "Um, you don't have mono, so that's good." I'd had a strange rash and general fatigue for months, and he'd been trying to figure out what was wrong.

"Oh good, that's good." I tilted a bottle of wine on the counter to read the label. I couldn't make it out, though; I was so nervous I couldn't focus.

"Or strep. That infection in your throat—how is it, by the way?"

"Uh, a little better, I guess. I've been drinking lots of fluids and maybe that's helped." I set the bottle back down on the marble counter.

"Good," he continued. "But the thing is, your blood work was still off, and, well, um, the HIV test…"

"Yes?"

"Well, it came back positive."

I froze. I'd been walking around in little circles, lifting the phone cord from the wall over my head with each circuit, like a cat following its tail. At his words, every inch of my body tingled. I trembled ever so slightly. I nearly dropped the phone from my clammy hand.

Could he possibly have just said what I think he said?

He continued speaking, but nothing else registered. I continued walking my circles, making so many turns I managed to wrap the cord around my neck until I was struggling to breathe. I unwound myself and tried to focus. At last I rejoined the conversation, now in a confused daze.

"...so here's the number for the clinic up in Novato. You should go there and have another test, to confirm the diagnosis," he said. "Martina? Are you still there?"

"Yes. But I kind of missed what you said, after the HIV part. I'm sorry, but could you start again?"

"Of course," he said. "I was just telling you that, since I've never dealt with this before, you should probably have another test to confirm. Then they can refer you to a specialist. I'm suggesting Planned Parenthood; they do excellent work."

"Oh, okay." My voice faint. My body stiff.

"Martina, I'm sorry. I've never had a patient before with a positive test. I'm just so sorry. I don't really even know what to say."

"Oh, all right, then. It's okay. Thanks."

I took down the clinic information from him, although it was illegible on the notepad, and hung up. My brain felt frozen, as if I'd eaten too much ice cream too fast. My head throbbed. Thoughts were impossible to process. I stood stationary in that sleek kitchen staring at the flat white wooden pantry door for what seemed like hours. I didn't cry or make a sound, just stared at the blank surface that reflected my new reality, as if my existence—my entire past—had just been wiped away. That was all I could manage to do, except sweat, until eventually the phone rang. I jumped, then slowly turned to answer it.

"Martina?" My sister Adrian was on the line. I'd been living with her and her family for a few months, an hour north of San Francisco, saving money so I could move overseas. Adrian and I had shared a room growing up. As adults, we'd lived in close geographic proximity, which let our relationship flourish into a deeper bond. She was the only person who knew I'd been tested for HIV, and she was the one who'd relayed the message to call the doctor earlier that afternoon. "Did you call him back? It's been an hour. Any news?"

"Yes. Well... I called and everything was positive. I mean, no, I don't have mono or strep, but I guess I have HIV. He said that. He said I have HIV."

"Oh, Martina. No, no. Oh, Martina..." Her breathing filled with sobs as she kept repeating my name. "I'm on my way, I'll be there as soon as possible. I love you so much."

"Okay."

I remained standing there, holding onto the cool marble counter, staring at the flat white pantry door. In under an hour my sister arrived from Novato, in northern Marin County, with a bottle of wine, which we drank—and then a few more that the owners of the house had left for me. The information was like a fly banging against a window screen, hitting and hitting but unable to find a gap where it could get through.

How can this be true? I'm only twenty-eight. Too young to have my life stolen.

Eventually the question crossed my mind: how had I been infected? I knew that like most people—over ninety percent worldwide—it must've been through unprotected sex. Probably, based on the preceding six months and the course of my illness, from a one-night stand in Italy. I'd joked that as a single straight woman in San Francisco, I had to go overseas to meet a straight man.

Beyond that moment, however, the details of the how and when and where made no difference. I never again gave it much thought. How the story started was no longer of any importance. What mattered was how it would end. And how I would live my life in between.

Somehow I made it to work each day for the rest of that week. I am nothing if not practical and needed the money. I was temping in a bank. A cute guy sat at the desk across from mine. Probably in his mid-thirties. He was married, had a child, and had just found out they were pregnant with a second baby.

He kept moaning, "My life's over. I can't believe this! I'm done. Now it's all about them. *My* life is over."

I wanted to scream and throw things at him. Listen, asshole, you think YOUR life is over? Wanna hear how MY Tuesday played out?

But I said nothing of the kind. I sat at my desk and did the most menial tasks possible to avoid having to switch on my brain. Filing and photocopying were ecstasy.

Each evening, I went back to The Garden House. There I'd sit on the master bed—a wacky arrangement surrounded by mirrors, even on the ceiling—and take my frustrations out on the pillows. I could watch myself fall apart from every possible angle.

The first time I'd visited there, the woman who owned it told me they'd bought it partially furnished, with that bed and mirrors in place. It was an extra-long California king that had, undoubtedly, been hard to get up the narrow circular stairs so many years earlier, so they just went with it.

"Yeah, the last owner actually died in this bed," she'd told me, patting one corner of the bedspread back into place. "Of AIDS. What a shame, such a nice man, according to his lover who sold us the house. I don't doubt it. This place has such amazing energy; he must've had a good soul. Never met him myself, of course. I mean, you know, he's dead."

This may be the place to explain things I didn't know then, but that I quickly learned. That everyone ought to know, but that, unfortunately, not everyone does, especially these days, when the blazing news of other epidemics has edged older ones (Polio, TB, Spanish Flu, West Nile) out of the limelight. At least for now.

HIV stands for Human Immunodeficiency Virus. If left untreated, it can lead to Acquired Immuno-Deficiency Syndrome, AIDS. The scientific consensus is that it jumped from some other primate to a human host early in the 20th Century. It's a "syndrome" because it is a combination of factors rather than the presence of the specific pathogen that warrants the more severe diagnosis. A person with AIDS definitely has HIV, but a person with HIV—thanks to advances in medications, and a better understanding of how to live with the chronic disease—may never progress further. I've had HIV since 1992, but have never been diagnosed with AIDS. Nor is it likely I ever will . . . knock on wood.

The retrovirus (so called because it replicates using RNA rather than DNA—I won't get more technical than that) is transmitted via bodily fluids. Specifically, through blood, semen (including pre-ejaculate fluids), vaginal fluids, rectal fluids, and breast milk. The risk comes when one person's bodily fluids contain HIV, and unprotected contact is made with an uninfected person. The uninfected person has now been exposed. If the virus takes hold, the person then becomes infected or HIV-positive.

The most common exposure is through unprotected sex—anal, vaginal, or oral. To avoid transmission, practice safer sex—always use a latex or polyurethane condom for each act—and get tested. Regularly.

Another common means of exposure is through sharing unsterilized needles. Ensure all needles and syringes are new and sterilized. Never share needles or syringes with anyone else.

Lastly, HIV can be transmitted from an HIV-positive mother to her fetus or baby during pregnancy, childbirth, or breastfeeding. Luckily, there are low cost interventions that prevent mother-to-child transmission. The first step is for the parents to each know their own status so they can make informed decisions for safe childbearing.

HIV is NOT transmitted through casual contact such as hugging, kissing, or sharing meals. Nor is it transmissible through coughs or sneezes, swimming pools, or by using public toilets. COVID-19 is far easier to contract.

Knowledge is definitely power.

Once the housesitting gig was over, I would return to my sister's. Novato, in northern Marin, was an hour north of San Francisco. On my way up the drive, I stopped to collect the mail. I went through the stack of letters as I sat in the car, idling next to the rickety old mailbox, always filled with spiders.

I'd received two letters: one from the Peace Corps and one from a language school in Prague. I'd applied to both organizations months prior as part of my plan to start living overseas. I'd been waiting anxiously for their decisions, hoping one would provide a chance to escape this harsh new reality.

Both announced I'd been accepted to their respective programs. Thank God.

Your French will be useful for a post in Senegal, the Peace Corps wrote. Yes!

Your willingness to venture to Eastern Europe is appreciated and will serve you well in the rapidly changing homeland of Vaclav Havel, stated the flowery text from the language school.

Excellent! Finally, something to look forward to. All I needed to do was complete and return the paperwork.

Upon closer examination of those forms, I realized both jobs required a test. A *negative* test. For HIV.

No, no, no. This cannot be.

At the time, then-Czechoslovakia refused visas to people living with HIV, no matter how healthy they still might be. And the Peace Corps categorically refused any HIV-positive volunteers.

That night I fell asleep clutching the envelopes that held two futures that would not be mine.

Comfortable with Death

A Murky Place, Frequently

I was always friends with the kid who'd died.

From as young as five or six, I was confronted with the deaths of others. I grew up in a town that has since grown into a city but felt very provincial in my youth. Fresno, California, the heart of the San Joaquin Valley, where much of the food America consumes is produced. Everyone seemed to know one another, and yet, I still knew more people who'd died than any of my three siblings who are, respectively, six, seven, and eight years older.

For reasons I've yet to understand, I rarely cried or grieved when someone died. I simply stuffed my feelings into some corner of my brain that got locked up behind the part that flooded me with a stoicism mismatched for one so young. Memories of them remain, but my grief goes unprocessed, even now.

Although I can't recall the specifics of his death, the disembodied head of the boy from my kindergarten Sunday school hovers in my

9

mind above the pair of sharp crosses that topped St. Therese's: one on the church, the other on the bell tower; my friend's face hovers just up and to the left, that much closer to God. They'd printed his image among the clouds on the flyer for his funeral mass. Even though I can't recall his name, his kind young face, dark hair and eyes, hangs there still, a life cut short and forever suspended in time.

A year or two later, a boy from my second-grade class grew smaller and more crumpled over the school year, until disease eventually took his life. Often, on my walk home from school, I would see his mother crouched next to his wheelchair, holding his hand, in his final days. I can still recall their house in the background, the street just ahead. Salmon-colored roses growing in the yard as they remain paused in that moment on their walkway that led only to sadness.

In April of 6th grade, just days after my eleventh birthday, my father came late to pick me up, as he often did.

"Sorry to keep you waiting, I was with your grandmother." At eighty, she was still witty and read voraciously in several languages. Most Sundays, we'd spend the day with her after attending mass at St. Therese's, and she'd make breakfast. She wasn't a fantastic cook, but the warmth of her small apartment and her love for me, my father, and my three older siblings, were a balm for our souls. My mother always opted out of going to mass or to my grandmother's place for the opportunity to enjoy some time on her own, which suited everyone.

"Oh well, I guess that's a good excuse…this time. How is she?"

My father grasped the wheel of our beige VW camper van and paused for a moment before pulling back out into traffic.

"I'm sorry to say she died last night. In her sleep."

I share a sense of gallows humor with my father and despite being shocked and deeply saddened by her unexpected passing, I simply said, "Then I guess this won't happen again."

He smiled ever so slightly. Still, I put my hand on his when he reached for the gearshift, feeling it my duty to comfort him.

In my late teens, I took a rather long *gap year* that turned into two—nearly three—years of traveling around Oceania. Among the many countries and places I visited was Tahiti, part of the overseas lands of France commonly referred to as French Polynesia.

"You're back early," I said to some travel acquaintances as they pulled their boat into harbor. Nobody replied. A local official arrived, boarded, then left, to do what, we weren't sure. Soon after the government agents went on board again, other travelers, who, like myself, were catching rides on sailboats around the South Pacific, pieced together what was happening with our friends from rumors and what we could overhear.

Many young college-age people start a band. Some start a business. These four Canadian young men, all with athletic builds, deep tans on what would otherwise be fair skin and with full heads of hair worn long either out of convenience or style, had saved their money, bought a sailboat and headed to Tahiti. They often went spear fishing. A day or two prior to their return to port, one had stayed down too long. When he didn't return, another went after him, and panicked. Ultimately both died, and the remaining friends, plus a girlfriend or two who'd joined them, suddenly found themselves not only with two bodies, but navigating the murky waters of reporting deaths at sea in a foreign country. Would their stories be believed? Would the families of the dead blame the living? How would they move forward in life, both literally and figuratively?

I felt for them; for their loss and the mess they had to deal with, which only delayed their grieving that much more. I barely knew them, having only shared a few evenings. But sadness permeated the air among our informal community. I don't remember crying, but I do recall losing any interest in scuba diving.

Decades later I went on a "try dive" and found it cathartic. I decided that underwater was about as beautiful a place to die as one could imagine. The combination of feeling afloat while simultaneously embraced by the water in the company of marine life and vibrant shades of blue and green all around somehow felt familiar, perhaps a return to the womb. The absolute calm, shutting out the usual sounds of life above, brought peace to my heart.

A few days after I returned to the US following more than two years abroad, I found that my closest friend from our sophomore year of high school had died. I was, of course, sad to realize I'd never see her again. And even sadder to learn she might've caused the car accident that killed her, by turning into on-coming traffic. But I remember mostly being angry that despite my regular correspondence and monthly calls home, nobody had told me of her passing even though she'd died the previous year. I learned of it one evening when I was at a club and a guy asked me to dance and as we were dancing and chatting we discovered things and friends we had in common. When I asked if he knew my friend, he said, "Yes, I mean, I did. She's dead. You know that, right?"

The next morning, I asked my mother if she'd heard the news "Did you know that Kelly died? Apparently, it was a car accident."

"I know. I went to her funeral," she said.

"What? Why didn't you tell me? We were inseparable sophomore year!"

"Well, sweetie, I didn't know how you'd take it. I didn't want to upset you."

"It would've been the same news then as it is now: She's dead. The only difference is I wouldn't have heard it so much later from a stranger in a bar."

It did explain why she hadn't written back to my last letters.

Another letter I'd written, to a young woman I'd traveled and become friends with in Western Australia, was answered by her mother. She'd invited me to stay at her parents' home in Perth, and I'd gratefully accepted their generous hospitality, a cherished and comfortable respite after months of cheap fleabag hostels and grueling bus journeys.

A month or so later, her mother wrote back to tell me my friend had died suddenly. In scratchy handwriting she explained how her daughter had been born with a hole in her heart and hadn't expected to live to see her teens. That she'd made it into her twenties was a miracle. She'd been determined to live fully, and so was forever giving her mother reasons to worry about her. But her mother was also proud she hadn't allowed herself to be defined or defeated by illness. Her mother thanked me for having helped create good memories for her daughter to enjoy in her last months. Although I felt sad such a spirited soul had passed, after writing a reply expressing my sympathy, I folded up her mother's letter and tucked it back in the envelope. I compartmentalized her death, and my grief, as I'd done so many times before.

By the time I was old enough to drink legally, I'd lost at least a dozen friends and family members. A few other kids in high school, plus all my grandparents, were gone. Even my first cat, whom we'd had only for a year or two. Maybe I'm just unsentimental. Or I'm simply practical, knowing that grieving the dead can equally include being glad to have known them and moving forward in life since they can't. Or maybe, since I'd been dealing with death from an early age, it simply seemed normal.

Just after my 21st birthday, I moved to San Francisco for college. In my sophomore year I moved to the Castro district, the heart of gay life in the City by the Bay. Far too frequently, my roommate and I would have a dialogue that went something like this:
"Did you hear that?" my roommate asked.
"What, the ambulance? Sure, why?"
"Yard sale next weekend!"
We'd smile, knowing our humor was morbid and could be construed as mean, but that it was also realistic. Gay men in the Castro were dying at alarming rates when I lived there in the mid-1980s. My upstairs neighbor. Coworkers. Friends from college. It seemed that everyone died.

Less than a decade later, when I was told that I too had HIV, this non-sentimentality kicked up a notch. My life experiences, compounded with knowing an inordinate number of people with the disease because of my own diagnosis, had made death seem the norm. Had that pragmatism wavered, I'm not sure how I would have coped. I stopped counting the number of people I knew who'd died of AIDS at fifty. That was in 1993, and I was just beginning to get involved in activism to fight the epidemic.

Until I had any reason to believe that my body was becoming ill, I chose not to obsess over the virus inside—an invisible thing I couldn't feel—and instead focused on what I could do to help stop the spread in any way possible. Activism became my defense mechanism; my way of staying one step ahead, of feeling life could still have meaning. This very non-sentimentality has helped me stay alive.

After all, when death lives inside you, it becomes absurd to fear it externally.

The Sea of Social Services: Trying Not to Drown

San Francisco Bay Area, California

The week after I'd learned my test had come back positive, I arranged for a follow-up at the local Planned Parenthood. I went for the blood draw on my own, but my sister Adrian came back with me ten days later for the results. In 1992, HIV results could take up to a month. By that point I'd put on my stoic suit—the attitude I project when I'm actually falling apart—and acted abnormally calm.

The caseworker—a gentle, curvy woman named Penny Chernow, with olive skin and kind eyes—began explaining my options and listing support organizations. I listened silently while my sister asked questions and kept a comforting hand on my knee. As they spoke, I turned my driver's license over and over in my hands. Eventually, I used my right thumbnail to scrape off the small pink dot on the corner, the dot that designated me an organ donor. The dot I no longer had a right to since even in death, my body was contaminated.

By the time we left, along with a list of organizations to call and a piece of paper indicating that my results had been confirmed, I held the number for a doctor who would become the first of many specialists I would meet.

My first visit to his office was surreal. Adrian waited outside in the car with her son. We'd be continuing on to the airport to fly to

Washington State, where our eldest sister, Alexandria, was about to have her first child.

I sat in the office on a white plastic chair wedged between the wall and the doctor's desk.

"So, I have your file from your referring doctor," he said as he straightened papers on his desk and avoided direct eye contact. "Do you understand what this means? To have a positive test."

"Yes. It means I have HIV." I felt insulted, and as though I was in an interrogation rather than with a care provider. Did he think I was an idiot?

"That's right. Do you have any questions?"

For fuck's sake, I have a million questions. How could I not? "Well, yes, lots. But my first question, I suppose, is if you know how long I have to live."

"I can't be sure," he said. "I've never had a female patient with this before. I'd have to say probably…maybe, a good five years. I really just don't know, but you've got some time. Yeah, probably five years."

I let that veil float down around me, taking a moment to absorb my prognosis before I continued. "So what now? I have to come back, right?"

"Yes. We'll do more labs today, then make an appointment at the front desk to come in next month. We'll see how you're feeling then. For now, try to get some rest and not worry too much. Stress is bad for you, might make the virus react more aggressively."

Fuck me. I'm twenty-eight and have five years to live. But sure, don't worry. Just stay calm. "I'll do that," I said through a forced smile.

The blood draw left a tiny plum of a bruise in the bend of my right elbow. I made the appointment and went out to my sister's car. On the passenger side, I sat quietly as my nephew walloped the back of my seat with bored kicks. Adrian waited for me to speak before starting the engine, so I could tell her how the visit went. Many thumps and a few minutes later, I soberly stated, "He says I probably have five years to live, and not to worry."

"Good God," my sister said. "Well, then we better not miss our flight. Christopher, quit kicking your aunt, she's having a bad day."

More like a bad life, I thought, staring out the window.

A few days later, I held my first niece, Genevieve, moments after her birth. I'd never held a baby so new before. I felt joy meeting the deep blue gaze of this amazing young life looking up at me. But also, deeply sorry for myself.

Genevieve was born on July 11, which also happened to be Adrian's fifth wedding anniversary. These were things I was sure I'd never have in my own life: a child, an anniversary, a marriage, husband, love, a family of my own. As yet, I couldn't begin to think of any of the things I *could* do in the years left to me. I was only able to register all that had been yanked away, leaving me raw and cold and shivering in a bleak and all too short new future.

My next challenge came with telling people I'd tested positive. Never underestimate the anguish of disclosure. For me, as for many living with this disease, it's the toughest part of dealing with it because every time is like getting the diagnosis all over again. Retelling the story. Reliving the pain. Then putting yourself out there in the face of possible rejection.

One of the best pieces of advice I got was from that first social worker—Penny Chernow, by now my hero. She told me to practice telling the story first, on my own, to the mirror.

"How you tell people, Martina, will determine how they take the information," she said. "The calmer you are, the calmer they'll be and the better able to handle it. If you're a mess, they'll be one too. It might scare them off. People are weird around this stuff."

I started with a few friends I could trust. They cried with me and swore they'd be there no matter what. Most took it pretty well. Some physically pulled away, though. Others never called again. And, for what it's worth, as I write this now, decades later, nothing has changed. Some people still recoil, and others make excuses to extract themselves from my life. The only difference is, now I no longer care what others think, so it hurts less.

After being diagnosed in May of 1992, it took me at least four months to gather the courage to tell my parents. When thinking about my dad, I kept recalling his comment when he interacted with a group of friends.

"Such a shame, those girls with girls and boys with boys and who even knows what. And AIDS, well, they deserve it. Only children are innocent." Perhaps since I was his child, he'd still love me? I can't recall what his initial reaction was, but I remember it having been kind. I'd had two bottles of wine to prepare myself.

My mother's words, however, stuck with me. She had a habit of saying hurtful things and this was no exception.

"So, I don't even know how to say this," I started. "But I tested positive for HIV. I have HIV." Hoping, as any child would, for some kind of calming words, I held the phone between my ear and shoulder as I hugged myself and rocked back and forth on the edge of the bed.

Barely missing a beat she replied, "Well, I guess I always knew something like that would happen to you. I've just been waiting for this call. You'll have to move out of your sister's house, of course."

"What? Why?" I asked.

"Because if you stay, you'll ruin your nephew's social life, making him live with your demons."

"Mama, he's *three*. He doesn't have a *social life*."

"Well, one day he will, and you'll ruin it."

Disappointed by her inability to show compassion, I proceeded to apologize profusely for ten minutes. There were no, "now, now, dear, it'll be okay," replies. There was simply shame. My shame for becoming infected. Her shame of having a "damaged" daughter. And more shame, on my end, for apparently being the cause of her misfortune. A spiral we'd never dig out of.

What I was not prepared for, whether from my mother or anyone else, was the inevitable next question.

"Wow. That's awful," was a typical response. Invariably followed up by "Do you know how you got it?"

What difference does that make? Why are you asking me this? In the beginning, this question would throw me. I'd feel like a child in confession for the first time in that horrible little black booth. Bad enough I had it; now I was expected to account for my actions to friends, family, and strangers alike.

You might think, sure, but it's normal for people to be curious. You can't blame them. Yet it still bothers me. Do we ask people how they got cancer or diabetes and demand they be at fault for it? The only people who really need that information are medical professionals—and only so they can make sure to consider any possible co-factors, such as hemophilia or addiction. Otherwise, it's absolutely nobody's business.

But I'll tell you that in my case, it was through unprotected heterosexual contact. I will also tell you that unprotected sex is how the vast majority of people worldwide contract it: As many as 85 percent to 90 percent of all cases, globally, result from unprotected sex with an infected person, whether consensual or forced. Once again, the ranking goes in this order:

Greatest risk of exposure: unprotected anal sex.

Second-greatest risk: unprotected vaginal sex.

Least risk: unprotected oral sex.

Now you know the stats and don't need to ask. Most importantly, not asking will be greatly appreciated by the other person. If they want to tell you, they will. If they do, you should feel honored. Trust me on this.

In the early years, we didn't much distinguish between HIV and AIDS, even though it's important to know that everyone living with AIDS has HIV, but not everyone living with HIV has—or even ever *will* have—AIDS. HIV is the virus, AIDS is the later manifestation of the disease. We now have viable treatments, so people diagnosed today are far less likely to progress to AIDS, *if* they can access quality health care and start treatment as soon as medically indicated. I live with HIV and always will be (unless a cure arrives), but I have never been given a diagnosis of AIDS. The distinction matters. Today, an HIV diagnosis, at least in most developed countries, means a normal life expectancy and is considered a chronic, manageable disease. Not an early-death sentence.

(As we go to press with this memoir in fall 2021, only about one in seven adults with HIV in the USA knows their status. Please be sure you know your own HIV status, get tested!)

After so many experiences of this nosiness, my standard answer to the "how'd you get it" question became "mosquito." That usually shut people up. But eventually even *that* I had to stop saying, because an alarming number of people believed me. Finally, I started saying I'd had sex with a mosquito, but that didn't work either.

Now I usually say, "Yes, I do know," and leave it at that. But increasingly, I tell people "through unprotected sex," and hope I don't need to explain the modes of transmission or statistics on how most people become infected or relate my whole life story.

The frankest response I ever gave was to a soft-spoken Zambian colleague. I ran into him on a bad day at a mandatory after-work reception. He'd innocently asked how I'd gotten into the work of HIV education.

"How? I screwed the wrong person," I snapped.

A kind man, he just smiled and said, "Let me get you another drink."

It is true, though, I got it from having unprotected sex with a man who, unbeknownst to me—perhaps even to him—already had the virus. That, and a big dose of bad luck mixed with equal parts desperation and low self-esteem.

As a young woman, and Catholic at that, I was woefully unprepared to interact with the opposite sex. I exuded *Run! Run away! I'm needy and don't know how to love myself.* And they would, after a quickie. Many of my encounters with men were one-night stands, but not by choice. The point being there was rarely a second date. Not even first dates were common. Often years would pass between them because it took a lot of courage for me to go out and try again.

At least testing positive cured that pattern. Once reality set in, I was so traumatized I couldn't imagine ever having sex again. Eventually I did, but for a long time I gave up on finding love from someone else and, at very long last, began to think more selfishly and about the possibility of learning to actually like—maybe even love—myself.

A few months after my diagnosis, I briefly dated a friend of a friend. Our relationship was not meant to evolve or last, but I mention it because, to his credit, he wanted to be educated. So he asked his doctor to test him. He'd never been tested and realized it was important to know his status. Much to his—and my—surprise, the doctor discouraged him.

"I can test you," the doc said, "but you probably don't want your insurance to know about it, and anyway, you're a straight man so you're not at risk. It's not like you're gay."

"No, but I'm dating a woman with HIV."

"Well, that's a surprise," the doctor said.

This was the same physician who'd tested me and delivered my positive results over the phone.

Another helpful thing that Penny, the social worker, said to me when we met was this:

"So, Martina, the good news is that HIV is not the end of the world. It's bad, but I'm sure we can help you find some ways to cope. The bad news is, you still have to go to work, pay the bills, eat, sleep and shit again tomorrow, and the day after that."

She made me laugh in that harsh moment. Her humor did me a huge service, by keeping me aligned with normal life. She had no patience for people who gave up. Through her, I found a support group that I attended a handful of times. Once a week, five or six positive women would meet after work hours at place so unremarkable that I don't even remember if it was a school or an office. What I do remember is that it was nowhere near the clinic because people didn't want to be seen going there. Like a Narcotics Anonymous meeting, I guess. A counselor or social worker would arrive and unlock the door. One by one, we'd get out of our respective cars, enter the building, and find a seat in our reserved room.

Someone would lead the group and ask us how we were all doing. Sometimes the stories people shared were funny. One thin strawberry-blonde told a story about Marinol, medical marijuana prescribed to stimulate the appetites of people with wasting syndrome—a symptom common in AIDS patients, who often lost their sense of hunger or were unable to keep food down.

"So there I am, minding my own business, when these friends dropped by, unannounced." She chuckled. "Here I thought these friends had come by to see *me*. But no. They stole my damn Marinol, so they could get high, and left!" Many of us giggled along with her.

Another woman, dark-haired and heavyset, always spoke about how angry she was at her husband. "I can't believe that fucker gave me this. Now I'm a widow with AIDS. Truthfully, I'm glad he's dead." Murmurs of support spread around the room. Then she added, "And the worst goddamn thing is that I still miss him. Shit. I'm so confused."

I once shared that I'd started dating someone and they all chimed in with "Oh. My. God. You're having sex?" I felt embarrassed.

Mostly, these women, understandably, were enraged. They complained each week about some new horror in their life. Their rage was palpable, and I found their fury toxic. I'd watch them, noticing how ill they looked, and felt I couldn't relate to them.

Perhaps I'd joined the wrong group—although back then there weren't a lot of options for positive women—or perhaps I joined too soon and simply wasn't ready to process. Ultimately, groups didn't work for me. I felt everyone was stuck in their wallowing and they'd never get beyond feeling sorry for themselves. Although that Marinol story was funny.

I'd always believed I needed to be of service to others to live a life of value. The bad thing about that was unless I put everyone else first, I felt unworthy of appreciation, or even of belonging. The good side of that equation is that it drove me to find a way to make use of my diagnosis by becoming an advocate and educator.

If even one other person heard my story and learned something, or better yet, got tested and lived a healthier life, then it would all be worth it. In the midst of being diagnosed with a life-threatening disease, I found a sense of purpose. A reason to get up again each day.

Like—I assume—most patients diagnosed with a life-threatening illness, I kept wondering, Why me? I felt sorry for myself with a passion. Eventually that wore off when I got bored with my whiny voice. I decided the most important thing was to make sure I got proper care. I wanted to stay a step ahead, if that was possible. As I entered the California state system for health care and benefits, I also started to educate myself about my illness.

And pretty soon, I got really pissed off.

I went to my first "intake" meeting with a public health care worker in the summer of that first year. Sitting in her simple square cubicle at the Marin Civic Center, a building so beautiful on the outside yet so sad on the inside, she slammed me with rapid-fire questions.

"Can you still brush your own hair?"

"Yes," I answered, thinking I'm not a toddler.

"Dress yourself in the morning?"

"Yes."

"Do you need assistance using the toilet?"

"No."

"Are you able to bathe and feed yourself?"

What the hell? In mere months I'd gone from "How do you think you'd manage if sent to work in Senegal?" to being asked if I could keep myself clean and wield a fork. But then I met other women with HIV, and other social workers. When I recounted my shock at the intake, they reminded me that many people with AIDS are *not* able to do these simple things the rest of us take for granted. And for a painful moment, I came face-to-face with my ignorance. The caseworker was just doing her job, checking off the boxes.

But I didn't want to be a statistic. I wanted to be the one who beat the odds and lived a normal life. Whatever that might mean. The thought of burdening someone else to feed or bathe me because I was too sick to do so was even more disturbing than the idea of dying young. That dread of being unable to look after myself still haunts me today, decades later.

Maybe if I ate more healthily, I thought, I wouldn't get wasting syndrome. Perhaps if I exercised more, my body would never fail. If I anticipated the things that could go wrong, perhaps I could prevent them. So, from that point on, I listened to others and learned as much as I could. I was determined to be armed with knowledge in this very personal battle against a remorseless and deadly speck of single-stranded RNA.

Sex Ed: The Things I'd Never Learned

The Wrong Place, At the Wrong Time, Far Too Often

I was raised by well-meaning parents in an era when self-esteem was frowned upon. The Catholic Church viewed this as self-glorification, which could lead to negating the need for God. The differentiation between self-worth, self-esteem, confidence, or self-absorption was never made in our home and the message us kids took away was that it was bad—very bad—to like yourself. It was worse to think you were excellent at something, or God forbid, someone whom others might admire or desire. We were also not allowed to have friends over to our house, ever, so our socialization skills were weak too.

At the same time, my mother endorsed the notion—still common in the 60s and 70s when I was a girl—that getting a husband was the primary measure of a woman's worth. Appearances mattered. Happiness, apparently, did not. With this, I found myself in a pretzel logic where I *should not* like myself, but I *should* make myself available to males, should they want me. None of this was helpful as I began to navigate adult life.

While my parents did eventually part ways—they were never well-suited—it was too late to modify their parenting. After sixty years of marriage, at the ages of 86 and 90, they were finally legally separated. To her dying day, my mother refused to finalize the divorce, to ensure my father couldn't remarry and there would never be a second Mrs. Frank S. Clark. And there never was.

My boy problems started early on.

When I was in the first grade, a kid from my class, Joey, made sexual advances. His attention made me uncomfortable, but I didn't know how to react, much less how to make him stop. Even at six, I thought boys noticing me was *always* a good thing. At first his actions seemed harmless, but because I didn't know how to protest—or even that I could—his behavior escalated.

Soon he was following me into the bathroom if I excused myself during class. He was clever, realizing nobody else would be there then. He would push me up against the wall, pin me with one hand, put the other up my skirt and grab me. Rub between my legs. Rub himself up against me. I was frozen. Tears came to my eyes, but I didn't scream. I didn't object. I didn't know how. I thought this must be normal, must be what I was expected to endure.

Once I mentioned it to an adult. I was told, "Joey sure must like you!" And that was the end of the discussion.

Then, one day on the playground, he pushed me to the ground, pinned me with his arms, and repeatedly thrust his pelvis against me. No clothes were removed, but other kids gathered to giggle and point and laugh. Half a century later, I still feel the indignity of that moment.

This time, I told my mother. Her response was "Aw, little Martina has a boyfriend. Isn't that cute." And it was never mentioned again.

No grown-up ever intervened—not a teacher, not a parent, nobody—and so I moved forward in life believing that his behavior, and that of other boys who would follow, was not only typical, it was normal. Acceptable. A sign I was liked.

Through my teens and twenties, I desperately wanted to be loved, but didn't feel worthy or even capable of finding a partner. As a result, my relationships amounted to little more than a succession of flings over the years. Men I'd met in college, at work, at clubs. A single kiss on a dance floor and I'd imagine a flourishing relationship while, I assume, they'd picture how I might look naked. This pattern persisted not because I was loose, not because I was liberated and wanted to have experiences, but because I had no idea there was another way to find companionship than in one night stands with men who'd never seek my company again. I truly believed that the only way I would ever have the love of a man was to allow him to do whatever he wanted with me. I grew detached from my body. The thought of protecting myself from anything other than pregnancy never crossed my mind.

When I look back, the number of these experiences that were actually assault are more than I can count on all my fingers and toes. The abuse started before my encounters with Joey, in fact. It just got worse, more invasive, more violent, and more damaging as the years went on.

One of my earliest memories is of a female adult relative touching my genitals, gently, and saying, "This is what ladies like." Another time, as a preschooler, I bled when I went to the toilet, and when I told my mother, she suggested I'd likely eaten too many strawberries. Long stretches of my youth between these memories are a blur. Like so many of us, I've blocked out years of my childhood. Years of things I must not want to remember.

The September I turned twenty-five, I was winding up an extended semester in Brussels, Belgium. During my last week there, I ended up with a man's hands around my neck, choking me as he proceeded to rape me. I heard the lyrics of Suzanne Vega's song "In the Eye."

If you were to kill me now...

And something snapped.

For once, I fought back. I bit his shoulder until I drew blood. He pulled back and accused me of being crazy. In the end he left, and I survived. It was the first time I started to take control of my life, of my body. Later, when I told friends about it, their only response was "You need another drink." Their dismissiveness of my experience reminded me of my childhood and, again, I shoved another sexual assault to the back of my mind.

By my late twenties, when I was told I had HIV, the only upside seemed to be that I could finally break the cycle of having sex I didn't want for love I wouldn't receive. In fact, I stopped having sex entirely, for years. Not due to a newly found sense of empowerment. But rather because now, added to the old I thought I was unworthy, I now felt dirty and repulsive. When what I really was, of course, was simply unlucky.

Growing up, I was never taught about sexual or reproductive health. My eldest sister, Alexandria, still in high school at the time, had been tasked with teaching me about sex when I was nine, maybe ten. My guess is she had very little experience herself, was still a virgin, and didn't have a clue as to how to talk to a child about it. To her credit, she bought me a copy of *Our Bodies, Ourselves*. I flipped through it, felt uncomfortable with the images, and hid it in a drawer. I never read it.

For the most part, I'd figured out birth control on my own in my late teens. I even made my way to Planned Parenthood in my early twenties, but my shame was still enormous. I felt ashamed even to ask questions of medical experts. I did not believe my life was worth protecting. Nor did I did believe sexually transmitted diseases were issues I'd ever need to consider.

All the science and research show that children who are taught about healthy sexuality from the earliest ages—beginning with "good touch, bad touch" as soon as they can speak, and adding more specific information as they grow up—delay their first sexual encounters longer, and make healthier decisions throughout their lives. If only we all had this advantage. Children should never be sexualized; they should be protected. But I grew up believing my body was here for others to enjoy. I am still trying to unlearn those lessons.

Have Tap Shoes, Will Travel

Wherever I Could Disappear from Reality, My Childhood

Despite those damaging emotional and sexual encounters early on, I had a comfortable, middle-class, privileged upbringing. My father provided for us. We were never hungry or without a roof. I spent much of my childhood in a ballet studio or theater. At age seven I was dancing in the Fresno Civic Ballet's annual production of *The Nutcracker*. By seventeen, I'd performed various roles in that ballet more than one hundred times.

Though there was always enough, my siblings and I all started working small jobs for spending money. I started babysitting at ten. It's mind-boggling, when I look back, to think anyone would hire a ten-year-old to watch even younger children, but times were different, I guess. Anyway, by fourteen I was hired for my first non-babysitting job, in a danceware store. My mother negotiated this for me in large part so I could get dance shoes, tights, and leotards for free or at a discount. At fifteen I was getting paid to dance—tap or jazz—and sing in a semi-professional troupe. The Good Company Players. We regularly performed musical comedies at Roger Rocka's Dinner Theater in Fresno. At sixteen I quit high school and took an equivalency exam to graduate early, thus skipping junior and senior years. Soon I was enrolled in junior college and working two jobs.

I still lived at home, so was able to save some money toward travel. I'd never yet really felt "at home" in my life, but like an outsider. The goal of traveling became my refuge. My father had caught the travel bug during World War II, returning soon after the end of the war before meeting and marrying my mother who, apparently, developed the same wanderlust. So I blame my parents, who'd spent the first four years of their marriage living in Spain, escaping their own families, and exploring the world beyond American borders. When traveling abroad, being different was expected, and that somehow helped put me at ease. Six months after I turned eighteen, I spent three months traveling the US and Canada alone, by Greyhound bus. I always refer to those days as my period of "traveling with the dog team." Riding a bus is a humbling way to see America.

At nineteen I bought a one-way plane ticket to Hawaii, then from there set out on nearly two years of solo travel through the South Pacific. The first eight months I crewed on sailboats and a tramp steamer, then switched to plane, bus, train or hitchhiking. Adrian and I overlapped for a month or two while crewing on sailboats—a wonderful, giggle-filled stint—but the rest of the extended trip I spent alone.

Just a few months into my journey, I happened, totally by chance, to be in Tahiti when they were filming a remake of the story of the mutiny on the *Bounty* titled, simply, *The Bounty*. The mostly-male film crew didn't speak French or Tahitian, so when an Anglophone was around—particularly a young blonde, I was pulled into the after-party and encouraged to stick around. Surprisingly, it wasn't even for sex. They just wanted someone to talk to, and I loved to listen.

One evening after dinner, a group of us—crew, actors, travelers like me—went to the beach with a bottle of rum. The Irish actor Liam Neeson, soft-spoken and the size of a giant, started singing. He taught me the words to the Gaelic folk song "Gypsy Rover." Another night, a similar group of bored Anglophones went for a nightcap at Club Med. After far too much to drink, a few took the stage, mooned the audience, and proceeded to get into a barroom brawl.

As we were escorted out, Mel Gibson, star of *The Bounty*, gave me a hug, then a peck on the mouth. "You're a good kid. Stay that way."

A few days later, I spent an hour or so speaking with the actor Anthony Hopkins on board the ship used in the film. We chatted about life and love. By this point, I was well beyond being starstruck. Meeting famous people and being in extraordinary situations started to seem the norm. Two months later, I continued my journey to other island nations, including New Zealand. Then Australia, so big it is *not* an island, but an entire continent.

Later, during college, I traveled to other parts of the world, almost always on my own. I spent my last semester of college between Belgium and France. Back in the States, during my first job post-graduation, I worked with politicians and dignitaries. I was a special-events planner for the World Affairs Council in San Francisco, a non-profit that organized educational events on international issues. I was given permission by George P. Shultz, the Secretary of State under Ronald Reagan from 1982 to 1989, to imitate his signature. He wrote a beautiful hand, and I enjoyed forging his name, even if it was just on appeal letters, asking donors to give to our organization.

By my late twenties, I felt worldlier than your average woman of my age from Central California. I'd held responsibilities, graduated from college, and worked at several jobs. I'd travelled to more than twenty countries and lived in four of them. I'd made acquaintances and friends around the globe. I felt special. Worldly. Different.

None of these experiences, however, could prepare me for my journey as a woman with HIV. Not one.

CHAPTER 2

testing the waters of activism

Finding My Voice

San Francisco, California

During my process of self-education, hearing other people's stories of living with the virus began to influence how I viewed myself. Within six months of my diagnosis, I sat in on another positive woman's testimonial before a group of high school students. When she shared the way she believed she'd become infected, and what had led her to be so vulnerable, the audience was engaged in a way I'd never seen before in a classroom. Those kids were listening as if their lives depended on taking in her words. For some, they no doubt did.

She was funny and smart, and although I don't recall the specifics of her story, she did explain all the ways a person could contract HIV. Those students left understanding the importance of knowing about sexually transmitted diseases, and that if everyone were tested, it would help break down the myths and stigma surrounding the pandemic.

Hearing women share their stories prompted me to do everything I could to educate others, too. That afternoon, in a high school up on some hill in San Francisco, I made a decision to be proactive. Even if I couldn't reverse my own situation, perhaps I could use it to help others.

29

Maybe if I'd met a woman with HIV before I'd been exposed, I would've realized the virus is not found only in the gay community. It seemed to be so in San Francisco, but it can infect anyone. I'd never really understood that, before. I'd thought that as a straight white middle-class woman, I was immune. Privilege personified.

People living with the virus sometimes say "HIV is a gift" because it requires a long, hard look at yourself and your life. You take account of where you stand. It forces you to contemplate your mortality. Perhaps. Still, I'd swap my "gift" for a nice pair of shoes! Yet there's some truth to the Panglossian outlook. Finding I had HIV made me consider my past, but it also made me think long and hard about what to do with the time ahead. Whether I had five years or more—or less—I wanted to make them count.

By early 1993, I'd become a speaker for Bay Area schools through a program called WEDGE. Telling my story again and again was transformative. It helped me release the virus's death grip. As I said the words, they became less painful. I let go, little by little, of the anger and sense of defeat. Gradually, I was finding a sense of purpose. More reasons to keep going.

The first time I spoke at a high school, I was scared to death. I mean, let's face it, high-schoolers can be brutal. And American society overall isn't too supportive of people perceived as sick, so I didn't expect a great reception even if my speech went well. I was terrified they'd ask a question I wouldn't be able to answer.

Those twenty minutes seemed to pass as if I were trapped in a Dali painting. Everything felt off and contorted. The classroom was stuffy, I was sweating hard under my arms and in the small of my back. Whether it was my nerves or shitty lighting, I couldn't actually see any of the students staring at me. But I could feel eyes like laser beams burning into my skin.

In my mind, they were all judging me as That Woman with AIDS. Although I was the speaker—the adult—in a sea of hormonal teens who were probably actually courteous and attentive, I felt like I was the thirteen-year-old version of myself trying to solve an equation on the blackboard in pre-algebra with an enormous blackhead between my eyebrows.

Eventually I finished. "Are there any questions?"

At first, the group was silent. Then a tentative hand lifted. A brunette a few rows back and to my left. "Excuse me, but…"

"Yes?" I said, trying to suppress the pondful of frogs jumping around in my throat.

"Do you know… Do you…"

"Yes?" I squeaked, even more nervous than before.

"Do you know you look *just* like Bridget Fonda?"

I smiled. Every muscle in my body relaxed. Maybe I could do this after all. I could speak to teenagers, and maybe they'd hear something. Maybe I'd just be "the woman with HIV who looks like Bridget Fonda" and not a scary monster.

Other questions followed. "How did your parents react when you told them?" "Do you still have to go to work?" "Are you afraid of dying?" Occasionally, a student would share that they'd had a loved one who'd died. San Francisco has always been a city of tolerance and those youngsters extended that kindness to me.

That day, in front of a room of curious teens, I peeled away another layer of fear, exposed myself, and survived. Pushing forth through the reality of my situation felt like a better option than hiding behind "what if."

On that day, I found my voice.

As I became a more seasoned public speaker, I'd perch on top of a table or desk, if possible. I thought it'd make me look cool. With rows of teens watching me with something between curiosity and *who is this circus freak*, I'd first share how I'd become infected, then gave a brief account of how my life was now. Some eyebrows would rise, while some shoulders would relax as their listening became more focused. I told them, "Even if you win the lotto, are given a Ferrari and get hired by MTV for your dream job, life will still be tough and throw you curves." I'd add that the last thing they should do was allow an incurable disease into their lives when they could prevent it. Often that made them giggle, but I believe it also made them think. Humor is a powerful tool in storytelling.

I explained that I was not yet sick, thank goodness, but it was probably just a matter of time. Even without overt illness, I was definitely dealing with the virus on a daily basis: I was tired a lot, and some of my friends had abandoned me.

And dating. Ouf. I told the students I hated telling men because they often physically recoiled, and that was painful. "I'll most likely live my life single, because I'm becoming convinced nobody will ever love me."

Being single is not something that appeals to teenagers, so I'm sure my messages registered at least with some of them.

Within the first year of my diagnosis, I met Rebecca Denison, who had started the WORLD organization in Oakland. She befriended me and invited me to work for her. I was the first paid employee (even before the founder) and took the job seriously. Rebecca saw I had a passion for international work and encouraged me to get involved on that level.

Thanks to her, I applied to attend an international conference of people living with HIV to be held in Mexico.

I'd been enrolled in a research study for a therapeutic vaccine called gp120, and as the only woman in the study, all the researchers knew who I was. They'd learned, for example, the importance of where the injection goes. Since women have more fat in our arms, they had to be that much more careful to find my muscle. This they learned when my shoulder became swollen after an injection and so inflamed my friends jokingly warmed their hands next to me.

As with the current research, clinical trials, and rollouts of COVID vaccines, it's critical that study participants reflect the population who'll be inoculated. Being inclusive is better science, but it also begins to break down the inequities between various demographics. My being part of that study mattered.

Their research was later discontinued, but I've always wondered if those shots had any impact on the length of time it took for my virus to manifest as serious illness in later years. When I asked if the drug company could support my travel to Mexico, they declined, but individual employees donated their own money to sponsor my travel, accommodation, and registration.

Rebecca also attended, as did a handful of other positive women I'd met through WORLD. I wasn't sure what I expected to find when I landed in Acapulco. I was just glad to be traveling again, and open to whatever might lie ahead.

How naïve I was.

A Kidnapping in Mexico

Acapulco, Mexico, 1993

Mexico: North America
Population: 127.6 million
Capital: Mexico City

Trying to drown out the shouting of conference attendees below and quiet my overwhelmed mind, I sat in the path of the daylight flooding my hotel room window for a long moment, my feet still on the adobe tile. The air conditioning was on high, but the warmth of the Acapulco sun felt like a much-needed hug. When I'd first been told I'd tested positive, I hadn't thought I'd live long enough to watch Oprah the next afternoon. Yet here I was, almost a year and a half later, at an international conference for people living with HIV.

Shy by nature (although I fake confidence), I was hesitant to go out and face the sea of angry activists outside my room. Some still looked and sounded healthy. Others appeared closer to death than anyone under eighty ever should. The stale stench of illness hung in the air amid the sweaty Act Up T-shirts, and the slap of flip-flops around the pool became our soundtrack. Punctuated now and then by shrieks of, "Oh my God! You're here! You're still alive!" or "Come here, princess, you look faaabulous!" Which might be said to a muscular six-foot-tall man.

These warriors were unlike the HIV-people I'd met so far. They were very pissed off. Not simply disenfranchised or disappointed or frustrated, or even like the perky ones determined to make their remaining years happy. These people felt the world owed them, and as I listened, I tended to agree. They were advocating for themselves and our global community in order to live. For access to better health care, affordable treatment and, perhaps most importantly, for their dignity to be acknowledged and the stigma and discrimination to end. Their activism went beyond the stereotypical marches, memorials, or campaigns. They were demanding a seat at the table alongside the decision makers. They wanted representation on local, national, and international advisory boards of pharmaceutical companies, medical networks, and governmental bodies, including the United Nations.

"You know, Mike Merson's going to be here," one lanky guy with spiky red hair said from across the breakfast table.

"Uh-huh." I nibbled some salty bacon and noted the slogan on his T-shirt: *SILENCE = DEATH.*

"You know who that is, right?"

"Um. No, not really," I said, looking back up into watery green eyes, like olives floating in gin.

"Girlfriend! Where have you been?" he yelped. "He's the head of GPA—you know, the Global Programme on AIDS at the WHO?"

I shrugged.

"Sorry, World Health Organization." He pronounced each word from the acronyms slowly, as if I had a hearing impairment.

"Of course," I said, pretending I'd known all along. "So is he going to speak or something?"

"Yeah, he's going to speak, all right. And so are we! We have some serious things to say to him, like, 'How dare you bureaucrats and doctors play with our lives, you arrogant prick?'"

"I see. Well, I'm sure that's going to be quite a session!"

I sat there imagining what I assumed to be a distinguished-looking doctor having it out with angry people fired up with more passion than their immune system could contain. I couldn't see how it would end well for these hard-core activists, but kept my mouth shut.

I was intimidated by their knowledge. Not only of the illness but also the history of the epidemic, and the workings of the bureaucracies guiding, or neglecting, the responses. I'd begun to educate myself, but hearing them discuss macrophages as eloquently as they dissected Big Pharma profit margins, I felt out of my depth.

Giving in to my survival tactic of silent watchfulness, I felt very much an outsider at the opening of this conference. What kind of nonstop chaos had I fallen into? I wanted to learn more about HIV, but mostly to know more about these people who wanted direct input into the decisions shaping their futures. Our futures.

My future.

Mothers, for example, wanted research trials to provide childcare so they could participate. The scientists apparently hadn't thought of that, and as a result, few women were enrolling in studies. So how could we be sure medications being tested on men would even work for half the population? I had so much to learn.

The fiercest activist I'd met so far was Bellona, who, like me, was a small, blue-eyed blonde. Five years younger, she not only spoke publicly about living with HIV, but was also candid about being a lesbian—not an easy label to wear in her rural Midwestern hometown. She'd been fighting like hell since having been infected in her early teens. Her mother's boyfriend had raped her, and that was a burning rage she'd never extinguish. But she also told me funny stories, which drew me to her gentler side. My favorite was about when she'd gone to her first support group and found herself surrounded by gay men. They listened, hugged her, and offered reassuring words. And, at the end of the night, one took her in his arms and said, "Bellona, darling, it's all going to be okay. Really, it is. Just don't *ever* wear that belt with those shoes again!"

She was already more involved and knowledgeable than I was and could help guide me through the madness. She'd been to one of the first world conferences, in Amsterdam, when the networks of people with HIV began to form. She knew many of the individuals and had trenchant opinions on them all. Her biting humor was a balm in the blistering rage that surrounded us.

At first, I'd wanted to go to the conference primarily for the opportunity to travel again. By 1993, scores of countries around the globe had imposed travel restrictions for people living with the virus (even today, many still do). In order to visit one, a test was required; if it was positive, the visa was denied. If the rules were somehow skirted but officials found related meds in your luggage, you'd be packed home on the next flight and blacklisted forever. This despite the fact that the HIV-1 retrovirus already exists in every country and continent. It is not airborne, it does not live long exposed to air, and it is extremely fragile. It's actually not that easily transmitted. It requires intimate contact with infected bodily fluids.

In short, such restrictions do nothing to stop the spread and everything to increase the stigma against positive individuals. As such, traveling again was a privilege, and I appreciated it that much more. Mexico was selected for the conference because it did not impose such restrictions. This trip was a glimmer of hope: maybe I could have a mostly normal life. My passport was my most prized possession. I still hoped I'd be able to use it frequently.

Also, I was eager to meet people with HIV from other countries, to see if their experiences were the same. Even as a child, I'd always been drawn to the new kid in school. If they came from another country, I felt I'd hit the jackpot. Though long since lost, one of my favorite childhood possessions was a handmade valentine from an Iranian boy whose family had escaped the revolution in the early 1970s. He'd written my name in Farsi with the script I'd later recognize as Arabic. I'd never seen my name written in another alphabet, much less cut out of red construction paper and pasted onto a blue background. I used to trace my fingers over this magical-looking depiction of my name so often, the edges became worn like those in a favorite book of poems. How a boy my age could know so many different things from a world so far from mine fascinated me. What he knew, of course was his own language, script, and culture, but I was too young to grasp that. My curiosity about the world beyond my hometown was piqued and has yet to subside.

The quiet Persian in grade school had been gentle and mysterious. But many of the participants at this conference scared the bejesus out of me. Some were so militant in their demands I found them off-putting. Like a diner straining to hear the daily specials in a crowded restaurant,

I tried to decipher the messages swirling around me, picking out a voice here and there to lock on to. Mostly, though, there rose a wall of vocalized irritation that I didn't have a way to make sense of.

Others seemed passionate in a way I could relate to though, because their fire stemmed from a place of hope—a desire to change things, rather than simply rage and accuse. They were *doers* and *fixers*. I tried to get closer, to absorb a dose of that strength. They sat quietly together in small groups, working on documents to circulate. Or drafting press releases. Or simply strategizing ways to make our collective voice clearer, so those who most needed to listen might actually be able to hear us.

The newer ones among us were lost, trying to navigate this new world of international activism. For me, that meant learning a new vocabulary. Acronyms were darting around like sandflies at the beach. GNP+. WHO. GPA. ICW. USAID. ICASO, CDC. ICASO, Picasso, Mi Casa, Su Casa. What the hell?

Many of those acronyms didn't sink in, but I discovered four were key. The first was the WHO—the World Health Organization—part of the United Nations, which, at that time, coordinated the response to AIDS. The second was the program within the WHO called GPA, or the Global Programme on AIDS.

WHO and GPA were easy enough to remember mostly because the activists had cast them as the enemy, the high and mighty medicos who would figure this all out *for* us rather that *with* us. And, though it looked like the WHO was about to reorganize and create a different program, which would certainly yield yet another acronym, I held on to those two abbreviations.

The other essential acronyms pertained to two international networks of people living with HIV who were trying to galvanize a collective voice, to build a stronger lobby to influence folks at the WHO. This conference had been organized by one of them: the GNP+: The Global Network of People Living with HIV. Acronym three. The other was the ICW, or International Community of Women Living with HIV. Acronym four. Like the GNP+ but exclusively for women. GNP+ and ICW worked together, and one of their goals in Mexico was to elect a new board of directors for each network and move the agenda forward in concrete ways to match the pandemic's rapid evolution.

They didn't want to merely write letters to the WHO. They wanted to ensure that the voices of positive people were given equal weight with the opinions of the scientists, doctors, and politicians who ran the international response. These individuals had gathered from around the globe to discuss our plight and plan for a less marginalized, longer, healthier future. Before we left Mexico, two people from each region of the world were to be selected to serve on the board of the GNP+. This was not your rich uncle's corporate board where people got paid to meet and greet. The appointment came without a salary (though some expenses might be covered if you were lucky). Members would become one of the global faces of HIV. While it was an honor to serve, these roles would entail personal and financial cost. Once a person went public with their status, anonymity could never be retrieved.

Between the many buffets of tame and tasteless food, there were how-to workshops on advocating for our needs, understanding treatment options (few though they were at the time), managing your doctor, and so on. There were support groups for women, for men, for parents, and even support groups for support groups! I heard speakers and attended panels. More interesting, however, were the stories in the hallways.

One day, in the shallow end of the swimming pool, a woman from Zimbabwe told a small gathering of female attendees about her travels from Africa to Mexico. She'd been questioned repeatedly by immigration officers across two continents, about why she was traveling. And thus, publicly humiliated at every turn. These government officials always made a showy affair of wrapping her luggage in industrial-strength trash bags so it would not "contaminate" other suitcases. She was assigned seats at the back of the planes on long-haul flights and told to stay there. To not get up to stretch her legs or to use the restroom. To not even ask for a blanket or pillow. Over the course of two days, she flew from Zimbabwe to South Africa to Brazil and then on to Mexico. She was treated like a leper, and she took it, because she was determined to speak her mind here.

A handful of women—one from Germany, another from Mexico, a few from various countries in Africa—told us they'd recently had babies who without medical intervention, miraculously, were not born HIV positive. Some of the Africans said that *not* breastfeeding—which was recommended—was simply not an option. Where they lived, a woman who didn't was already an outcast. So they could never risk drawing attention to themselves and their babies by raising suspicions as to why they weren't nursing.

Of course, that was only one issue for those living in developing nations. There was also having to haul water in rural areas and then boil it, which required a stove, which not everyone had. I learned that many of the early medications (none of which I'd had to take) required refrigeration. Again, a huge problem, because not everyone has access to reliable electricity.

I'd already traveled a fair bit before my diagnosis. But never in order to learn the reality for someone dealing with such issues, so these stories were illustrative of life beyond my privileges. I'd never gone hungry or been unable to afford a safe, warm place to live. These issues, and more, compounded and accelerated the fatality rates in developing nations. There was so much I'd been taking for granted.

Another impressive speaker was one of the first women diagnosed in the United Kingdom (U.K.). Kate had co-founded the first women's group there, Positively Women. Later she helped start the International Community of Women Living with HIV (ICW), the sister organization to the GNP+. She'd been diagnosed nearly a decade earlier and I was astonished she'd survived so long. She was a striking beauty. Half Indian, half English, her enormous blue eyes were set against olive skin and black hair. I may have had a girl crush on her, but I certainly developed an activist crush.

One night she came out to the edge of the pool, where a bunch of us were lounging. Eyes bloodshot, slurring her words, smoking and waving a glass of liquor in her hands, she made her way toward us. "Thaaas it," she said, "Can't do this... anymore."

"Why? What happened? What are you talking about?" we asked, pulling our feet from the pool, or rising from our lounge chairs to form a circle around her.

"The lasssss one died. The lasss woman I started Positively Women with... has died. Sss no one left. I jusss don' have it in me... to continue."

I watched her swollen eyes spill over with tears and feared she might collapse right there on the patio. She looked broken, exhausted. So frail and tiny. I wondered if I'd ever see her again.

I knew why she was crying in that particular moment. But it also started to sink in that many of these people were angry not just because of the issues, but because they were tired. Tired of their friends dying. Tired of being told no. Tired of being rejected. Tired of fighting for their lives.

As I watched Kate slump in exhaustion, I felt my thinking shift. Maybe I could play a role. Maybe I belonged in this movement as well. If I could work with people like her on concrete issues, perhaps we could help make life better for women in our situation—at least for future generations, if not for ourselves.

Between these hallway and poolside discussions, I managed to attend a few of the actual conference sessions. Unfortunately, I remember little of what was said. Dr. Michael Merson, director of the WHO Global Program on AIDS, a nondescript man in his fifties, made his speech, and not a word sank in. My brain was on overload. Most of what he said floated away like passing clouds.

What I do remember clearly was the day a near-riot broke out during one of the plenaries. The group had been discussing, in English, the financial state of the GNP+ and the fact it was in debt. The Spanish language translators had not quite caught the gist of the conversation, however, and were relaying a discussion of "*la muerta*" of the organization and its members.

One of the Spanish-speaking delegates stood, removed his headphones and in broken English demanded, "Stop speaking of our precious lives as if we were mere statistics. We are here. We are alive this day. Stop to disrespect our humanity! *Por favor.*"

Startled glances flew around the room like a game of laser tag, each of us looking for someone who might calm the insulted man. Pairs of heads leaned together. Soon, giggles erupted as we realized the translators had confused *debt* with *death*, sending us all into an unintended tizzy. Calm was restored, and the drone of speakers resumed.

On the last night, we held a Miss GNP+ contest. Most of the contestants were guys in drag. I lent my favorite black leather belt to one to secure his toga—ultimately the winning costume—only to watch him take a celebratory leap into the pool. My belt was ruined. Oh, well. At least I helped him win. I was already beginning to collaborate and, to my surprise, having fun in the process.

The music for this closing event was DJ'd by Yolanda, a wry woman from Trinidad. I heard Caribbean carnival music for the first time. "The Ballad of Hulsie X" and another called "Tayee Ayee" that employed beats I'd never heard before. Calypso. Soca. Steel pan. No wonder these grinding rhythms propel the famous carnival spirit and parades of Trinidad and Tobago. I couldn't keep my hips still. We danced into the night and celebrated our lives, crazy and challenged though they were.

Meanwhile, unbeknownst to me, another event was occurring nearby that would go down as one of the wackiest on the timeline of AIDS activism.

From our poolside vantage point, the tops of heads could be seen through a window in a suite overlooking the pool area where we were dancing. There, several of the more militant activists had skipped the party to waylay Dr. Merson. As the man in charge of the global response to the pandemic, he had disappointed the more seasoned activists. They felt he owed our community a fuller explanation of his intentions. There were rumors that a new United Nations (UN) entity was being set up to replace his program, and these activists wanted to make sure people with HIV would be involved from the outset. Not as puppets in a tokenistic way, but as respected decision makers in our own right.

Merson's hotel room was blocked at the door by the very people he was tasked to help. They canceled his taxi and told the airline he'd miss his flight. His luggage stood outside his room untouched, until eventually he retrieved it under the watchful eye of a man wearing that same *Silence = Death* tee. Lights from his room stayed lit long after the party outside wound down as the activists and the bureaucrat deliberated. The sky turned lavender shades of sunrise, then rose overhead, and eventually sank down again for the evening. But Merson listened. He vowed to take the messages back to the WHO and others at the UN to see if things couldn't be different in the future.

The redhead I'd met at breakfast my first day—the one with the olive martini eyes—and other activists demanded that never again should the medical community alone make decisions on a much broader-reaching social and health issue. HIV was more than a virus; it epitomized a chasm in society—an unwillingness to discuss sex and sexuality or to respect those deemed "different" by the mainstream "norm". The gay rights movement had merged with AIDS activism.

The downside of the union was that the epidemic was labeled as a "gay disease," associated with what many perceived to be immoral behavior, compounding the stigma. The upside was that this powerful lobby used years of organizing skills to change the face of patient rights for many illnesses to follow.

From that impromptu kidnapping, a movement was born. That night set into motion GIPA, or The Greater Involvement of People Living with HIV or AIDS. The term had first been coined years earlier, as a part of the Denver Principles in 1983, although it wouldn't be formalized until 1994. After those living with and facing the day-to-day reality of the disease joined forces to shape the global agenda, more informed decisions might be made. While I'd been shaking my booty, these activists had been blazing a trail I'd soon walk, and widen, in my own small way.

Ultimately, I agreed to be nominated for the board of the GNP+. I don't think any others even stood for the position, so I was easily voted in. I'd never before been on the board of anything. I mean, I was class president once, but that was in the sixth grade. I'd run on a platform of "legalizing" chewing gum. My brain, however, was three steps ahead, committing me to tasks I felt compelled to take on simply because someone had to. My inner activist apparently was eager to emerge, so she gave herself a coming-out party in Mexico.

There was no guidebook, no rules. We were all making it up as we went along. But I always like a challenge, and the possibility of more travel was enough for me to agree. The job would be unpaid, but I was already working as a temp, so I wasn't exactly tied up in any fast-track career. Somehow, I'd make it work.

I'd arrived from San Francisco as just another woman living with HIV, but returned with a purpose. I had new friends, renewed vigor and—let's not forget—a new appreciation of Caribbean music! Along with Eric Sawyer—a pioneer in the movement as one of the founders of Act Up and later Housing Works—and Stefan Collins, a community outreach worker from Canada, I was now a North American board member of the Global Network of People Living with HIV and AIDS. I felt that I mattered and knew, with relief, that I was not only not alone, I was in excellent company.

Poster Child

Yokohama

Japan: East Asia
Population: 126.3 million
Capital: Tokyo

The best part about flying west from Japan *to* California is that, with the right flights, you can arrive before you left. The flip side is going to Japan *from* California, the jet lag from crossing the international dateline is so disorienting it takes days to clear the fuzz from your brain.

So as I rode up the escalator at the 10th International AIDS Conference, after my very long journey across the Pacific, I had to do a triple take to be sure I wasn't imagining things. There, at the top of the escalator, I spotted my face. Not just a snapshot, but a larger-than-life three-by-five-foot photograph. A friend stood next to the it, pointed to it, and said, "Hey, Martina! Look at you. You look great!" Only then did I realize he wasn't talking about me, in person, but about the image. In less than a year of international activism, and two years after my diagnosis, I'd somehow become a poster child for AIDS.

The preceding winter, a team had come to San Francisco from Asia to do a photo essay on Women Living with AIDS. The quiet, tall photographer was referred to as the Annie Leibovitz of Japan. The short, well-dressed fellow who accompanied her was always talking, and they both smoked incessantly. Over the course of ten days, twenty positive women were scheduled to be photographed in various places in San Francisco. For my shoot, I met them at the house of another activist whom they were also photographing that day. The sun was bright, but it was very cold. I remember because they decided to do my shoot outside, to take advantage of the light.

I was wearing a jacket, but they insisted my black turtleneck was more striking on its own. "It makes your blue eyes and blond hair pop," said the photographer. This was good, they said, because I would break the Japanese stereotype of people living with HIV as all being African. I agreed with at least the second part of their logic—the Japanese were not alone in holding that stereotype—so I pulled off my jacket. I sat on a metal-backed chair in front of a garage door, trying not to shiver, for what felt like hours.

The result was a series of photos of me with both hands covering my mouth, then cradling the sides of my face, and another with eyes closed. Together, the set looked like the classic "hear no evil, see no evil, speak no evil" monkeys, but I'd simply been trying to stay warm.

The team was organizing an event in Tokyo to happen concurrently with the 10th International AIDS Conference, which would be farther south in the port city of Yokohama. They'd asked if any of us would be attending and, if so, whether we would sit on a few panels to raise awareness. Again, I agreed. Surely educating others could only be a good thing. I still believed I could stay one step ahead of the infection if I remained vigilant in my activism. If nothing else, it was a way to channel my anger into something useful, rather than beating myself up for having contracted the virus or consuming my energy with destructive thoughts and needless stress.

A month or two before the conference, a dear friend and former colleague contacted me to say she was in town and asked if we could meet for lunch. I adored Susan and was delighted to catch up. We met at a café near our old workplace downtown. I quickly found my friend seated in a booth near the entrance of the café. She was impeccably dressed, and her black hair was in a sharp bob.

"Susan, you look fantastic—as always, of course! What are you up to these days?"

"Living in Japan and working as a journalist. It's my dream come true. I'm finally getting to learn my native language properly—crazy how I could grow up with Japanese parents yet speak better Hawaiian surfer lingo than Japanese!"

"That's great! Your family must be proud."

"They are, they definitely are. Crazy thing is, I am actually working on the International AIDS Conference. Part of their media team."

I felt the blood drain from my face. My skin went cold and clammy. I hadn't disclosed my status to many ex-colleagues yet. I hadn't exactly decided to keep it a secret; it's just that my focus had turned almost entirely toward the world of AIDS, and I rarely saw people from earlier chapters in my life. Truthfully, the people I'd worked with when I did special events for the World Affairs Council—a nonprofit that promotes learning about international issues—were the group I'd avoided the most. They all knew I'd left that job so I could travel more. They were happy for my next chapter in life, yet I felt like I'd failed them all. I was embarrassed and ashamed.

"Really. Wow. I, uh, I think I'm probably going to that conference, too, actually."

"I know." She took my hand and gently squeezed as if to banish of my unease. "I saw the book, and I've been in touch with their creative team."

I frowned, "The book?"

"Yes, it's beautiful. I brought you a copy." She reached into a large satchel and handed me a sleek paperback about nine by twelve inches. On the cover, a number one in a circle, seemed to indicate that more issues would be coming. Without a word, I set it on the table and opened it as I had a million books before. Inside I immediately recognized the photo of another woman from San Francisco, then a few of some Asian women I'd never seen before. The photos were stunning. I couldn't read the Kanji text. Even so, it made a powerful impression.

45

Names, birthdates, hometowns and a blurb, I assumed, were what the characters revealed about each subject.

"It's in Japanese, Martina."

"I can see that." I was confused about what she meant.

She took the book from me. "We read from right to left. You have the book in the wrong direction." She flipped it over, revealing the actual cover, which read boldly in English, in bright colors, *Em:Bridge SPECIAL - AIDS + HIV: Part I, Women Living with AIDS—Part II, AIDS in Asia.* As I opened it again, from the proper side, she said, "You're the second picture. As in second at the beginning. Not second to last."

I stared down at my face, both amazed at how beautiful the photo was, yet also disturbed and shocked to know I'd been included in a book I didn't know existed. We'd all signed releases, so they had the right to publish our photos and stories. I'd had an idea they were planning a publication, but hadn't realized it had come to fruition.

Susan sensed my discomfort. Again, she took my hand. "I'm so sorry. But, my dear, you do look beautiful! How could you not? You *are* beautiful."

Tears welled up. I bit my lip and gripped her hand tightly for a moment, then gave her a hug.

Seated side by side, we proceeded to catch up. Clearly there was a lot to talk about. Susan was saddened, above all, but also proud I was trying to help others. She said that the stigma in Japan was very marked. My participation was a good thing and would certainly help others living with the virus, particularly women.

We agreed to meet in Yokohama and exchanged long hugs before parting. I cared what Susan thought of me, and she'd taken it well. Each time I disclosed my diagnosis without someone freaking out, I gained more strength and courage. I left the restaurant carrying the volume under one arm. Walking a tiny bit taller than when I'd arrived.

When I'd first seen that image in the book, back in San Francisco, I'd been stunned. Now, when I saw it again in Yokohama, I was again surprised. When I later saw it on a street corner in Tokyo, I felt paralyzed.

After taking the bullet train to Tokyo (at the expense of the exhibit organizers, no less) I, along with two other women from San Francisco, emerged to ground level. There, I caught a glimpse of that same image just outside the station. *No, it can't be.* I walked toward the kiosk as if drawn by a magnet, slowly realizing that indeed the woman in the poster with the big blue eyes was me.

I'd had no idea they'd used my image for promotion of the exhibit or that I'd find my face, five feet high, on the street corners of one of the busiest cities in the world. They'd used the shot of me covering my mouth with one hand. Without realizing it, I mimicked the image and stood, hand over my mouth. In shock, eyes widened in disbelief. After a moment or two, a small group of Japanese gathered. Pointing and giggling, realizing that I was the woman in the poster. The woman "Living with AIDS + HIV."

I froze. What had my life become?

One of the other women from the conference shouted, "Martina, this way! The gallery is over here."

When I didn't move, she looked past me and spotted the poster. "Holy shit!"

She took my hand and pulled me toward the gallery, as a mother would tow away a child transfixed by a toy or TV show.

As we descended the wide steps of the light-filled gallery I saw two more photos, both with me covering my mouth; one with my eyes open, the other with my eyes closed. At some point I stood between the two and covered my ears to complete the troika in a snapshot, taken by another woman in the photoshoot who'd also agreed to join the panels.

Several times during that week, I took the train north to Tokyo and spoke at the gallery, followed by a Q & A. A variety of journalists and other interested parties asked about what it was like to live with HIV. The organizers had asked us to speak because so far the media had identified only four citizens in the country willing to publicly admit to being positive. Only eight hundred cases had been reported there at the time, so the public perception was that HIV was a disease of foreigners. And while we might've looked the stereotype of "foreigners," we also allowed reporters and regular citizens to ask us about our lives, to gain information they might not have been able to gather otherwise.

One evening after a day of interviews, the exhibit organizers took a few of us to a traditional restaurant. One woman in our group—the one whose photo I'd first seen in the book—happened to be a professional chef. She knew the restaurant was a good choice. Each course was displayed like a work of art, and each was more delicious than the last. When at last our host excused himself to pay, she whispered, "This is the most expensive meal I've ever had. The most expensive *you've* ever had."

I laughed. "How do you know?"

"I read about this place in a guidebook. He is now paying at least a thousand dollars for our meal."

"*One thousand dollars*? Are you sure? There are only four of us, and he didn't eat."

"At least. This is one of the nicest restaurants in Tokyo."

I couldn't decide if the food now seemed more delicious, or less so with that layer of guilt topping. But it really was an extraordinary experience, so I set my upbringing aside and embraced the perks of being a pseudo-star—if only for a few hours.

On the last day of the conference, after the closing ceremonies, the gallery folks organized an outing for us to visit a few temples and a bamboo forest. While strolling through the cool, serene, seemingly mile-high stalks, I spoke with my friend Bellona. I'd been with her in Mexico too. We mused about how odd our lives had become.

Walking through that forest, or visiting a fifty-foot Buddha, were not things either of us had expected to be doing, particularly not on someone else's dime. Issues that had seemed important pre-diagnosis had been replaced with an entirely new agenda.

She, for example, had also been very public about her status in hopes of letting women in her rural Midwest community know that they were not alone.

One result was threats from the Ku Klux Klan, including a burning cross on her lawn, for speaking about such sinful things as sex and drugs. Another was finding *AIDS FAG* spray-painted across her windows. She'd lost track of the number of threats she'd received. All because she'd dared to speak up. The media swallowed her stories like candy and left her to pick up the garbage after they moved on to the next "hot topic."

And who was there to support her on the other end of these acts of courage and determination? Mostly, other positive women and men from around the US and, increasingly, the globe. Our support systems were tethered across continents and phone lines, held together by a lifeline of emails. Many of the women I was meeting in my new role as an activist had been ostracized; isolated by their efforts to help others.

Bellona and I sat silently for a long while in that bamboo forest to absorb the calm of the faintly rustling, constantly growing shoots. In the right conditions, bamboo can add two feet per day. And while *we* weren't any taller when we left the forest, we definitely felt renewed.

That was a good thing. We would need every ounce of strength we could muster to make the world a more AIDS-friendly place.

CHAPTER 3

breaking down barriers

Finding My Inner Negotiator

few months after Yokohama, in my role as a board member of the GNP+, I was invited to Paris to help prepare for a high-level international meeting of heads of state. They would be discussing global priorities for mitigating the AIDS pandemic.

On December 1st, 1994, The Paris AIDS Summit took place. There 42 representatives of national governments signed the Paris Declaration. Certainly, it wasn't the first declaration by governments, nor the first piece of paper about AIDS. But it was the first time that the rights of people living with HIV would be explicitly addressed in a meaningful and supportive manner at such a high level.

The Declaration, notably, included a phrase that indicated the necessity of including us in all governmental and international deliberations.

That notion soon became known as the GIPA Principle. Later it would be expanded to include those others impacted by the disease, such as partners and caregivers, who often carried on the work after their loved one was gone. We needed all hands on deck in this fight, but we needed to ensure the focus remained on positive people being allowed to speak for themselves, first and foremost.

As I mentioned in the previous chapter, the idea of GIPA was first voiced in 1983 at the 5th Annual Gay and Lesbian Health Conference in Denver. It's included in documentation called The Denver Principles. I'd learned about it in Mexico. A key section reads as follows:

> We condemn attempts to label us as "victims," a term which implies defeat, and we are only occasionally "patients," a term which implies passivity, helplessness, and dependence upon the care of others. We are "People With AIDS."

Also included, among other things, were three recommendations for people living with HIV/AIDS:

1.) Form caucuses to choose their own representatives, to deal with the media, to choose their own agenda and to plan their own strategies.

2.) Be involved at every level of decision-making and specifically serve on the boards of directors of provider organizations.

3.) Be included in all AIDS forums with equal credibility as other participants, to share their own experiences and knowledge.

Formalization and recognition from the broader AIDS community, however, did not happen until eleven years later, at the Paris AIDS Summit.

A few days prior to the summit, I sat in a small room with some other representatives of nongovernmental organizations. We met with some United Nations representatives (from the original Global Programme on AIDS, which functioned as a part of the World Health Organization) as well as representatives of the French government. Together, we hashed over the language of the Paris Declaration. Maintaining the wording on including people living with HIV/AIDS at the forefront was our goal, and we succeeded. As with many negotiations, the real work that sparked change took place in side meetings and hallways, prior to the official event recorded in the history books.

A day or two before the summit, I was interviewed by Jim Bitterman of CNN. We talked about the importance of involving people living with HIV, both at the Paris Summit and in all future official deliberations. I called my mother to forewarn her. "Hi, I might be on national news talking about having HIV. I thought you might want to know."

"We don't get the same news here," she replied, denying the fact Central California got the exact same nightly news as every other place in America. She apparently lived in an alternate universe. The piece never aired in the US so it was ultimately a moot point.

I and the other activists were invited to a reception one evening at the residence of the American Ambassador to France, Pamela Harriman. From that event, I only recall three things:

1.) Pamela Harriman was polite and had very big hair.

2.) The residence was like a palace with an entryway large enough to host a ball.

3.) Much of the artwork had been removed because they were afraid activists might splatter blood to protest lack of action by the US government—particularly under presidents Bush, Sr. and Reagan.

However, we behaved in a civilized fashion, and did not scream epithets or splatter blood or deface any property. We did giggle throughout the evening at the diplomats' obvious fear.

When the Paris AIDS Summit took place, on December 1, 1994—World AIDS Day—I was napping in a small apartment where I'd been hosted by a local. That night we marched through the streets wearing T-shirts that read *Paris Is Burning* (a hat-tip to the documentary of the same name by Jennie Livingston) while chanting Act Up slogans in English and French. The weather was cold, the gathering wonderful, and I felt very much alive.

A Seat at Table Mountain

Cape Town

South Africa: Africa
Population: 58.6 million
Capital: Pretoria

Another event that would change my life was the seventh annual conference of the Global Network of People Living with HIV/AIDS (GNP+) in Cape Town. All I knew at the time, though, was that I'd been invited to attend the meeting in March 1995. Since I was the GNP+ board member representing North America, the organizers of this conference, I'd have to be there. In addition to the agenda, we'd also hold board meetings, since we'd all be in one place.

During my time in Cape Town, the ICW (International Community of Women Living with HIV) also held meetings, and I decided to put myself forward as a board member of the ICW—Key Contacts, we were called—instead of continuing with the GNP+.

The needs of a woman living with HIV are very specific. As I met more positive women, I realized there were major concerns I wasn't dealing with—pregnancy, childbirth, breast-feeding, motherhood, being a wife. These, too, required focused attention. I felt I could be more helpful to the greater struggle by working to raise awareness about these issues.

Basically, I arrived in South Africa as a board member for GNP+ and left as a Key Contact for the ICW. During our conference, Dr. Peter Piot, who'd been appointed the first leader of what would become UNAIDS, gave a presentation. Although the new organization would not be formally launched until the next year, logistical preparations to shift the global response from the World Health Organization to UNAIDS, an interagency program, were well under way.

Before, during, and after our conference, Dr. Piot frequently spoke about the importance of GIPA and how he valued the role that only people living with HIV could play in keeping UNAIDS honest. He not only articulated what we'd been lobbying for for years, but his obvious passion made us believe he meant every word. UNAIDS was going to be a different type of entity, one that embraced the community it was built to serve. Indeed, until the creation of UNAIDS, no UN entity had ever included nongovernmental representation in its organizing bodies, beyond affording a courtesy seat as a silent observer.

I found Piot a likeable man with a good sense of humor. Over cocktails one evening as we watched the sun set behind majestic Table Mountain, he told a group of us, "I feel a little nervous being here, you know. I mean, will you at least let me know when you're planning to hold me hostage so I can get another beer?" He was, of course, alluding to the so-called kidnapping of his predecessor, Mike Merson. We promised him that we were kind to our detainees but that, so far, his words were working, and we'd likely allow him to leave on his scheduled day of departure.

That conference was key, I believe, to fostering a relationship between the UN and our community that would forever change the global response to the pandemic. While we didn't yet have all the answers—and perhaps we never will—at last we felt we'd been heard. We felt respected.

A month or two later, Kate Thomson at the ICW called me. The group had been asked to nominate a representative to the governing board of UNAIDS, to be known as the Programme Coordinating Board, or PCB. For the first time in history, as I said earlier, a UN entity would grant full membership privileges to nongovernmental organizations and, in particular, people living with the disease being addressed. We wouldn't be allowed to vote—only governments can do that—but we'd have a seat at the table so we could be recognized, speak, and submit recommendations on behalf of our community.

We'd have our voices heard and considered as equal to all the others on the governing board.

Kate said, "The ICW's decided to nominate you. You studied international relations in college, and speak French. You'll be a good spokeswoman for the cause."

Truth be told, I didn't fully appreciate what was being proposed. I knew roughly what UNAIDS was going to be, as much as anyone did at that point. Certainly, I understood what a governing board was. But the importance of the role did not fully sink in until I found myself a month or so later at a meeting in Venice, Italy, where preliminary discussions were being held on how the PCB's governance mechanism would work.

I'd been to Venice six years before—three years prior to my diagnosis—with an old boyfriend. I'd met him in San Francisco when he was an exchange student from France. I'd been disappointed when he didn't turn out to be as romantic as I'd hoped, not even in such a supremely romantic city.

At the time, we were visiting his brother who lived in Trieste, so we'd made a day trip to La Serenissima. Enamored by the magical floating city, I delighted at every turn. I grinned at the pigeons in the Piazza San Marco. Didier worried he'd step in their droppings and ruin his expensive shoes. I wanted us to cuddle in a gondola and be rowed along the canals. He thought this a contemptible tourist cliché. My own charm as the American girlfriend had clearly begun to wane. We'd broken up soon after. Now, as I walked over the bridges and along the canals, I found myself wondering what my life would've been like if that relationship had endured.

Most likely I would've become a French housewife in pearls and low heels and button-down shirts with simple skirts. I'd have had two or three children, vacationed on the Côte d'Azur, and learned to cook excellent ratatouille. And possibly, would never have contracted HIV, nor wound up on the board of a UN body.

Life is strange. Sometimes awful, sometimes amazing. But never, never dull.

Gathered Around the Round Table

Geneva

Switzerland: Central Europe

Population: 8.5 million

Capital: Bern

A cool draft flowed along white marble floors, up the two-story vaulted ceiling, and back down again. It brushed my face as we walked the seemingly endless trek from the entrance of the International Labor Organization (ILO) toward the back, where the conference rooms were situated. It was only about seventy five degrees out—a typical July day in Geneva—but I was nervous, perspiring under my conservative blue linen suit.

Weeks before, friends who worked in the US government had briefed me for my first meeting of the Programme Coordinating Board of UNAIDS. They'd explained that the room would likely have seating with fixed desks arranged in a circle, like the Security Council we see on television, but on a smaller scale.

Once inside, I took in the space. It seemed oddly dim and it took a moment for my eyes to adjust in the windowless room. Five chairs, at a curved desk with placards reading NGO, for nongovernmental organization. Where my colleagues and I were to sit. To my right was another section with six seats, placarded CCO: Committee of Co-Sponsoring Organizations.

I knew that there was one seat for each acronym in the United Nations alphabet soup: UNICEF, UNDP, UNFPA, UNESCO, WHO, and The World Bank. Beyond them, completing the circle with a seat designated "Chair" were seats marked for Algeria, Australia, Barbados, Bulgaria, Canada, China, Congo, Côte d'Ivoire, France, India, Japan, Mexico, Netherlands, Pakistan, Paraguay, Russia, South Africa, Sweden,

Thailand, Uganda, The United Kingdom and the USA. Ordered alphabetically, the world had been brought together to formalize a program to address the global pandemic.

This would be its first meeting. Although UNAIDS had already been approved for creation by the General Assembly in New York, this would be the first formal gathering. Here, the initial structure would be voted on. Then recruitment and hiring could begin, in advance of the 1996 launch of the program.

UNAIDS was novel on many levels. It was an interagency program, so in addition to the regular delegations from nation states, as all UN entities have, there were also representatives of the co-sponsoring agencies, funds, and programs of UNAIDS. But, unlike any other before it, the UNAIDS PCB also included our five-member delegation of NGOs.

I barely understood what any of this meant. I felt intimidated walking those halls among powerful world leaders. There was no UN funding for our participation, nor should there have been, as it could've been perceived as attempting to sway our input. I was grateful I'd been briefed by friends in the USA before arriving. They wanted to make sure I wouldn't be overwhelmed and feel too nervous to speak up. Still, I don't think anyone can ever be truly prepared for such an overwhelming experience.

I made my way to our delegation's area and found the heavy engraved plaque that said *NGO—North America*. The ICW had nominated me to represent North America, but also to be a voice for all the HIV-positive women around the globe. Sure, no problem. I checked my sleeves to make sure they didn't have any visible sweat stains. Not that I could've done much about them at that point, but I was grateful for the powerful air conditioning.

Taking my place in the somber, cold, too-dim space, I was glad the molded plastic chair had built-in cushions and ample armrests. We'd be here for two days of eight-hour sessions. I picked up the foot-long NGO plaque and practiced standing it up on one edge. This was how I'd signal I wanted to speak. Only then would I be called on and given the floor. When a red light glowed on my microphone box, it was my turn.

I rummaged in the cubby built into the wooden desk, following the coiled mic cord to its white plastic ear cup (probably not the official term). I hung it over my ear and fiddled with the channel knob to the right of the cubby. The six official languages (English, French, Spanish, Arabic, Russian and Chinese) and their corresponding channels were marked so I could listen to the translations. I turned my knob to 1 for English and tucked the ear cup back inside the cubby.

My colleagues were doing much the same as we all tried to calm our nerves with mundane tasks. I found it comforting that Arnaud Marty-Lavauzelle, from France, Mazuwa Banda, from Zambia, Bai Bagasao, from the Philippines, and Luis Gauthier, from Chile, all highly respected in their areas of expertise, looked just as overwhelmed as I felt.

Prior to this arrangement, NGOs had only been allowed to sit in as observers during UN board meetings. Occasionally representatives might have been allowed to speak, but usually not. This was groundbreaking. But more important was that we—the community most directly impacted by the work to be undertaken to reverse the pandemic—were suddenly considered near-peers among the decision makers.

Those first moments waiting there, as other delegates slowly filed in, were surreal. I might've been watching myself in a film, considering how detached I felt. I'd studied international relations, sure, and had always wanted to travel. But after my diagnosis I'd been convinced those options were behind me. Yet here I was on the board of a UN program, just three years later.

As my thoughts darted about in confusion and reverie, a slight Ugandan tapped me on the shoulder. "Hello, how do you do?" he said.

"Oh, hello. I'm well, and you?"

"Very well, thank you. Might I ask a question?"

"Of course," I said, and stood, so we were face to face.

"Yes, well, you see," he murmured, "I was led to believe there might be some individuals living with HIV amongst your delegation, and I was wondering if you could point them out. I wanted to make sure they know how glad I am that they are here. That they will speak for those who cannot be present today."

I smiled and extended a hand. "Martina Clark."

"Miss Clark, it is nice to meet you. Could you tell me who is who?"

"Indeed, I am. I mean *I* am one of those living with HIV."

He stepped back ever so slightly, straightened and stared at me before speaking. "Ah, my sister, *asante sanaa*. Thank you. You are brave. And very white!"

I smiled and we hugged awkwardly.

At that time, his country had the highest rates in Africa, and it was clear from our brief chat that he'd had firsthand experience dealing with the epidemic. For him, like me, that first official meeting of the PCB was more than just a bureaucratic gathering; it was history in the making.

At a subsequent meeting of the PCB, at the headquarters of the World Health Organization later that year, I spoke with one of the senior UNAIDS staff members during the coffee break.

"So, Martina, tell me a little about yourself," he said.

"Well, I live in San Francisco."

"Oh, wow. My wife and I both went to medical school at UCSF!"

"Small world," I said. "That's where I go for my health care. They're fantastic. Their clinic for positive women is amazing."

We smiled and chatted, selected cookies from a long table to eat with our *cafés* as we stood among the other delegates. "So, what else?" I mused. "I guess I can tell you I studied international relations at San Francisco State."

"That's convenient." He smiled.

Later, when the meeting reconvened, it was suggested that UNAIDS consider relocating its headquarters to somewhere less expensive than Switzerland. The United States representative quickly suggested our government might be interested in hosting it.

Up went my placard. And then my hand as, like a schoolgirl, I indicated I wanted to speak.

"With all due respect," I countered, "the United States cannot, must not, host this organization until it changes its laws prohibiting the entry of foreign nationals and nonresidents living with HIV."

The room fell silent. In that moment, it became more evident than ever that it was crucial those of us living with HIV continue to sit at the table. These well-intended officials were zealous to see UNAIDS succeed. Yet they'd still overlooked the basic rights of the people they were supposed to be helping.

"Just as no international conference on AIDS can be held in the US, until the laws change, so too must UNAIDS stay on neutral territory," I added. "At least Switzerland does not forbid us entry."

What resulted next was something only a little short of chaos. Ultimately, one of the governmental officials proposed a massive (and expensive) study to determine where UNAIDS would best be located. Because of the intervention of our five-member delegation, the other members had been forced to look at the actual human rights issues surrounding what they saw mainly as a pandemic.

As of today, UNAIDS remains in Switzerland. The law banning entry of people with HIV remained in place until it was lifted by President Barack Obama. Fourteen years from the day of that meeting passed before the US government corrected that draconian law. Had we not been sitting there, our community might have ended up not having a voice. On that day, we made a meaningful and lasting difference.

Soon after that meeting concluded and I'd left Geneva, I was invited by the director of Policy, Evidence, and Partnership to interview for a full-time job with UNAIDS. Being told one has five years to live had upped my level of 'why the fuck not.' I was thoroughly enjoying my work as an activist and I wanted to do more. But, of course, I also needed a paycheck, so I could cover my bills. My role on the PCB had convinced me UNAIDS was serious about involving HIV-positive people, so I felt I had nothing to lose by applying.

I often joked that they'd only considered hiring me to get me to stop making trouble on the PCB.

I Was On C-SPAN Before It Was Cool
(Okay, It Was Never Cool)

Washington, DC

United States of America: North America
Population: 328.2 million
Capital: Washington, DC

Because of my work on UNAIDS, I got to know Patsy Fleming, a soft-spoken Black woman who served as the AIDS Czar under the Clinton administration. She led the US delegation to the UNAIDS meetings and was an advocate for everyone, domestically and abroad. She also saw the importance of going the extra distance to raise awareness for women, in particular, who were far less visible in the global response to the pandemic.

When the planning was underway for the first ever White House Conference on AIDS, Patsy called me at home. "Hi, Martina. I wanted to touch base with you on the conference and who we're inviting."

"Sure, I'm all ears."

"It will be an all-day event at the Treasury Building with working groups in the morning, then lunch. In the afternoon we'll have a round-table with President Clinton. That part will be covered live on C-SPAN."

"Uh, what? C-Who?"

"C-SPAN. It's a non-profit cable channel that covers government proceedings. I don't think anyone outside of DC watches it, but, it's better than nothing."

"Gotcha."

"Later in the evening," Patsy continued, "there'll be some sort of cocktail event with the First Lady."

"Sounds great."

"We're anticipating three hundred participants, front-line individuals in our domestic work. We'll break you up into nine concurrent workshops for the morning session."

I caught the word *you*, but didn't ask. "Makes sense. What are the groups?"

Papers rustled on her end. "Let's see, we'll have three on research, one on therapeutics and two around prevention. Then one each on substance abuse, housing, services, primary care, international issues, and discrimination."

"Who will you have for the international workshop?" She rattled off a number of names being considered. Some I knew, like Michael Merson and Jonathan Mann—Merson's predecessor who'd notably resigned from his position as creator and director of the Global Programme on AIDS at the WHO citing lack of commitment from the greater UN family. Many others I did not. She added, "I'd like you to be the reporter for the International Workshop."

"I guess you're inviting me, then?" I added in a half-laugh.

"Of course we are, Martina! That's why I want you to be the reporter."

"To take notes, sure, I'd be honored."

"Yes, then report back to the President and other guests during the round table."

"Oh. Wow. Okay, sure."

We had follow up calls as the day neared. On one I shared an anecdote from my then six-year-old nephew, Chris, Adrian's son. "I told my nephew I was going to meet the President. He wants me to ask President Clinton if we could bring the dinosaurs back."

Patsy laughed and promised she'd get right on that.

In early December, I flew to Washington. I'd purchased a red suit for the occasion. Back then I could still walk in heels, so I looked professional. A stark contrast to my preferred jeans and t-shirts.

Early on the morning of Wednesday, December 6th, I met a few people who worked for the United States Agency for International Development, USAID, who'd also be attending the conference, at a coffee shop near the Treasury Building. In particular, I looked for Dr. Jacob Gayle. At that time, he was the Chief of the HIV/AIDS division of USAID. I knew him from my board work at UNAIDS. As a government employee, he was allowed to escort me into the building.

Just before entering, I reached up and gave a hug and kisses on the cheeks to my dear, very tall, friend, Eric Sawyer. We'd first met in Mexico and served together on the board of the GNP+. As I headed inside to advocate, Eric stood outside with a bullhorn, surrounded by a hundred and fifty others from ACT-Up, as they protested the government's lack of work on the issue. Both inside and outside this historic meeting, we each had our role.

Once inside, I joined my working group in a poorly-lit conference room. Many of us sat at a long row of tables. When there weren't enough chairs, others dropped to the floor. I recognized Dr. Michael Merson seated on the floor against the wall, across from me. He was now the Dean of Public Health at Yale. I'd been granted a place at the table because people like him gave us their seats. He'd listened and I appreciated that.

During our two-hour working group, I took copious notes, which I then distilled and shaped into five minutes of remarks over the lunch break. I hoped I'd be able to read my own handwriting. Around one in the afternoon, we were escorted through the Secret Service's underground passageways and into the Cash Room of the Treasury Building, where we took our seats at a U-shaped arrangement of tables, covered with red cloths that matched my suit.

When the President arrived, we all stood and were introduced, one by one. Bill Clinton seemed backlit, as if he glowed, his charisma was so effusive. He shook my hand with both of his. "So great to meet you, Ms…uh…Clark," he said after Patsy whispered my name in his ear and explained who I was and why I was there. He repeated the hand-shaking ritual with each speaker. He then spoke at a podium set just inside the U. Many remarks. Many. One in particular, however, remained with me. Clinton said, "I do not want to wait until every single family has somebody die before we have a good policy." We could certainly have used such leadership at the beginning of the COVID pandemic. Alas, I digress.

Eventually, we nine reporters were invited to give summaries of our respective working groups. Speaking last, I first addressed diversity.

"Thank you. Mr. President. We live in a global community. Most people in this country are descended from somewhere else. The faces of AIDS, both in this country and abroad, clearly reflect this diversity. We at this table who are positive are but a handful of the eighteen million people worldwide who are living with HIV."

Using current events—sending 20,000 troops to Bosnia—to bring statistics to life, I explained that by conservative estimates, at least that many would die of AIDS by the end of the following week. I then shifted to the fact that the face of the disease was rapidly becoming female.

"In many areas, more than sixteen percent of all new infections are occurring in young women between the ages of fifteen and twenty-four years old. Worldwide, this epidemic is overwhelmingly spread through heterosexual contact, and men and women of all sexual orientations from all cultures continue to become infected. The epidemic affects individuals in their most productive years. It is a family issue. Who will give birth to the children? Who will care for the orphans? Who will raise the food so that countries can eat, survive and not become dependent on the United States in future years?" I asked.

Knowing that compliments are always worth slipping in, I congratulated the President and his administration on having taken a much stronger stance, and a global role, in fighting the pandemic. I then criticized his travel restrictions.

"We cannot isolate the United States. HIV has already successfully penetrated every border of every nation. Our current immigration policy will do absolutely nothing to decrease the spread of AIDS. It only increases the stigma, fear, denial and discrimination already so rampant in this pandemic." The other speakers and the audience—several hundred people sitting in rows of chairs, facing us—applauded. Encouraging the administration to continue, and expand, its efforts to mitigate the pandemic, I added, "We must share our advances with other nations so that all people, not just the privileged few living in the northern hemisphere, can live longer, more productive lives."

As we navigate the current COVID-19 crisis, these same issues have resurfaced—indeed, they never went away. They need to be addressed, yet again. Still.

Before sitting down, after concluding my remarks, I said, "And finally, if I may, I would like to invite all of the HIV-positive people in this room, who so wish, to stand up and show the true diversity and reality of this epidemic."

To quote David W. Dunlap's December 7, 1995 piece in *The New York Times*, "The immediacy of [these speakers'] concerns became clear when Martina Clark...asked for a show of people in the room who had HIV. More than forty stood up." The President, clearly moved, applauded our courage.

An hour later, the participants joined a cocktail reception at the Renwick Gallery of Art—a branch of the Smithsonian—just steps from the White House. It was co-hosted by the White House Office of National AIDS Policy and The David Geffen Foundation. As we entered, we were all given sterling silver bracelets with ribbons etched into the ends, symbolizing the red ribbons now emblematic of the fight against AIDS. Inside, the date and name of the conference were engraved. I still have the bracelet, decades later, although I've never actually worn it.

Once inside, after enough time had passed for everyone to have a drink and a requisite cube of cheese, then-First Lady Hillary Clinton addressed the crowd. I found her remarks more focused, poignant, and sincere than those her husband had delivered earlier.

Twenty minutes or so after her speech, Patsy Fleming, who'd organized the day's events, came up to me and said, "I want you to meet someone." She tugged me over to Hillary Clinton, and introduced us.

"Martina, nice to meet you. I appreciated your remarks today at the round-table," Mrs. Clinton said warmly.

"Thank you." I shook her hand. "I think you may have met a friend of mine once. At the Fourth World Conference on Women, in Beijing."

Despite having just met me, having no idea I'd make that comment, and without skipping a beat, she replied, "Cindy? Of course! She's also with the ICW, I believe. She's lovely."

Cindy was one of many extraordinary women with HIV I'd met by that point in my life and she'd represented our community at the Beijing event.

The then-First Lady and I chatted for a few more minutes, until a staffer pulled her away to meet other participants. I was floored by her acuity. It was as if she had some sort of supersonic search engine in her brain. I was seriously impressed.

"Oh, Patsy, thank you so much for introducing me to her. She seems amazing."

"She is," Patsy said as she gave me a quick hug. "Oh, before I forget, I asked the President about the dinosaurs."

Chuckling, I said, "You did not!"

"I did. He said to tell your nephew that we couldn't bring the dinosaurs back because they'd just make a mess of traffic, stepping on all the cars and trucks."

We both smiled, laughed, and hugged again. At the end of that very long day, I wasn't sure how much impact our interventions would make, but at least I had a great story for my nephew next time we spoke. Exhausted, I eventually returned to my hotel room and slept soundly. They next day I would head to East Africa, for the IX Annual International Conference on AIDS and STDs in Africa, in Kampala, the capital of Uganda.

CHAPTER 4

transitioning toward a sense of belonging

Stars, Drifting into Place

Tororo

Uganda: East Africa
Population: 44.3 million
Capital: Kampala

"Martina, you awake?" Julie whispered from the doorway of the hut.

With a full bladder, and after the heaving pounding of the storm just passed, I was very much awake. Only lying still, waiting my turn to pee. I was staying with several Ugandan women just outside of Tororo in the eastern part of the country.

On the drive from the airport, I'd been struck by the mile after mile of rows and rows of coffins for sale. They were upright, unopened portals to the netherworld, lining the roadside.

The conference center, a large complex with 1970s wood paneling, was riddled with bullet holes. Beams of light seeped through the walls like eyes from another time. They reminded me of the civil unrest that now competed with the battle against AIDS. At that time, Uganda had the highest rate of infection per capita in the world.

During this conference I met doctors, researchers, activists and other HIV-positive individuals from around the continent. David from Zambia, Lynde from Zimbabwe, Stephen, a soldier from Uganda, the two Dorothys from Kenya, Milly from Malawi. They were woven into my own global tapestry, friends who would shape my future and reappear in years to come.

Noerine Kaleeba, who had started the first AIDS service organization in Africa, TASO, had arranged for me to stay an additional few days afterward to get to know some of the local women and understand their needs. "Martina, I want you to see how we live and spend time with your positive sisters. Listen to their stories. Learn from them."

She saw that my trajectory was pointing toward an international position and wanted to be sure I would consider their concerns. What she might not have known was how much they would help me.

"Yes, I'm awake, but I was waiting," I said now to Julie.

"Waiting for what?"

"You know, for you to finish so I wouldn't interrupt. In case you or any of the others were having a pee."

She laughed. "My dear, if you have to, you have to. Plus, it is the middle of the night, nobody will see. But you must come outside now. We're all out here."

"Why?"

"To see the stars in the grass," she said. "Don't forget your shoes. You wouldn't want to step on a snake."

Confused, I sat up and felt for my shoes, shaking them out, in case any creepy-crawlies had taken up residence. Although my eyes had adjusted to the dim, I was disoriented by the circular shape of the mud-walled house. I was, however, impressed that despite the heavy rain that just passed, not a drop had seeped through the thatch. I shuffled toward the wooden door, stepping on the backs of my sneakers as my toes wiggled forward to secure my feet. The pungent scent of wet earth filled my nose with a damp freshness as I stepped outside.

Before joining the others a short distance away, I relieved myself on the other side of the hut in relative privacy. During the day, everyone used the toilet in the nearby house where the elders lived. At night, nature was quieter, closer, and more convenient.

"Sister, look," Julie said, as she pointed east toward the border with Kenya, where the storm was now letting loose with full force. Bolts of lightning appeared intermittently in the distance like stitches holding together the earth and sky. Directly above us, the clouds were scudding past to reveal a moonless sky dense with stars. A slab of glistening marble with glints of mica and scarves of galaxies streaming above.

Down at our feet, and for at least the length of a football field all around us, fireflies rose out of the damp ground en masse. Indeed, it did appear as if some of the night stars had dropped from the sky and were now drifting back up into place.

I stood motionless in awe, listening to thunder in the distance and the muffled rustling of the grass. As the fireflies—and who knows what else—resumed life, post-rainfall. Despite this likely being a common occurrence, my Ugandan sisters clearly enjoyed nature's performance as much as I did. The women smiled, pointing at constellations, speaking softly in the local dialect. They spoke English, Swahili and Luganda, all of which had been used at the conference, but this was a language I'd only heard amongst them.

Eventually we returned to our cots. But now, all fully awake, we chatted about life and love and the reality of living with HIV as a woman. At some point I brought up dating. All of them happened to be widows who, most likely, had been infected by their husbands. But, as is often the case, they'd been blamed for bringing the virus into their families when their babies had been born HIV-infected. Some children died within a year or two.

"Me? I am so happy to be single at long last," Julie said. "Financially, things are more difficult, but emotionally, I finally feel free."

"Me too, me too," added another woman, then another.

They spoke quickly, one cutting off the next, about how their marriages were expected—not necessarily desired—and at times abusive, so when their husbands had died, they were relieved of the duty to serve and obey them. Being widowed allowed them a chance to reclaim their power. Being widowed by AIDS gave them a chance to speak their truths and become activists. Like so many of us diagnosed in those earlier years, we felt we had nothing to lose and everything to gain—if not for ourselves, then at least for future generations.

"It is so much easier because now nobody expects me to be someone's wife," one woman said. "I no longer belong to anyone."

Someone else said, "Because we are widowed and everyone knows it is from AIDS, we get to just be alone for the first time as adults, and to only look after our children. It is hard but, somehow, easier."

Another added, "Sex got me into this problem, so honestly, that is the last thing on earth I want now. I want freedom, not more illness. Not more death."

It was surprising to hear them speak so candidly, but also understandable. Hearing them vocalize their feelings about being single afforded me a deep sense of comfort and relief. When I had begun to navigate my own new reality, a few surprises removed some of the societal pressures in my life as well.

People assumed, for example, that now I would never have children. Effective mother-to-child prevention of HIV was not yet available. In North America, a positive woman choosing to get pregnant was tantamount to a murderess in the eyes of many. Once, soon after my diagnosis, a well-intentioned friend brought up the subject as we cleaned up after a meal.

"So, I just want you to know that if anything happens and you have a baby," she said, drying a serving platter, "that I'll help. I mean, I assume you'll do everything to avoid that, but just in case it happens, I will step in."

"And what exactly does that mean?" I asked, stacking glasses in the top rack of the dishwasher.

"I'll raise the baby for you, you know, if you won't be able to. If you die."

I don't remember my answer. I think I *tried* to look appreciative, knowing that by these comments she meant only love and kindness. And was unaware of how much it hurt to be reminded I was now considered unfit to bear children.

And so, like so many others diagnosed in those earlier years, I mourned my presumed loss of the experience of motherhood.

Next on that list was the notion of marriage. Who would ever want me—a broken model—when they could find someone "healthy" who could give them children? I was born in an era when marrying a reasonably good man was the prime measurement of a woman's success. At the time of diagnosis, however, having been given a life expectancy of about five years, I was pretty sure that knocked me out of the running for anything even vaguely resembling a long-term relationship.

In some strange way, though, those "losses" were not entirely awful. On many levels, like the women in Uganda, I felt liberated by no longer being expected to fulfill those roles imposed by society. Dating's complicated in the best of situations. Dating with HIV, I suspected, would be far more difficult to navigate, so I gladly put that low on my wish list. If science came up with a cure, or a way to keep me alive longer, and either children or marriage happened… well, then I'd figure it out. It was cathartic to reorder my priorities.

I found an inner strength I hadn't known I even possessed. A deep peace and purpose in the rewards of the activism and work that was consuming more and more of my time. Like some students who forgo relationships to focus on their studies, I too felt driven to concentrate my energy on fighting. I'd found support and solidarity in the new sisterhood I'd been welcomed into. Certainly not a group I'd sought to join, but once I had, they became my pillars of strength.

Just like those women that night in Uganda, all I was expected to do now was fight to stay alive. With each passing year, I threw myself more fully into activism, and learned to be happy with my self. Fully at ease in my own company, while always trying to stay one step ahead of the Reaper.

Honestly, for the time being, that was enough.

My Return to Reality

San Francisco, California

Just before Christmas, I returned home. The trip to East Africa had come on the heels of the White House Conference on AIDS and I was spent. What I most needed was rest, and a chance to digest all I'd experienced in those few weeks.

What I came home to, however, broke me.

Three and a half years post-diagnosis, I'd already lost so many acquaintances to AIDS: neighbors, colleagues, friends of friends, and, of course, people I'd met through my own journey. There were too many deaths to count. But they weren't *my people.* They weren't the people I hung out with on my free time. They weren't my closest friends from my life pre-HIV.

Carlos was. And he died while I was in Uganda.

Indeed, Carlos was the first to test positive in my immediate friend group. He was handsome, funny, gregarious, and hosted fabulous parties. He didn't want to talk about the virus, not even after my diagnosis, but we had a silent bond. We were in this together.

As I set down my luggage, I listened to my answering machine. An unsteady voice told me Carlos had passed. It took me several listens to grasp what I'd heard, and recognize the grief-stricken voice of our mutual friend, Irma.

A day later—maybe two, I can't recall—I attended his funeral, in the Castro district. Most Holy Redeemer was one of the few churches that welcomed the LGBTQ community and embraced HIV-positive people.

My worlds had collided. I cried for days. Until my grief shifted to anger. Then I got back up and continued to fight for our rights, for my life.

A Misfit in Search of Community

Could've Been Anywhere, A Long Time Ago

I remember leaning against my mother on a warm summer day somewhere in the Pacific Northwest during one of our few family vacations. Her ample weight made her feel like a giant pillow as I rested my four-year-old self against her. My eldest sister, Alexandria—eight years my senior—and my brother Christopher—six years my senior—were both brunettes. Alexandria was—still is—short, and Chris was already taller than his sisters. Adrian, my second sister with whom I shared a room for much of my childhood, was seven years older and, like me, blond, though, ultimately, several inches taller. All of us were blue-eyed like our parents.

Mama and I were sitting on a wooden bench twenty yards from a still lake, woods all around. I watched as my older siblings, probably ten to twelve years old at the time, boarded a seaplane. It taxied backward, then lifted off the water into the sky. Or maybe it turned and then took off; I don't really know how seaplanes work even now. I just recall I was too young and maybe scared to join the flight, so my mother and I waited for their return.

"Look at them, Mama, they're up over the water!"

"Yes, they are."

We sat in silence for a few moments until she added, "If it weren't for you, *I* could be having fun, too."

Shame, like death, was a familiar emotion. I'd been reminded regularly, as we kids all were, that we were the cause of our mother's misery. She should never have had children. She was talented and extremely intelligent, but maternal she was not. She managed as best she could, but never developed a filter for voicing how much she resented having to care for us. Each child heard a different version of *how* we had ruined her life, but we all got one.

"You were an accident," I was told as a young child, which didn't seem much of a surprise given the six years between me and my brother, Chris. I carried that myth for more than fifty years: That by accidentally being born, I'd been the final blow to my mother's dreams. Her chance at happiness. I kept her tethered that much longer.

"Papa, what was I like as a baby?" I often asked.

"You were an angel sent from heaven. I was always afraid we'd lose you," he consistently answered.

I'd never understood his comments as, to the best of my knowledge, I was not sickly. Much later, the year I turned fifty, our family had been celebrating the college graduation of Genevieve, my eldest niece. Sandy—one of my father's closest friends—pulled two of us aside for a private chat.

"Martina. Adrian. If *I* don't tell you, you'll never know. Your parents plan to take this to their graves," Sandy told us. "You have another brother."

"What?" Adrian's eyes widened.

"I knew it!" I blurted out.

It is my understanding that during gestation, due to a phenomenon known as fetal micro-chimerism, a trace of the baby's DNA can remain in the mother's blood. The next baby can then actually acquire a trace of that baby's DNA. I'd always believed there'd been another between me and my oldest brother. My suspicions were confirmed.

In the early 1960s we lived in a municipality in New Mexico so small I don't even know how to label it. The population of Vanadium is currently estimated to be about two thousand souls. Apparently it's grown. A lot. My father worked for the Kennecott Mining Company at the Santa Rita mine across the street.

In 1963, my mother gave birth to my second brother at Mimbres Memorial Hospital in Deming—where I was born one year and two weeks later—an hour south of Vanadium. He was healthy, fair skinned and blue-eyed like the rest of us. But for reasons we'll never fully understand, my parents put him up for adoption.

When she returned home without a baby, apparently she told the few people who knew of her pregnancy—mostly neighbors—that the newborn had died. She never told any of our extended family she was pregnant. My siblings were then five, six, and seven, and only remember her being pregnant for a long time, likely merging the two back-to-back pregnancies in their minds. We had never once heard any utterance of his existence. Not one word.

Within a few hours of Sandy's revelation, my tall namesake niece, Stretch Martina, as I like to call her, located our long-lost brother on an adoption database. The rest of this story is not yet ripe for the telling, but suffice it to say that finding an additional awesome brother was the greatest gift of my fiftieth year. He was the last of my mother's children to be with her before she died.

My father later shared that he was surprised when my mother wanted to be intimate with him again, after my brother's birth, and that I had been a sort of conciliatory baby. His odd comment about being afraid they'd lose me now made sense. He probably feared she'd give me away, as well. I was supposed to heal their fractured marriage, I suppose. Perhaps she did want me, then, but for the wrong reasons. I'll never know. The result of her mixed messages, however, is that I never really felt wanted, or that I belonged. Sometimes Mama left me at home alone when she'd take the other kids to school. Though I was not old enough for kindergarten, I'd make my way down the brick stairs to find an empty house. Other times she'd leave me in the bath and go to another room. When the leaky drain would suck out the last of the water, I'd sit, shivering. Waiting for someone to help me out because I was too small to climb over the edge and out of the tub.

So later, when people *did* like me or seem to want me around, I didn't trust it, or them. I still don't, entirely. The upside of this, however, is that I've always felt at ease traveling or in situations where being different or "other" is the norm. Those were the times and places I felt most at home because belonging was not expected. Making my way quietly through life without drawing attention was the modus operandi that most closely suited my soul.

When I learned I had HIV, although I clearly would have rather *not* worn that scarlet H, there was finally a legitimate reason for people not to like me. So much stigma still surrounded it then that it was common for people who had it to be shunned. Friends disappeared from my life suddenly. Worse, they occasionally pulled away from me physically, in disgust, on hearing the news. The stigma remains today, though it's less palpable. But since feeling I'd never belonged was my normal, the added burden didn't perturb me as much as it might have others. Now, at least, it just felt easier to explain.

Although I haven't thought much about that stigma in recent years, as I write this and the world is currently in the midst of the COVID-19 pandemic, some of these memories are resurging. I am reminded that as humans, we often fear the person with the virus, rather than the virus itself. We're quick to blame individuals, yet don't always do our part to protect ourselves. With HIV, many people resisted—and still resist—using condoms. Today, people resist wearing a mask. In February 2021, Dr. Tom Frieden, a former director of the CDC, tweeted, *Nobody has a right to infect other people avoidably. If you don't want to wear a mask, don't get near other people indoors.* The obstinance of humans being willing to risk their lives for preventable diseases remains mindboggling. By now, we should all know better. Dr. Frieden's words should not be needed. Science should be our guide.

After learning of my new reality in 1992, I was quickly encouraged by a case worker to join a support group, of others living with the virus. It was good to meet other HIV-positive women because I, like so many others, had not previously been aware of them. (They are still less visible in this country.)

But soon I felt I didn't quite belong there, either.

I wasn't sick, nor did I have any co-factors, like hemophilia or addiction. It was as if I only *sort of* had HIV, like sitting in the uppermost section of arena, watching events unfold down below from a great distance.

From those first support group meetings to my involvement with WORLD, Rebecca Denison, whom I met through an introduction from my case worker, Penny Chernow, became a role model for me. Following her own HIV-diagnosis, Rebecca started WORLD (Women Organized to Respond to Life-threatening Disease) with some of her HIV-positive peers to provide support to positive women in the San Francisco Bay Area. The organization started in Rebecca's living room in Oakland,

California in 1991. Starting just with holding retreats and establishing a newsletter, WORLD has grown to support women in 87 countries. Rebecca's pioneering work and early vision of connecting positive women world-wide has helped the global response to the pandemic in myriad ways. She remains one of my inspirations to this day.

Working with WORLD gave me the chance to interact with many women with HIV, all over the planet—for which I was grateful. My role was to help build an organization and community with them, so they could in turn support one another. For example, in San Francisco women advocated early on for childcare for research participants and in health care facilities for people with HIV. In New York City, even as I write this in 2021, there is no clinic devoted specifically to the care of women with HIV. Yet, again, I still feel like an outsider.

At Rebecca's suggestion I became more involved as an activist. The activism in San Francisco in the early 1990s was led overwhelmingly by gay men, which made sense, considering the devastating impact of the pandemic on the gay community, but theirs was a place I also didn't fit in. Frequent comments from male activists, like "It is entirely up to us in the gay community to fight this, because it is our issue" made me feel like I was not a part of that struggle.

In meetings with gay—mostly male—activists in San Francisco in those early days, I would raise concerns about women living with HIV, but these often fell on deaf ears.

As I turned toward international activism, I began to feel more included. Trying to fight the bigger fight made sense, particularly since the epidemic outside of San Francisco and New York remains overwhelmingly a heterosexual one. Out in the wider world, my being a straight woman was no longer an oddity.

By the time that activism led me to work within the United Nations, I had finally found my tribe. These were people also trying to make the world a better place. They were passionate about global issues and the big picture as much as the individual struggles.

One of my early UNAIDS colleagues, Monica Wernette, called us the FuhKaWee tribe, as in "Where the fuck are we?" We all seemed to have the common trait of going forth into the unknown with a full heart and very little idea of how we were going to pull off whatever our given assignment was.

Halfway around the globe, sitting at a desk in Geneva, I at last felt like I had found a place where I belonged. One where I could be of use, right alongside all the other misfits that make up the forces for change we know as international civil servants.

At long last, I felt I'd come home.

Disclaimer: I'm A Jerk

Ubiquitously, Often

In those early years, and probably still today, I'm pretty sure I was an asshole to a lot of people. And for that, I apologize. I was confused. Overwhelmed. I felt somehow responsible for everyone's pain yet barely able to recognize my own. Trying to sort out a combination of already being a jerk as a twentysomething who thought she knew everything; fearing I was going to die young; then being catapulted into the limelight, was beyond dizzying. I would alternate from feeling on top of the world one minute to thinking the pain in my foot was going to lead to amputation within hours.

When I find myself in complete doubt, I often go into fake-it mode, in which I overcompensate my know-it-all-ness to convince myself I am still one step ahead of the virus. Or at least I did then.

I hope I've mellowed over the years. Become more humble. I no longer fear I'll be dead in a matter of days because we—I—now know the science and we—I—have medications to boost my immune system, and I'm able to sort things out more clearly.

To all the people I've ignored, avoided, or hurt along the way, I'm sorry.

CHAPTER 5

at your [civil] service

Joining My UN Tribe

Geneva, Switzerland

n March, 1996, I accepted a full-time position with UNAIDS as the NGO Liaison. I often say they offered me the job because I was becoming too vocal as a board member, but I'd like to think they actually did it because they thought I was valuable. The truth is probably somewhere in between.

Initially I stayed in an efficiency apartment in downtown Geneva. 'Efficiency' meant it had a kitchenette with a microwave and a doll-house-sized fridge. It was efficient, as long as you didn't want to eat much, or have friends over. The view was of other buildings, none that registered enough for a memory.

Once outside my building, smells of grilled lamb and beef from the many Middle Eastern restaurants always made me hungry. I'd walk past the sex workers on their corners, greeting them as I emerged onto the main street, where there seemed to be more sunlight. I'd take a bus up to the campus of the World Health Organization. Although I'd visited the city before, the view from the bus of Lake Geneva, with its famous fountain jetting water into the air for no apparent reason, always made me smile.

The city lies in a valley, surrounded by mountains. The Jura, on one side, are the Alpine foreland, geologic cousins to the Alps beyond. On a clear day, Mont Blanc juts above the other peaks, majestic and iconic. I will not lie, however. For several months I mistook it for the Matterhorn. I thought I was looking at the same mountain as the Toblerone logo on their triangular chocolate boxes. Chocolate cannot replace an atlas.

As a city, Geneva is fairly small, with only about two hundred thousand residents. Because of a diverse semitransient population, due partly to the United Nations organizations and international headquarters of various banks, however, it is extraordinarily cosmopolitan. And clean. Hanging baskets of flowers line the major streets and are changed regularly before the flora wilts. They joke that flights are never delayed in Geneva because they have machines to catch the snow before it lands. While that's not (entirely) true, planes, trains, and buses run on schedule, and tardiness is frowned upon. Even the seedier neighborhoods are tidy in their debauchery. UN personnel complain Geneva is boring, but I find it to be a fascinating crossroads of cultures, unparalleled for people-watching.

Following the twenty minute bus ride up to the Avenue Appia, past the main UN Office, then the International Red Cross, and the International Labor Organization, we at last pulled in front of the World Health Organization. It's a long modular block of windowed offices, allowing staff to enjoy glimpses of nature from many vantage points. On my first day of work on that campus, I was giddy.

In elementary school, I somehow fell into a tradition of wearing brown on the first day of school each year. In keeping with that, I wore a brown pants suit with a light blue blouse. And, much like the first day of a new school year, I was nervous about what was to come, but also thrilled with my new adventure. At thirty-two, I was the first openly HIV-positive employee of UNAIDS. Some staff simply transitioned over from the now defunct Global Programme, but many of us were new and, like me, non-traditional picks. The GPA had been overwhelmingly staffed by medical doctors, predominately white, European, and male. Our staff was much more diverse geographically, and also represented more of those impacted by the pandemic, so as to better address the issue holistically.

In my first months at UNAIDS, I worked long hours—ten to twelve-hour days, sometimes more—as we began configuring this new worldwide response. My primary job was to be the link between all NGOs working on AIDS around the world and the United Nations system. It was an impossible job for one, but I was not deterred. Additionally, I wore down the senior management with my insistence we institute an HIV in the Workplace program to educate our own staff.

"But we're UNAIDS, we don't need that," they'd say.

"No. We're UNAIDS, we *absolutely* need this," I would answer. "We may be a part of a huge bureaucracy, but at the end of the day, we're still made up of individuals. We come to this work with very different life experiences and beliefs."

It seemed irresponsible to employ more and more very smart folks each month who went home as representatives of the program but weren't afforded training to learn everything they could about the disease. How dare we? Granted, many already knew a tremendous amount. But even among those who knew the most, that information was often very specific or limited to a narrow aspect, such as the biochemistry of the virus or the science of creating and testing possible drugs and vaccines. It didn't guarantee that they, or any other member, would feel a hundred percent comfortable educating even their own children about how to avoid infection.

Upon joining the staff, I had to check in with our in-house medical services, to be cleared for a fixed-term contract. Note that this was not a clinic somewhere down the road, nor a local hospital, but the internal clinic tasked to support UNAIDS. Our offices were hosted in the complex of the World Health Organization—the organization responsible for issuing "universal" precautions medical personnel everywhere should follow.

When the clinician (a doctor, if I recall correctly, but certainly at least an RN) drew my blood, she didn't wear gloves. Sometimes medical professionals choose not to because they can't feel what they're doing through the latex, or because they know there's treatment in case of an accidental needle stick to minimize the risk of infection. But, really . . .

"So, you're not wearing gloves," I said.

"No, why do you ask?"

Her response left me speechless. Finally I added, "Well, I guess because where I'm from, everyone wears gloves, so I'm surprised."

"Oh. And where are you from, exactly?"

"San Francisco, in California. The US, you know."

"Oh, well, that explains it." She smiled.

I blinked at her, confused.

"Everyone there has AIDS," she said. "This is Switzerland. We don't worry about that here."

Somehow I managed to bite my tongue.

When I reported this encounter to my colleagues, they shook their heads. They'd already advised me not to disclose my status on any paperwork with medical services. As the first openly positive recruit, they weren't sure if I'd make it through. I was the guinea pig.

I'd agreed to keep mum, but I was stunned.

As it turned out, I *was* hired, on a two-year contract, and it became abundantly clear we had an enormous amount of work to do in-house. If our own professionals were lackadaisical about the epidemic, how could we expect better beyond the borders of tidy Switzerland?

We needed to bring people in line with reality. We needed condoms made available in the workplace, so they'd seem commonplace. That would help people realize practicing safer sex was in no way related to promiscuity. When children are educated early, they tend to delay their first experience and employ safer practices. It also holds true that the more educated adults are about protecting themselves—and the less we stigmatize it—the more likely they are to know their status through testing and, in turn, make informed decisions.

Early on, I did battle with one human resources manager, who told me, "You were only hired because they feel sorry for you." He claimed I wasn't qualified. That I only filled a diversity quota so they could say they had someone with HIV on staff.

In my insistence on breaking down the stigma within the walls of UNAIDS, and beginning to implement a workplace program, I held a workshop with senior management to explore the various ways they would work with colleagues living with HIV.

At that half-day workshop, in an as-yet-unfurnished office, as we perched in a circle on hard steel chairs, I felt exposed without a table or desk to hide behind. I asked that same senior HR manager if he would attend an event hosted by people living with HIV, if invited.

"Sure. I'd go. But, obviously, I wouldn't eat any food they'd prepared, or anything like that," he said.

As I fumed, the others chuckled a low, embarrassed laugh. Nobody called him out, though. The only good side of that day was that senior management had seen my point. Slowly but surely, we began half-day workshops, to ensure everyone had not just a minimum basic knowledge about the virus, but also knew how to begin breaking down the discrimination surrounding the disease.

That manager's inappropriate comments were far from an isolated incident. Actually, they were sadly representative of the attitudes of some early UNAIDS employees. Most were kind and open to working with positive colleagues, but some were not. I'll never know if they were afraid because of past experiences or simply lacked empathy in general. By then I knew my official job was not nearly as important as my unofficial one, which was to keep the organization itself honest. To be a daily reminder that people living with HIV are to be respected and treated as equals.

Our workplace housed a microcosm of humanity. We needed to model what we were trying to impose on the world. If we were going forth to make the planet a better, safer place for people living with, impacted by, or at risk of contracting HIV, the least we could do was to behave with respect and sensitivity among our peers.

One night I woke with a phrase in my head that I jotted down on a piece of paper next to my bed before returning to sleep. The next day I typed and printed it out, then posted it boldly above my desk.

Be the model, not the judge.

A few other colleagues rallied to the cause because they too had been directly affected by the pandemic. Noerine Kaleeba and Kim Ali and, later, Sinead Ryan, joined me in lobbying for in-house learning. Noerine and Kim knew people who were living with or had died from AIDS.

Sinead shared my office. I'm sure she was forever changed by surviving the daily rants of a frustrated woman living with HIV.

Laissez Passer: The Diplomatic Lane

Here, There, and Everywhere

When people muse about what they would take along if their home caught fire, my first thought is my cat and my passports. My cat is my boss. My passports are my most prized inanimate possessions. When joining UNAIDS earned me the privilege of a United Nations Laissez Passer—a diplomatic passport—I was ecstatic. Within weeks, I began collecting stamps in my precious light blue authorization.

In just my first seven months on the job, I traveled to at least eight countries on four continents. I actually lost count. After arriving in Geneva in mid-March, I went to Cyprus in April. Easy. My next trip was to Vancouver, Canada, for the XI International AIDS Conference in early July. Lovely. I had a chance to visit my eldest sister, Alexandria, who—at the time—lived on Whidbey Island in Washington state, just a few hours south. In late July I traveled to India for three weeks. Whew. Ten days later, Colombia, then immediately on to Venezuela, returning to Geneva in late September. Ouf. Three weeks later, I traveled to Botswana, then Malawi. Where the fuck am I?

Sadly, for my wanderlusting soul, much of that time was spent in conference rooms. I've been to many countries and sat in a lot of chairs in nondescript venues. Those first months were a blur and many of the details remain fuzzy but there were, of course, memorable moments.

In Cyprus, we met at a simple hotel near the beach in Larnaca. While, I imagined, its other guests were heading out for a day of sea, surf, and sun, I found my way to the UNICEF-hosted meeting on the impact of HIV on sexual exploitation of children in the Middle East. I was there to elaborate as needed. The other delegates, aside from the UNICEF personnel, were NGO or government health officials from half a dozen countries. Jordan, Egypt, Iran, and, more I can't recall.

"Good morning, I'm Martina Clark from UNAIDS, Geneva."

"Welcome! Are you an intern? You're so...young," asked the meeting chair.

As we sat around the large heavy mahogany table, there was no refreshing breeze from the Mediterranean. There were no aquatic birds swooping past. There were no windows in that basement room. When discussing punishment for sexual assault of children, one delegate said, "We imposed a law that a man's hand shall be cut off if he rapes a child. Unfortunately, the perpetrators generally just tell the children to not tell anyone, so no amputations will occur. The children fear the men, so they keep quiet."

After I asked the group about the infection rates in their countries, the Iranian Minister of Health said, "We don't have an HIV pandemic in Iran, so we don't have this concern."

Later, at a coffee break, he pulled me aside to say, "Actually, we have a huge problem, but I am not allowed to say that officially. I'd love to chat more about it more, off the record, of course."

In the evenings I sat on my balcony and watched at the waves lap at the shore, trying to clear my mind of the horrific images conjured up by the day's deliberations.

As would become the norm on most work trips, before leaving that country I made a courtesy call on its national AIDS program. A UN vehicle picked me up for the drive to Nicosia, the capitol. I only recall noticing that the vegetation along the highway lacked vibrancy. At the end of my meeting with the Cypriote program manager, a tall, prim doctor with glasses, hair worn in a bun, she said she had one last question.

"Miss Clark, I need to exchange a shipment of condoms the WHO sent us."

"Of course. I can certainly relay the request. Did they arrive damaged?"

"Oh no, not at all. They are perfectly fine, and I've stored them properly, so they can be used elsewhere."

"Okay?"

"You see, they're too small."

"Oh." I felt my eyes widen.

"What can I say? We're big!"

I promised her I would not forget her request. Ever.

In Vancouver, at the International XI AIDS Conference in July, UNAIDS was the new kid on the block. In a sleek modern conference center with stunning views over the Pacific on one side, and the city I'd never have time to visit on the other, everyone wanted something from us. From me. They wanted a job. Funding for their work. Introductions to the senior directors. Access to the new medications that were announced at that same conference. I wanted to hide.

In India, a few weeks later, I met with the national officials in Delhi. Outside an office without A/C, despite the oppressive heat, monkeys played in the trees beyond the open windows.

"Let us be practical," said the director. "We have more than a billion people. If we lose one million to AIDS..." He shrugged.

On that trip I visited Delhi, Pune, Mumbai, and Kolkata, before returning to Delhi as my last stop. On the legs of the trip to Kolkata and Pune, I travelled with the UNAIDS Country Programme Advisor from neighboring Bangladesh, Dr. Lisa Messersmith, a medical anthropologist and public health specialist. While the heat in Delhi had been horrendous, the weather in Kolkata was worse. The combination of the heat and humidity along with the smog felt like we could have been swimming in bong water, without the high. I was, nonetheless, delighted to visit the city. The influence of the British Empire remained prominent with colonial buildings and manicured gardens peeping through unexpectedly, and often, between the gray, brown, and ocher tones of the smog.

We'd requested a meeting with Mother Teresa, who was reportedly in town that week. We wanted to discuss her reluctance to provide pain medicines to hospice patients. It would not be a simple conversation, but we also doubted we'd actually get to meet. That week, we visited

Sonagachi—the red-light district, HIV-dedicated medical facilities, and NGOs, as well as the British Council, which worked to provide funding and educational program for work on AIDS.

By the time we'd return to our hotels in the evenings, we were struggling to process the difficulties of mounting a pandemic response amid so much abject poverty. The splendid smells of local food mixed with the round-the-clock cacophony of an overcrowded city. The opulence of British Council offices was stark against the dark labyrinths of unadorned brothels in Sonagachi. Between the spicy food and the sensory overload, my sleep was restless.

One morning over breakfast, Lisa and I were alerted that our meeting had been confirmed. We left immediately for Mother House, the headquarters of the Missionaries of Charity. After a taxi ride through narrow crowded back streets, we were escorted to the second floor of the unadorned building. As we fidgeted on a wooden bench in an outdoor hallway, we took in the courtyard below. Nuns and volunteers moved through the space quietly, but with obvious purpose.

About thirty minutes later, an elderly nun approached and stretched out her arm. "My business card," she said.

Mother Teresa was very, very, short. In her iconic white robes with three light blue stripes edging the hem, she said, "Let me first offer you my blessing." We bowed. With her unexpectedly strong hands on our heads, as she recited a prayer, it felt as if an electrical shock ran through me. When she removed her hands, we all straightened. She said, "I understand you'd like to talk about AIDS."

Overwhelmed, I never managed to explicitly raise the importance of easing the pain of the dying with medication. I did, however, suggest that UNAIDS would be happy to partner with her organization to procure the recently-announced antivirals as they became available, as well as drugs for pain or other related issues. To this day, I periodically take out her 'business card' and reread it:

The fruit of SILENCE is Prayer
The fruit of PRAYER is Faith
The fruit of FAITH is Love
The fruit of LOVE is Service
The fruit of SERVICE is Peace

-Mother Teresa

I remain in disagreement with some of her beliefs on letting God alone heal one's pain, but her resolve, grounding in love, and dedication to service of others, inspires me still.

Following the other legs of my trip, I returned to Delhi for a debriefing with our national program coordinator, Patrick Brenny, who'd invited me to stay my last few days at his home with his wife, Mei Zegers, and their children. Exhausted, I thanked him and accepted, saying I looked forward to a chance to unwind. The day before my departure, he insisted I wake early. He drove me to a tour company and handed me a ticket for a full-day excursion to Agra. "I don't care how tired you are, Martina, you cannot leave India without seeing the Taj Mahal."

The day was glorious. Clear skies and blissfully cooler than usual. The bus ride to and from Agra was unremarkable, but the building itself was magical. Up close, the white marble holds glints of rainbows and may have been mixed with unicorn horns. If one can block out the obvious disparities in wealth on display, and the human toll involved in the construction of the Taj Mahal, and just relax into the moment, it is awe inspiring. I am forever grateful for Patrick and Mei's thoughtful generosity.

In Colombia, ten days later, I joined a regional meeting of networks of people with HIV from across South America. Again, I sat at tables, this time wondering what Bogota looked like. Much of the conversation involved the challenge of strict Catholicism throughout Latin America, which forced homosexuality underground.

My perfunctory visit to the national program involved the local WHO representative who'd invited himself to the meeting. He was

Venezuelan, a medical doctor. He blamed the problem of HIV in the sub-region on Colombians and their supposed loose morals, and said the local organizations didn't deserve funding.

"Excuse me?" I blurted.

"These people with AIDS are worthless. So dirty," he said.

I retrieved my light blue laissez-passer from my bag and held it up. "Sir, I have the same diplomatic passport as you do. Am I dirty?"

He looked puzzled. "No, but you're not one of *them*."

"But I am. I have HIV and I am deeply disappointed by your comments. You seriously need to consider your viewpoints if you continue working for the UN. Shame on you."

We concluded our meeting and left for a quick walk along the wide tree-lined boulevards in the cool air. At nearly nine thousand feet above sea level, Bogota, claimed by the Spanish in 1538, is the third-highest capital in the world, after Quito in Ecuador and La Paz in Bolivia. Consequently, the weather is chillier than one might expect so near the equator.

The next day, we heard that the WHO representative had allocated US $10,000 to support the work of the local network of people with HIV. Apparently, as he agreed to the payment, he said, "That woman from Geneva, from UNAIDS... she's short, but she's mean." I beamed with pride.

In Venezuela, the following week, I joined my colleagues—also my hosts—in an overnight tour of nightclubs in Caracas to witness their impressive outreach programs, including condom distribution and the circulation of educational leaflets on the basics of safer practices. As the sun was rising, they dropped me off at their guest house, where I showered as a symphony of tropical birds serenaded the morning in the verdant trees outside the bathroom window.

Three weeks later, in Botswana, I was taken aback by the absolute denial of the pandemic by a group of students. My colleague, Noerine Kaleeba, and I spoke to a seemingly well-informed group of young people at a local typing school. They knew the importance of a high CD4 count—the marker of a strong immune system—and that condoms were effective in reducing the chance of infection during intercourse. And yet, after we spoke for some time about the basics of the virus and the current epidemic in Africa, when I asked the kids how they felt when they're in the same room as someone with HIV, their answers surprised me.

"What? What do you mean?" asked one person.

"We don't know anyone with HIV," added another.

"Miss, we are good girls and boys, we don't associate with such people." And on it went with a half dozen chiming in that they did not, personally, know anyone with HIV or AIDS.

This they said despite the horrendous rates in their country—well over fifteen percent of the adult population.

"Well, I'm pretty sure you do, considering how many of your citizens already have it."

"No, those are not people we know."

"Okay, well, how about *me*? Now you know me, and I have HIV."

To this the room fell silent. Then a few chairs scraped linoleum as their occupants pushed away from me.

"How could you come here today?" one young man shouted. "Now we are all going to die!"

I'd experienced denial from audiences before, but never in a place with such high prevalence. They weren't denying my status, they were denying the reality of the epidemic where they lived. I was stunned.

Noerine gave me a hug and stood. "Look at yourselves! You know so much yet you know so little. This is my friend. I am not afraid to hug her. In fact, we share an office in Geneva, so I sit with her every day and I have not yet died. I am verrry much alive."

The group watched her, a robust African woman with a subtle power in her kind voice that could probably stop traffic at rush hour.

"You need to apologize to *my friend*," she continued. "But you also need to be honest with yourselves. You all have neighbors and family and friends with this disease. We all do. Stop pretending this isn't about you. This is about all of us."

She gave me another hug and the group began to disperse. They seemed both embarrassed and humbled. Noerine's words had struck a nerve they could not ignore.

The following week, in Malawi, I joined an international team to conduct an assessment of their national prevention program. It was a remarkable group, comprised mostly of physicians, and I felt out of my depth. I didn't know any of them prior to arrival. A kind young doctor from Zambia, Moses, sensed my nervousness. "Martina, you have a lot to contribute. The perspective of civil society is just as important, if not more, than those of us doctors."

Over dinner that first evening, another doctor, this one from Belgium, caught me off guard. Jens, who'd worked in various countries in Africa as well as in Belgium, said, "Don't you think it would help our assessment team if someone would share their own experience of living with HIV?"

Was my status tattooed on my forehead, and someone forgot to tell me? "Maybe. It's helpful. It brings the work into perspective in a more profound manner," I replied.

"That's what I've been thinking. I think this is critical."

"Are you suggesting I share my own story?" I finally asked.

He furrowed his brow. "You? No. Why?"

"Well, because I'm HIV-positive."

"Wow! No. I mean, I'm sorry to hear that. But, no, I was talking about myself. I also have HIV."

We raised our beers in a mutual toast to this unexpected moment.

The following day, we both shared our experiences of having HIV, and how we felt the Malawian program could be shifted to better serve their population. For me, I was accustomed to sharing my story. For Jens, this was one of the first time he'd spoken in a professional setting about himself. Our openness was helpful, to be sure, but mostly it was liberating.

Much to my surprise, after I began my job at UNAIDS, I was rarely asked to go out and publicly represent it. I attended meetings as a staff member, but only three times during my two-and-a-half-year tenure was I asked to speak officially on behalf of the organization. Much of my work time was spent quietly lobbying for the rights of HIV-positive people globally. And also trying to figure out ways to broaden the role of people living with HIV/AIDS (PLHIV) at all levels around the world.

One of those three times I would be asked to speak was in 1996, at the UN General Assembly in New York.

AIDS Star Syndrome: United Nations General Assembly

New York, New York

As I sat onstage in the cavernous hall that houses the General Assembly for their deliberations, I fingered my new earrings: Marvin the Martian, encased in an antique-looking setting. They went with my Bugs Bunny watch. Unless they moved in for close inspection of my ears, nobody but me would know I was wearing cartoon characters at such a momentous gathering. To my right was Elizabeth Taylor, who looked stoned out of her mind. Probably from the pain meds she took for her famously bad back. To my left was the Spanish-language television personality Cristina Saralegui. I didn't know much about her, but she seemed to have quite a following, and abnormally tiny hands. On her right was Marina Mahathir, president of the Malaysian AIDS Council; she'd been a friend for a few years, since we'd both served on the PCB. At the far right was Noerine Kaleeba, my officemate. She'd started the first-ever service organization on the continent of Africa—in Uganda—after her husband had died of AIDS a decade before.

I was reflecting how the past years had brought me to that moment. I would be speaking as the first—and at the time, only—openly HIV-positive UNAIDS staff member. I was the first person the UN system had ever recruited *because* of being HIV-positive. I had other skills and qualifications, but that was one of the requirements. UNAIDS was determined to have in-house representation of the people it was tasked to serve, a milestone in staffing protocol for any UN organization.

This was the first time I'd been asked to speak since I'd joined the staff.

94

I was known as an advocate, but ever since being brought on board, it felt like I'd basically been silenced. And I didn't think it mattered much that I'd be speaking that day, anyway, because the audience looked sadly sparse.

A few countries' delegations were scattered about. Some seemed engaged, but many seemed unclear as to what the session was about as they searched through documents, presumably looking for an agenda. Perhaps they didn't know this session wasn't mandatory.

Some activists and UN staff sat at the back. Notably, my friend Eric Sawyer was there, as he'd often been during my activist years. Eric was also around when I spoke at the White House Conference the year before, but he'd been outside, protesting with Act Up. It was a beautiful moment when we two hugged by the entrance before I went inside to speak and he stood outside with his bullhorn. Both voices were needed. Both voices were loud.

Another friend in the audience that day was Nick Fucile. I'd met him at the first PCB meeting in Geneva when he'd come as a representative of the staff unions of the United Nations. Nick and I quickly became close because of a mutual love of music and dry senses of humor, but his story also stuck with me. Openly gay, Nick had taken it upon himself to be trained as an HIV counselor in New York at the Gay Man's Health Crisis (GMHC). Somehow this information became known around the Secretariat, where he worked.

His job there, officially, had been in the trades and crafts division, specifically to lay and maintain the carpet in the offices. Slowly at first, and more frequently as time passed, he received calls requesting him, by name, for help with carpet issues in various offices. When he'd arrive, though, it would turn out that the floor covering was fine. People wanted to ask him questions about HIV. They were embarrassed to go to our in-house medical services, or afraid to venture out to the clinics and testing sites in New York, so they turned to Nick.

Rumors of his counseling spread quickly. Toshi Niwa, a senior manager within the Secretariat, decided Nick's side work was more important than carpeting. He helped secure a private office and a phone so Nick could start what is now the UN HIV Hotline. Nick ended up working full-time on HIV for the UN Secretariat, but those first many years were completely of his own design and volition. He was one of my unsung heroes for the work he'd started.

Another colleague, Mark Hamilton from UNDP, was, however, absent. When I asked about him later, a mutual friend said he was hurt because he'd been trying to speak within the system but nobody ever listened. Mark had taken to calling me "Little Miss HIV" and was annoyed I was in the limelight that day. I could imagine him huffing and puffing in frustration. He was one of the few UN personnel—already on staff for many years before my tenure—who'd dared to speak openly within the system, and in particular to our medical services. A true pioneer, he'd fought internally for support for staff living with HIV before I'd ever set foot in a UN building. I was the cowgirl who'd ridden in on the coattails of his duster.

The UN, notoriously conservative, wouldn't listen to a gay man. It took a straight, blue-eyed blonde to make them pay attention. I was no threat to their conventional notions of sexuality. They perceived me as "normal," albeit diseased. A sad state but, I believe, the truth back then. Homophobia was very much alive in the United Nations. The dregs still remain but, twenty-five years later, some steps have been made—small but important ones.

As then–Secretary General Boutros Boutros-Ghali introduced me, I stood to approach the podium where so many world leaders had addressed the body before me. As I walked the few yards toward it, I noticed a light-haired middle-aged woman enter and sit off to the right-hand side of the front row. I don't see well at a distance, but even so, I recognized Madeleine Albright, then–US Ambassador to the UN. She listened intently to my message, about the need to involve people living with HIV in the decisions being made about our lives, how the UN must be the role model, and how being a model must start from within.

I thanked my scant audience and returned to my seat next to Ms. Taylor. I noticed Ms. Albright had only then left the room.

Madeline Albright came just to hear me speak. Wow.

I was excited to speak there on that day, but my oomph was gone. I felt tired, and feared I'd been suffering from an acute case of "AIDS Star Syndrome." This was a condition I'd seen before, where a person from an otherwise unremarkable background was catapulted into the public eye, simply because he or she had HIV and could string a few sentences together in a coherent manner. I had been diagnosed only four and a half years prior, and there I was, addressing the UN with Liz Taylor.

Who was I? What had I become?

Many of my fellow activists would say I had sold out. My siblings would say I'd turned lemons into lemonade. Luckily, my studies of foreign relations had, in some tiny way, prepared me for a new career as an international civil servant. The day-to-day work was not entirely overwhelming. But many of us who've been shot through the cosmos into AIDS Star roles were unprepared for the emotional toll. We often ended up crashing and burning. Badly.

Did anyone ever wonder what would happen to that person on the far end of their fifteen minutes of fame? After the next star came along to replace them, and they'd land, *splat,* back in an old life that no longer fit their new reality?

Yet again, I was luckier than most; my fifteen minutes seemed to be turning into a behind-the-scenes role with only a handful of front-and-center appearances.

Besides, by the time I was finally hired by the UN, I was already jaded and bitter. It was like I'd been fighting a war with no end in sight. The casualties were piling up too quickly to process. I felt a personal responsibility for every HIV-positive person in the world, an absurd notion in retrospect, but one I burdened myself with then. The pandemic, my life, my work, was all evolving so quickly I couldn't cope. It was spilling out of me like foam from the mouth of a rabid dog. I'd jumped forward to the frontline without having ever really grieved my own diagnosis. I was overwhelmed, but afraid to ask for help.

In 1998, my second year in Geneva, though I wasn't ill, I felt run down. When I went to see my doctor, Dr. Renold-Moynier gave me two months of sick leave and a stern talking-to. "Now, you go straight home," she snapped. "I will fax this to your office and make sure they know you're not coming back. If you need anything, we'll have someone bring it to you. No work, understand?"

I nodded but felt guilty. As the first openly HIV-positive person ever hired to work full-time at UNAIDS, I felt I was letting everyone down—especially the millions living with the virus—by not being able to do my job. But the truth was, I was so tired that I was no longer doing it properly anyway. I'd lost my fire, my internal will to fight. So when she spoke, I took heed of her words.

"As I see it, you have two options, Martina," Dr. Renold-Moynier said, "and this is what I want you to think about. One is that you start treatment, but personally, I think it's too soon for that, so I'm hoping you don't make that choice. I can prescribe the pills, but I don't think it is what is medically indicated nor really what is best for you in the long run. Your other option, the one I *would* recommend, is that you change your life and learn to take better care of yourself. Quit trying to help everyone else at your own expense."

Nobody had ever given me a directive, let alone permission, to take care of myself before. Her words sounded strange, but I knew she was right. I took those two months, rested and got better (without treatment), and returned to work. Then I handed in my resignation.

I'd stopped speaking up in meetings and knew it was time to step aside. Leaving that job was the best thing for everyone because my case of AIDS Star Syndrome was untenable.

The last time I spoke on behalf of UNAIDS, in May or June of 1998, was, ironically, at a conference in former Czechoslovakia, now the Czech Republic—where I'd been offered a job at the same time I'd been diagnosed. Not only had I been invited into their country, I was treated with respect, and my visit and words were appreciated.

Before my departure in July 1998, a few other HIV-positive staff members had been brought on board, and those same people, who'd suggested I'd sold out, apologized and even thanked me.

"You had an impossible job, I had no idea how hard it was to navigate this system until I came on board myself," one man said. "Thank you for opening the door for the rest of us."

A positive woman told me, "We totally underestimated how it must have been to be that first person, the one responsible for always bringing up our issues as people living with HIV."

"You've had an arduous task, Martina," another man added. "To be the first one inside—we all relied on you, but few of us truly supported you. That's not right. You're stronger than you know. Thank you."

I was grateful for their words because, even though I still felt I hadn't done enough, at least my community had reclaimed me as one of their own. But I had to move on with my life. And, more important, make space for others to fill my shoes. But now I felt less alone.

The job I vacated was quickly replaced by what is now a team…of ten.

On the Saturday following my last day, I signed into the WHO complex as Marge Simpson. I'd parked my car outside my ground floor office so I could remove my personal belongings. I left through the window and never signed back out.

I privately vowed never to work full-time for the UN again unless I could address HIV within that body. We needed to practice what we preached if we were going to tell the rest of the world how to respond to the pandemic. I don't think I ever imagined that actually happening—but, of course, it was a worthy dream.

CHAPTER 6

my fairytale phase

Painting, Sculpture, and Rock-n-Roll

Carouge, Switzerland

fter following the advice of sage Dr. Renold-Moynier, I started taking better care of myself. For me, that meant taking on more artistic endeavors.

On July 4, 1998, I had an art exhibit, my first ever, of sculptures I'd made from plaster and then painted. I called it "EmanciPainted: A Woman of Purpose." It was a perfect way to mark my departure from UNAIDS and the beginning of my new life as a creative… something-as-yet-undefined. I also enrolled at the University of Geneva, so I could extend my visa for another year. I never went to class, but nobody seemed to care.

This period was, ultimately, the first time I'd ever taken to really process my diagnosis. I used creative outlets to make beauty out of the chaos that was still my mind. By that point it had been six years since that day, and while I'd never exactly been in denial, the complexity still hadn't quite sunk in. I'd been living as if I'd keel over at any moment. What I hadn't considered was the fact that I might not actually die from AIDS. I believe that is in large part because I never had any major physical illness.

I'd had a bout of shingles and certainly been run down, but nothing that could be directly attributed to HIV. In fact, my lab results consistently showed that my immune system remained intact without treatment and was functioning as it should have been. What had really been damaged was my emotional well-being. My self-confidence, which hadn't been great to start with. During that first year post-UNAIDS, I wasn't looking for the next career move or trying to prove anything; I merely lived my life without a traditional job because I had the luxury of a healthy savings account and plenty of time. The ability to stay home, particularly not needing to travel for work, was a much needed respite.

My entire time in Switzerland, I lived in Carouge, the neighborhood sometimes referred to as the Greenwich Village of Geneva. Carouge, an independent city until 1816, had alternated rule by France and Sardinia before joining the municipality of Geneva. The architecture is notable because most buildings look alike and none are more than four stories, all with dormer windows on the top floors. The feeling is more hip, bohemian, and lively than most other parts of town.

Some evenings I'd have dinner with friends in the neighborhood. They, like me, were also artists who embraced their inner silly. One night we ended up loading up our water guns (because, you know, as adults we all had them), and chasing each other around the streets, hiding in corners, only to leap out and soak one another.

We were a band of overgrown children, and it was heaven.

My first task when I had joined UNAIDS had been to work with local NGOs as we planned an international conference to be held in Geneva, and that assignment had made the difference in my experience of living in that city. From day one, I had local friends, Swiss friends, so when I left the UN, I still had a community separate from my work. I cherished these friends and they helped me get to know who I was.

As is often the case when one leaves a color-inside-the-lines career for a creative life, everything seemed to bloom. At long last, I allowed myself to feel my feels. Either through creative channels, or over dinner with friends, or with a glass of wine (okay, a bottle) as I soaked in my tub, I gave myself permission slow down. No longer distracted by the hectic pace and demanding requirements of my previous job, I finally focused on myself.

I decided I actually kind of liked myself, and that was liberating. At that gallery opening, I began to connect with a long suppressed side of myself: *Martina the artist*. She painted plaster sculptures and learned how to make lamps out of repurposed metal objects. Forks became hands, a ladle set over a hand-cranked cheese grater made a perfect incense burner. And a three-by-five index-card box became a treasure chest for a mischievous make-believe boy with an ice cream cone made from a pastry funnel and a ball-bearing in one of his cocktail-forked hands.

One day my friend Jennifer Weatherly, a successful country singer with waist-length blond hair and a huge smile, came by the atelier for a visit.

"Well, hell, Martina. I thought *I* was the happiest person I knew, but I'll be damned if you don't seem happier than anyone I know! Looooook at *you*!"

She hugged me and planted soft pink-lipstick kisses on my smiling face. I showed her some of the photographs from my recent opening. There was one of the two of us.

She asked if she could keep it. "I need to keep this on my wall to remember I always have to stay this happy."

It was my only copy and I'd wanted to keep it myself, for the same reason. I gave it to her anyway, knowing I'd always have that moment, between us.

My former colleague, Kim, also was a musician, and she'd become very worried about my health, mental and physical. She'd actually seen the burnout coming before I did. One day, she sat me down for a good talking-to.

"Martina, you know what I think? I think you should join a band. Start staying up too late, smokin' fags, drinkin' beers, feelin' shite the next day—I think you'll be much happier!"

So I started singing and even played guitar, albeit poorly. I also wrote lyrics to songs.

My friend Janet, who I'd met through a colleague in my first days in Geneva, pushed me even further once I'd taken Kim's advice. She invited me to sing backup in her band and soon saw, or rather heard, that I was blocked. One evening at rehearsal, I stood timidly in front of the mic, emitting semblances of sound. Janet, who stood next to me, simultaneously smacked one hand on my soft belly, the other on my lower back and yelled, "*Sing*, damn it! Stand up properly and sing!"

She never got me to shut up after that.

This new, artistic Martina resembled the little girl I once knew who loved playing piano and making things out of pieces of bark or stamping paint patterns with cut up potatoes. She was a happy weirdo.

A year into my life as an artist, I was getting ready for an evening gig with the band I was singing with. My eldest sister, Alexandria, was visiting with her husband Thom, and their two daughters, Genevieve, and Spencer. My youngest niece—five or so—assisted me in getting dressed. I'd opted for overalls with a crop top underneath.

Spencer frowned, hands on hips. "Auntie M, you can't possibly be thinking of wearing that?"

"Why not? I like it."

"This is a very important night. You need to be pretty. You need to wear something…something red."

They rummaged through my closet and pulled out a red wrap skirt with a geometric print I'd bought in India. Then paired it with a snug black T-shirt that showed off my curves, and red heels.

"I sing barefoot, you know," I told them.

"Well, you'll still need shoes to get to and from the stage, so wear these." Even at that young age they already had a better sense of fashion than I'd mustered in three decades.

They guided the makeup application, as well. Since my hair was short at the time, they simply brushed it with remarkably long fingers on tiny hands, standing on my bed while I stood on the floor, so they could reach it. At last they grasped my shoulders and proclaimed me "ready for the ball where you shall meet your prince." I smiled, hugged them, and swung them around. Finally, we headed to the Haute Savoie, in France, for the concert. My sister and her husband drove their rental car, while I drove mine, my niece as co-pilot.

Properly dressed, with my pint-sized fashion coach in tow, I never could have guessed that that night would indeed turn out to be an important one for me.

Meeting My Prince

Haute Savoie, France

Once at the venue, a community center with a rustic outdoor stage and plenty of space for dancing in the parking lot, we began unloading the cars. Almost immediately, I spotted a man in the small crowd I'd never seen before. He was with a group of people, one I recognized as the girlfriend of our guitarist, but I didn't know who he was.

He was gorgeous, though his age was hard to guess. While he had youthful skin, he also had the demeanor of someone older. Most of us in the band were in our thirties and forties, so I guessed, by association, he was in his early thirties. Against my thirty-five, that seemed fair game. He noticed me just as quickly.

As on a television wildlife program, we were like two big cats who'd spotted each other in the jungle, then stalked each other from a distance, slowly closing in until one of us either pounced or ran. With lush green foothills all around, and the majestic Alps in the background, our hunting ground was pastoral.

After depositing my bag and music folder on the stage, and checking the height of my mic stand, I wandered over to my sister and her family. They were taking in the scene, enjoying the beauty of the setting and looking forward to the music. My brother-in-law, Thom, was a proficient drummer and both he and my sister loved rock-'n'-roll.

Eventually the mystery man came over. I felt immediately at ease in his presence.

He was about five-eleven with long dark brown hair gathered in a loose ponytail. He wore black jeans and a dark blue shirt, tucked in, adorned with little white embroidered flowers. I noticed his shoes—shoes that did not match the occasion, leather old-man shoes. Most of the other guys were in shorts or jeans, sneakers, and t-shirts. His rosy cheeks flushed more deeply when he introduced himself. I could see

105

my reflection in those shining dark eyes.

In French he said, "Good evening. I saw you looking at me. My name is Genrebear."

"Good evening. My name is Martina," I said, before turning to introduce my sister and her family. "I'm sorry, but could you tell me your name again?"

"Genrebear."

I smiled. My nieces giggled, watching their Auntie M flirting in French.

My French is excellent, but at times I couldn't quite follow his words. "Sorry, one more time? Your name. Slower."

"It's a double-barreled name, Jean *et* Robert. Jrr...o...berrr. The T is silent." He smiled.

"Ah, got it. Thank you."

His beauty and charm won me over immediately. I was at one of the best junctures of my life and I'm sure he was drawn to that—my joy in that moment. An art exhibit going on in town—my second, where I was selling more pieces along with my lamps—singing with a wonderful rock band in the foothills of the Alps on a glorious summer evening. I sang Janis Joplin covers. We interpreted the Scottish band, Texas, Jimi Hendrix, and the Doobie Brothers. We called our red-headed lead guitarist the Ginger-Carlos Santana. I had money in the bank and projects in mind. The only thing missing was a lover, a partner—and now, it seemed, perhaps here he was. My niece had been right; I'd met my prince.

We couldn't take our eyes off each other. After my set with the band we danced, and he kissed me. Not the most extraordinary kiss I'd ever had, but it felt familiar; warm and manageable.

As the music shifted from live to the boom box, we kept dancing. We even danced in the rain, after the music had stopped. Finally, someone came out and told us to go home. I'd lost track of time. My sister and her family had already left, and I realized that, indeed, I needed to go home. Or at least get out of the rain.

"Where are you staying? Would you like to come back to Geneva with me? I can drive you back tomorrow."

"We were going to camp out here. I'd much rather be with you than in a tent in the rain." On the drive home we talked about things I can't recall. I kept speaking mostly to make sure this wasn't a dream. To reassure myself that we were both really present.

Once at my place, we cuddled in my bed, but didn't have sex. "I hope it's okay, but I like to really get to know a person before becoming intimate," he said.

"That absolutely works for me."

I actually welcomed that. His words were reassuring.

At some point during that first night at my place, I told him I was living with HIV.

"Aaaaahhhh, now I understand," he said. "One of the guys told me to 'be careful' with you. I wasn't sure what he meant exactly since he didn't stop me, and clearly they all adore you. Now I get it, thaaaaat's what he meant."

He looked over and stroked my face. "It's okay, it's not that big a deal," he said.

I breathed a deep sigh of relief and smiled, thinking, *Whew, this man is a keeper. He hasn't called me names or tried to hurt me or anything. He must be okay.*

Apparently, my smile confused him. "I'm surprised you're not crying," he said. "It must be a hard thing to deal with and tell people. Why aren't you more upset?"

I'd learned early on that how you tell people, and what frame of mind you're in when you deliver the news, is key to how *they* cope with the information. So I was surprised by his reaction. I thought he'd see me as strong and able to deal with the situation. Instead he questioned it and implied I must be hiding something. He'd apparently expected me to break down and didn't know how to react when I didn't.

I felt confused but, as was often the case, I smashed down that worry and embraced only the fact I hadn't scared him away. I wasn't craving sex, I was craving companionship.

I didn't want someone to *fuck* me ever again.

I wanted someone to love me.

I'd always been the other woman in my few and far between relationships. My first real boyfriend was a French exchange student I'd met when I was twenty-four, during my junior year at San Francisco State. He'd been cheating on his girlfriend with me. Sure enough, he was soon cheating on me too before we broke up. I knew this in my gut but also because I'd smelled hairspray on his pillow, and the scent wasn't mine. Within two years of our breakup, he was married and had a six-month-old.

My most recent relationship had ended in 1997. He and his wife had been 'separated'. I was too naïve then to see he was simply working in a different country and wanted a relationship. Or that he'd never leave her, because of their son. I believe he did care for me, but wasn't strong enough to say no. In my red convertible cabriolet, we'd put the top down and drive up into the mountains on a weekend afternoon. We'd just pick a destination and go. Taking in the fresh air as we navigated winding roads among the Swiss chalets, lush green farms, and grazing cows with their giant, sonorous bells.

"It's so beautiful here," I'd say.

"Let's keep driving. I'm serious. Martina, let's just escape together."

After his contract ended, he returned home. He had two more children with his wife and tried to make his marriage work. They did eventually divorce, but decades later. Ours had been merely stolen moments, which never felt entirely satisfying or true.

I can't blame anyone for these situations. I'd gotten myself into them. But then, I'd never learned about boundaries. Partly because I didn't understand the confines of healthy love, but also because I grew up in an era when women were still valued based on the status of men they married. Despite my professional successes and luck in terms of surviving my illness, I was still weighed down by low self-esteem. The happy weirdo was still deeply insecure, and fell into relationships for the wrong reasons. My capacity to love others still felt real and intact. It was my capacity to love myself that was in need of nurturing.

On a side note, I once had a conversation with two female coworkers on a related topic. The end result was mutual sad agreement that it was, in many ways, easier for a woman to be divorced than to have never married.

"At least she'd been wanted at some point," I said. Whereas a woman who'd never found a man was somehow defective. A single woman over twenty-five was a conundrum, apparently. And perhaps still is.

After that relationship with the married man, I dated a few guys who'd presented as single, though I'm not sure they actually were. At least they weren't legally married. This seemed like an improvement at the time. I never felt I deserved better, though, and felt lucky just to have someone pay attention. Really; anyone.

One guy had scarred me deeply. After we'd dated a few times, he'd come over for dinner and we had a bit too much to drink. I'd decided, before our date, that for once, I'd just insist he use a condom if we had sex, and not tell him I had HIV. Although I'd never not disclosed my status beforehand to a potential lover, this had been the advice of so many friends and even other people with the virus. I thought I'd give it a try.

He was attractive, though not someone I thought had long-term potential; we had little in common. So I thought, *What the hell, it'll be a fling. As long as I don't put him at risk, what's the harm?* That night we did have sex and I'd requested he use a condom. He probably presumed my only concern was not getting pregnant. But then things all happened very—*very*—quickly, and he never put it on. Nor did he ejaculate inside me, so in his mind, no doubt, everything was fine.

Mortified, I froze, imagining him finding out my status and sending me to prison for attempted murder. In some countries there are laws that would lock me up for years. And, God forbid, if he *did* become infected, I could never forgive myself. I'd not allowed him the opportunity to make an informed choice. I'd acted irresponsibly.

I panicked, already unable to live with the guilt. The next day I called and said I had to see him. I went to his apartment and told him the truth.

He screamed at me. "What, are you trying to kill me? You bitch! How can you live with yourself? You don't deserve to live. You're just another dirty fucking slut."

He grabbed me and shook me.

I tried to explain that the risk was nearly nonexistent because I was in excellent health. That it was harder for a man to get HIV from a woman, anyway. That he should have listened in the first place. "Please, calm down. I'm so sorry. Please, just calm down."

Luckily, he had to be somewhere else soon, so he let go. Aside from the shaking, he didn't hurt me.

After he left, I sat in my car paralyzed with fear, behind the wheel but unable to drive away. Hugging myself for what felt like hours. A few weeks later he called to apologize, saying he'd overreacted. He'd been tested. The counselors had assured him he shouldn't worry if I was really as healthy as I'd said. "Since I know you worked with the World Health Organization and UNAIDS, I feel inclined to believe you," he added.

Sometime later, he called again to confirm that the results had been negative. And then, I was thankful to never hear from him again. But the episode frightened me. I understood I could never again become intimate with someone who didn't know *all* about me. I'd only tried to conceal my diagnosis just that once and was never going to do it again.

And so, when my "prince" came along on that rainy June night and wanted to delay sex and first really get to know me, I was *relieved*. I felt safe.

Sunday morning, when we got up, I again introduced him to my sister and her daughters. Much to my surprise and delight, he spoke English to them. Up until then we'd spoken only French. It'd not even occurred to me that he *could* speak English. His grasp wasn't great, but I appreciated he at least tried.

My sister, Alexandria, had actually worked in Belgium, his home country, many years back. She'd been a quality assurance specialist for an American chain of department stores which also had locations across Europe. They chatted about this town and that place. Both were comfortable striking up conversations with strangers, so my sister and Jean-Robert were soon well on their way to getting to know each other.

Later that day we walked over to the gallery so I could show him my exhibit. The gallery was normally closed on Sundays, like most places in Switzerland, but since I worked there, the owner allowed us in. During the day, the atelier was lit naturally by the sunshine flowing in through the floor-to-ceiling windows. Jean-Robert wandered around and looked at my artwork positioned against the yellow and blue striped walls. The plaster casts I'd made were mostly body parts; I'd made molds of my breasts, for instance, and then painted their plaster sisters with scenes or patterns (these were a popular item), and I'd also done my stomach, into which I'd integrated a battery-operated clock and upon which I'd painted a frog known in many cultures as a symbol of fertility. I painted the numbers starting at 31 and ending at 42 (rather than 1 to 12) and titled it "My Biological Clock."

Generally, he liked the work. "They're interesting," he said, "but it's a shame they're not smooth. Smooth things are more appealing. You should work on that."

"But I *like* the texture—that's sort of the point." I felt deflated.

"Oh, yeah, well, I still think you should make them smooth; they'll be nicer."

I brushed off the comments, just feeling happy that he hadn't said, "These suck." I wasn't hard to please. My art was an extension of myself. Sadly, I felt it was also unworthy of praise.

Jean-Robert ended up staying over another night. By the time I'd dropped him off Monday morning in France, at our lead guitarist's house, we'd decided to see each other again. He would return to Geneva in a few weeks. Meanwhile, I was going to vacation with my sisters in the south of France, so this worked out perfectly. We exchanged emails and he phoned a few times. A beautiful young man was interested in me. Everyone else was happy, but I'm guessing they also thought it would be a passing thing.

In the two short days we'd spent together, I'd learned that he was not quite twenty-five, a good ten years younger than I. I wanted to think that didn't matter; he seemed mature. Had our ages been reversed, no one would consider it an issue.

Our other differences were many: cultural, language, life experience and education, to name a few. But I was sure love would conquer all. I'd soak in a tub of other happy clichés if I just held on to this man. I still had the emotional maturity of an adolescent when it came to relationships, and that's pretty much how I proceeded: as if at the end I'd go home with a corsage, sore feet and smudged lipstick.

I'd never even been to a prom, but I was good at dreaming.

When I returned from France, Jean-Robert came to Geneva to visit me. I was stunned and overjoyed.

I sat in my car near the train station, awaiting his arrival. Remembering a time in college when I'd gone to a theater production with a guy I liked. After the show, I told him I was going to the ladies' room. When I came out and he was still standing there, I felt truly astonished he'd waited. Now, many years later, I was still astonished someone would return—or wait—for me.

Once back in my apartment, we sat in my long, narrow kitchen at the round Indonesian cherrywood table, in matching slatted chairs. As we looked over the courtyard below, through the open windows, he took my hands in his.

"I know you must be worried about what I think about you having HIV. I want you to know that it's okay. I want you to know I'm not afraid."

In fact, I had already assumed it was not an issue simply because he was there. He'd said as much the night I'd met him. So when he felt a need to reiterate it, I was taken aback. It almost felt as if *he* had wanted it to be a big deal. I convinced myself the red flag was a heart being shot through the air by Cupid.

He stayed for two weeks. We got along. He had a sense of humor that made me laugh. One day he said, "I would love to live in a house with plastic furniture."

"Oh? Okay."

"Yes, but I'd fill it with helium and put strings on the bottom."

"Helium?"

"That way you just pull it down when you need it. You'd have a lot more floor space." I giggled, imaging a house filled with balloon chairs and an inflatable sofa hovering near the ceiling.

I enjoyed introducing him to my friends, and everyone was impressed with how comfortable he seemed with so many new people.

He was charming and knew he was attractive.

"My friends love you!"

"Of course they do. Have you seen me?" He winked.

He struck just the right mix of being attentive to me while making my friends feel special. He commanded attention but didn't abuse it. In many ways he was arrogant, but he seemed self-aware enough to dampen the impact. He was like a Renaissance man, able to comment on any topic.

One evening, he'd stopped me on the street when we were walking home after drinks with some friends of mine, and on a well-lit corner, held me in his arms as he leaned against a lamppost and said, "You know, I'm going to marry you; you're going to be my wife."

And in that instant, I knew he was right. I knew I'd say yes because I felt he was already my partner in life. I did not want to envision a future without him.

On the 14th of July, that same summer, three weeks after we'd met, we drove to the top of the Salève, a mountain that backdrops Geneva, to watch the sunset. As I sat cross-legged on a picnic table, the sun setting as the lights of the city flickered on below us, he stood before me. The last of the sunshine lit his broad face. Wisps of dark brown hair catching in the evening breeze. Solidly built, he took my hands in his and squared his broad shoulders. "I want to ask you something. But I also want to know the answer before I ask."

I smiled and nodded, ever so slightly.

"Okay. Martina Clark, will you marry me?"

"Yes!" I blurted out nearly before he'd finished the question.

It was as if I'd flipped ahead to the end of the chapter and knew no matter how it played out, that was going to be the result. I wanted desperately to be married. I wanted to be normal and for society to stop questioning if I could ever be wanted.

"This is insane because I barely know you, but yes, I'll marry you," I said.

"Ah, we've only just met now, but you can't forget all of our previous lifetimes together, I think they add up to a lot!"

His comment made me laugh and somehow resonated as true.

I felt sure, on that momentous evening, we'd go home and finally make love. If he wanted to marry me, then certainly he was feeling comfortable enough to have sex with me.

We made our way back down the mountain and to my place. Again, though, we shared my bed and snuggled together for warmth and safety, but in no way like lovers. Still, no one had ever asked me to marry him before, so I allowed myself the joy of basking in the moment. Finally, somebody wanted me. Somebody wanted to announce to the world that he'd chosen me, that I belonged to him. I had never felt so special. I felt at peace.

My life now felt complete. I had my writing and my music and my art and great friends, now I had my prince. What more could a woman want?

But we couldn't stay in Switzerland. We'd have to live in Belgium. He was on unemployment there so he couldn't afford to leave. A work permit for him would have been difficult—primarily because that would have required him to work. He cherished his ability to 'live off the system'. But the Swiss didn't give out permits easily, either. He'd need a job offer first, so that wasn't going to happen. My student visa was running out, so we decided it made sense to start our life together in Belgium.

When I announced to my family that I was going to move to Belgium and get married, I suspect they took a collective gasp and then held their tongues. They all expressed delight I'd found someone. Nobody questioned my thinking, or my sanity. At least not to my face.

During my first weeks there, we looked into the necessary paperwork for marriage and learned a few illuminating facts. At the time, people from outside the European Union who wanted to marry Belgians were required to submit an HIV test result. A *negative* HIV test result. When we casually asked a government official about the test, her answer was unexpected.

"Sure, we require an HIV test, but, let's face it, you don't need to worry. You're an American moving here from Switzerland after a UN career. We're not worried about you."

"So, I don't need to submit test results to get married here?" I asked.

"No, really, between us—that's just for Africans. Don't worry, nobody will ask you for that."

I found all of this disturbing and racist, but I kept my mouth shut. The head of UNAIDS, Peter Piot, was Belgian, so I hadn't imagined such discrimination existed in his country. Then again, discriminatory applications of laws were common around the world. As just one man, he couldn't fix everything. A reminder of why UNAIDS was important.

Even if my work there was behind me, there was still much to be done. In retrospect, I am ashamed for having kept silent.

Between applying for documents and researching work options (for me), we found a beautiful house to rent in Spa. It's a charming place, settled centuries before because of the healing waters. The word that is now globally synonymous with a place of healing is derived from the name of the town. In Roman times, the location was known as Aquae Spadanee. In the late 1500s, an English visitor returned to Yorkshire in the U.K. and eventually founded the country's first resort, known as *The English Spaw*, which brought the word into our vernacular.

Our house dated from the 1600s. There was a small long-defunct fountain built into the gray stone façade. The front door, painted green and with glass panes on the top half, led to a grand white marble stairway that ascended in a Hollywoodesque curve. While we had the downstairs, which included a room I'd use as my office, we lived on the second floor, above what had once been stables.

By leaving Geneva, however, I somehow ceased to be the woman he'd fallen in love with. I was still me, of course. But he'd loved my life, my world, my creativity and the joy I exuded while doing the things that made me so happy. He'd loved my friends and their open-minded acceptance of everyone. He was drawn to my life in Geneva and me in that life.

Moving to Belgium to be with him meant leaving that all behind. And though I tried to re-create it there, I was starting from scratch. I didn't have years of friendships to draw upon or contacts in the music or art worlds. And I was trying to be responsible and make everything work because I thought that was also something about me that he'd been attracted to.

With such dramatic changes to our lives in such a short span of time, we seemed to be out of sync. Each of us was processing in our own way. I was starting to realize there were things about Jean-Robert I didn't like, but I was too ashamed to admit I'd moved too quickly.

Five months after we'd met, we were married, and from that day forward, things were never the same. My own personal Bluebeard had trapped me in his castle.

Parc de Quatre Heures

Spa, Belgium

Belgium: Western Europe
Population: 11.5 million
Capital: Brussels

I've always assumed that in the first months of living together, most couples spent a lot of time having wild sex. Instead, we watched American television shows with English subtitles. Jean-Robert explained that, in Belgium, movies are always dubbed because the country has three official languages to consider (French, Flemish, and German), which would make subtitling in them all prohibitively expensive. Most movies he saw came from France, and the only English radio or TV Belgians were exposed to was the BBC, so he'd truly never listened to American accents. "I want to feel comfortable with your language," he told me.

He learned remarkably quickly and, for a short time, began speaking in what I referred to as his "late-eighties English," asking me to "pump up the volume" on the TV or announcing that he was "hungry, like the wolf" at dinnertime. We watched documentaries and old episodes of *Friends* and *Seinfeld*. I'd never owned a television, so his method of learning language through a twenty three-inch screen was strange, but amusing. We were planning a trip to the States so he could meet my family. I appreciated the effort and was impressed by his progress.

Spa is situated in the forested Ardennes, the only part of Belgium that's not perfectly flat. After years of apartments, I was delighted with our spacious three-bedroom house. Dating from the 1600's, as I said, it had a pitched red tile roof, and had once served as living quarters above the carriage house of a mansion. It faced a wooded hill, and a 1,000-square-foot terrace opened off our 1,000-square-foot living room. We had skylights and solar heating, although the latter was not very efficient in rain-drenched Belgium. That year we had eleven months of rain days.

The fact that it was nestled in the cul-de-sac of a private park, the *Parc de Quatre Heures*—so named because the aristocrats of yore took their afternoon strolls there, centuries before—just made it that much more delightful.

When the truck arrived from Geneva with my furniture, I told Jean-Robert, "This is so exciting! I love setting up a new house. Is it all right with you if I just do what I think works and then we take it from there?"

While it's true organizing a home is something I enjoy, I was disappointed when he offered zero resistance. "Okay, that works, I'll let you do it."

He then proceeded to lie on the sofa for a week, maybe two, while I put together bookcases. He went for a walk while I organized closets or alphabetized books. Even though doing nothing whatsoever to help, he seemed annoyed at me for reasons I could not understand. And so I did what I always do: I tried to fix it. I made our home as beautiful as possible to ease the eye-daggers increasingly aimed my way. I made furniture and decorated with my whimsical artwork to lighten the mood.

I also suggested we have dinner parties so I could integrate into his world. There I met some of his friends. I liked a few, but many struck me as odd, though. They seemed untethered to reality, but I passed it off as a consequence of cultural, language, or age differences. Many were also unemployed, like Jean-Robert. I quickly learned that screwing the system was a major pastime of theirs. In Belgium, once a person went on unemployment, at least back then, he could stay on it for life. And it paid pretty well. Jean-Robert, like so many of his friends, had worked briefly in his late teens. Then, following an illness due to ulcers, he went on disability, then unemployment. He hadn't worked since.

With substantial savings in the bank, I offered to be the bread-winner, for now, and encouraged him to take classes and discover what he'd like to do for a living, to finish his GED and get a college degree so he could qualify for a job that would make him happy.

He started a million things—classes, projects, internships—and finished none.

We set a date to marry at the end of October, after five months of courting in our strange hands-off fashion. My papers had run out in Switzerland. We'd done our homework, and knew an official marriage would allow me to get Belgian citizenship, access to free health care, and a European Union passport. The latter two I valued highly.

I organized our little wedding, planning finger foods for the reception we'd hold in our beautiful home before continuing on to a local restaurant for dinner for his closest friends and relatives. I sampled cakes, found little statuettes that resembled us, and had the baker paint them to match our wedding outfits. I'd already found my dress, and had it fitted. Everything was ready.

My second sister, Adrian, with whom I'd been living when I first tested positive, decided at the last minute she needed to be there and flew over from California. She was the only one from my side who'd be at the wedding.

The night before our wedding, Jean-Robert went to Liège to spend the night at his mother's place. Why we felt this tradition needed to be honored, I'll never know. My sister and I went out for a gorgeous meal to mark my last night as a single woman. I had "boulet à la Liègeoise"—a regional dish of seasoned meatballs that are first lightly fried and then cooked in a sweet and savory dark-brown sauce. Like many Belgian dishes, it's served with thick fries and is heavy, hearty and delicious. I don't love everything about Belgium, but the people certainly can cook.

As we savored our meals, Adrian finally plucked up the courage to question me. "Are you reeeeeeeeeally sure you want to go through with this? I mean, Jean-Robert seems lovely, and he certainly is funny, but... don't you think you're jumping into this a bit too quickly? I know it feels impossible to think about this now, the night before your wedding, but you *can* just postpone it. Live together for a while longer, and *then* do it. Be sure."

Aside from a few harmless fabrications when we were children, I've always been truthful with my sister. But on that particular night over our candle-lit table for two, I looked her straight in the eyes and lied. "I've never been so sure. I *am* sure. I am going to do this, and it's all going to be wonderful. I'm so happy you're here, Adrian, I love you!" I said, trying hard for a sincere tone as I transformed this piece of fiction into a truth I so desperately needed to create.

We jokingly toasted with the bubbly mineral water of Spa, to be more local and authentic. I believe she swallowed the story because she didn't want to shatter my fairy tale. We both surely knew I was lying, but we also knew I was very stubborn and would insist on going through with it. I felt I'd failed in so many other areas of my life, I needed to do this one *normal* thing—and make it a success.

Our wedding took place on a crisp autumn day. The turning leaves, red, orange, yellow, brown, carpeted the ground.

As Jean-Robert drove up from his mother's house that morning, I'd just finished buttoning up the fitted, long-sleeved, low-cut champagne dress I'd had made in nearby Maastricht, Holland. It was raw silk, and I wore it with a red silk scarf from India and vintage gold pumps. My sister, my maid of honor, lent me her blue Tahitian pearls.

Something old, something new, something borrowed, something blue.

We walked from our old stone house through the private park to the city hall, where we were married by our landlord, who was conveniently also a minister in the government. In his speech, he talked about how the night Jean-Robert and I met, we'd danced in the rain—and now we'd ended up in the town where healing waters had gained great notoriety.

If Adrian hadn't been there to serve as my witness, I might not have believed it actually happened. The ceremony, reception, and dinner came and went so quickly, it all felt surreal.

That night the skies let loose again. Barely able to see the roads though the downpour, we drove two and half hours through the flood to Bruges. The "Venice of the North," as they call the picturesque city famous for its canals and fine lace, was where we spent our honeymoon.

If one could call it that. Jean-Robert was angry because he'd misplaced my credit card, claiming *I'd* lost it after I paid for our wedding dinner. We'd left Spa late; the hotel was ready to give away our rooms to eager tourists when we arrived drenched at the front desk. Yes, *rooms*. He'd insisted my sister come with us since she'd never been to Belgium. In fact, I missed my family and was happy to have her along even if the trip there in the pounding rain was hair-raising.

On the night before Halloween, our first together as husband and wife, he stayed down in the restaurant. "I'm stressed from the drive. I'm going to relax here for a while. You go up."

Exhausted, I was nearly asleep when he finally arrived. He quietly slipped into bed as far away as possible. We didn't even cuddle. I'd become used to the absence of sex, but in my fantasy, this was to be the night we'd finally and truly give ourselves to each other. Feeling more alone than ever before, I told myself: This is the beginning of your marriage.

I eventually fell asleep, my pillow damp and heavy with sadness.

Before we were married, he'd often said he wanted to take care of me. His words reminded me of a visit I'd had with my friend Kate and her husband Steve in London. While Kate and I bent over a laptop to work, Steve made tea and roasted nuts for us to snack on. I envisioned moments like this when Jean-Robert wanted to take classes in massage so he could knead my every ache. Unlike Steve, who was nurturing, however, Jean-Robert said, "I want to fix you." Only once we lived together and he got to know me better, he realized I didn't need fixing. I wasn't sick, and while I'd always have HIV, it wasn't something anyone needed to or could fix.

When he broke one of my favorite little red etched cordial glasses from the Czech Republic, it was my fault for leaving it near the edge of the sink. When we flew to the United States for Christmas and he caught the 'flu, that was somehow my fault, too.

"Where is my suitcase?" he asked once we arrived at Adrian's.

"Our luggage is delayed. It will be delivered tomorrow."

"How the fuck did you let *that* happen? How am I supposed to brush my teeth?"

It was all my fault.

That same year, in an attempt to share my culture and better get to know his friends and his mother, I'd prepared Thanksgiving dinner. For fourteen. As the standard ingredients for an American Thanksgiving are not readily available in small-town Belgium, it had taken me a week to prepare everything from scratch. I special-ordered the turkey, which I brined in a storage tub for two days on our patio. I baked the pumpkin and yams to be nestled in homemade crusts. I found just the right "chocolat noir" to mix into my signature chocolate pecan pie. I stewed the cranberries to make the sauce and let bread go a little hard on the windowsill so I could make the homemade stuffing.

When it was time to serve the meal on that snowy bitter-cold night, I was removing a final side dish from the oven when Jean-Robert came into the kitchen and announced, "You know, it's all cold. I don't know how we can even eat this food."

I was so stunned by his spiteful words I lost my balance for a split second. My right hand raised a fraction and I seared it, halfway between the base of my thumb and my wrist, on the four hundred degree broiling rack above. I bit my lip and pinched back the pain. A welt emerged that remains as a scar today.

On our first Christmas together, I presented him with an expensive, fancy Palm Pilot to help him put order in his life. He gave me a spare card he'd gotten from my sister and a scribbled note: "Good for one visit to the spa in Spa—original, no?! Kiss, your husband." After I'd spent too much money and all my frequent flyer miles on our six-week trip to New York City and Northern California, I was deeply hurt he couldn't think of something more appropriate.

He never came through with the spa visit.

Once we returned to Spa from our trip to the US, our lives got even crazier. As if a sexless, anger-filled marriage wasn't bad enough, we found ourselves caregivers to a teenager.

Before we'd met, Jean-Robert had lived in Liège, where he'd become friends with a neighbor, Marc, down the street. Marc's younger sister, Charlotte, had been living with him and his wife. Life with her mother had become unsafe and the two were estranged. What ensued is Charlotte's story and the specific details are not mine to tell. But when she no longer felt safe in Marc's home either, and was unsure where else to go, Charlotte turned to Jean-Robert and me.

She'd been to our house a few times and felt safe there. Once she'd even spent a weekend with us, on her own, and she and I had bonded.

She had fits of crying, but what teenager didn't.

The day after we returned from the United States, Charlotte called Jean-Robert and told him what had been going on. That Friday in mid-January, he screamed, "Get your coat! We're going to see Charlotte." We drove the normal three-quarters of an hour to nearby Liège in under thirty minutes.

We met her in the back booth at a café where she sat with her father. He was a kind man but had long struggled with mental illness and had been deemed unfit to parent her. She'd been raised primarily by her mother, but they were no longer on speaking terms.

My French was fluent but spending weeks in California had shoved it to a back shelf. I was struggling to follow the conversation. I ordered a Diet Coke and a side of fries with mayonnaise and tried to piece things together in my jet-lagged mind, mostly keeping quiet, listening, and hugging Charlotte.

She shivered uncontrollably as she explained that her brother had become abusive, emotionally and sexually. Having also been sexually assaulted—remember Joey, and the guy who'd raped and choked me in Brussels, and other violations and betrayals I don't really care to revisit—I immediately recognized the truth in her words from her demeanor. I just held her, rocked her, and whispered, "Shhhhhhh, ça va aller." This will pass. And prayed I wasn't lying.

Marc's actions had made it unsafe for Charlotte to stay in his home. Along with her father, we agreed the immediate solution was that she stay with us, at least for now.

That afternoon Charlotte came home with us. She stayed for nearly a year. Now I had two immature people to look after. Something happened to me then that I could only liken to wearing a burka. I was there, but it felt as if I had become invisible. I supported the now enlarged family and tried to hold everything together. But I felt absent in my own story.

My fantasy that being married would make me happy was definitively smashed to fragments by this point. I sleepwalked through life like a zombie. I completed all of duties and found money—at first borrowed from my parents, later earned as a consultant to support the three of us. The income from my husband's unemployment went towards utilities. My savings were running out, fast.

Charlotte clung to me emotionally and physically, even though we barely knew one another. I don't know if she realized how much she supported me, as well. I did my best not to burden her with my own emotional needs, but being able to simply sit next to someone, touch shoulders on the sofa during a movie—was the only human contact I had. It fed the shred of life-energy in my hungry soul.

She stayed home from school in the first few weeks as we sorted out her legal placement by the state, through countless interviews with child-protection officers, social workers and even medical personnel. We were all trying to figure out what was best for her.

Clearly, I could not say, "Hey, folks, could this traumatized, abused teenager just come back in a few years? We're not ready for this. It's not a good time." Perhaps I should have protested. But in an emergency, I turn into a machine and do what is asked of me.

During one of the interviews, I explained that although I was between jobs at the moment, I'd recently left a senior position at the UN, where I had to manage a multimillion-dollar budget with far-reaching global responsibilities. I thought this made me sound trustworthy and, therefore, suitable to care for Charlotte.

My husband later yelled, "Why do you *always* have to show off? You're such a snob! 'I work for the UN. I'm sooo special,'" he ended in a high-pitched squeal.

Frustrated, I explained my motive and went to the kitchen to start cooking. He stormed out and went to the library to borrow more comic books. This is how we'd each escape into our respective domains, mine in the kitchen, his in the library with cartoons.

I remain remarkably calm in very difficult situations. In childhood, my mother's emotional instability required us to remain composed and alert to avoid her wrath. This allows me to soldier on and help everyone else before considering whether I really have the strength to carry the burden. I usually end up buckling under the pressure—but by that point, everyone else is usually on their way to recovery. Then I'm left alone with my silence and pain. I've done this from the time I was able to walk, trying to massage my mother's unpredictable moods into normalcy, and have never stopped. My life goal is to become bored, if only for a few moments.

And so, three months into an already-rocky marriage, I became the legal foster mother of a fifteen-year old. I had a lot to learn in a very short period of time. My sisters both have children so I'd spent time in the caregiver role, but nothing had prepared me for this. Babies are born tiny and cute for a reason: you immediately fall in love with them. When they come to you in a gangly adolescent body with pimples and problems—not to mention traumatized—they're much harder to manage.

Luckily, Charlotte and I found a common love of music. When we were home alone, which was fairly often, we'd blast the stereo and dance around the living room to Björk or her favorite trance music. We made jewelry with beads from broken necklaces and orphaned earrings. We drew pictures and made cookies. She told me about her friends and school and subjects she liked, and I listened and encouraged her to open up. When she slept or was at school, I read books on abuse, family relations, and parenting.

She started learning English with me. We'd try to decipher song lyrics and figure out the meanings, she in English and me in French. We made up ridiculous phrases and started to create our own little language. When I would present her with some small gift, I knew would make her happy, she'd smile up at me and say, "Thank you very *mouche*, Mama Bear. *C'est très fly!*" *Mouche* is the French word for *fly*, so I enjoyed her play on words, since I knew in hip-hop terms, something fly was cool.

We both loved language, one of many things that brought us closer. She'd started calling me Mama Bear because we were a sort of made-up family, I suppose. Her manic-depressive father, on the other hand, would call the house and reintroduce himself each and every time we spoke—several times a week. He addressed me as "Madame, the Director" and referred to Jean-Robert simply as "Thingy."

I think he was on to something.

When the day arrived Charlotte was ready to return to school, I drove her to the train for the hour's journey to Liège. We'd made the trip several times together, but it was the first time she'd gone alone. As the train pulled away at half past six in the cold, damp winter morning air, my heart felt severed. She gazed out the window, huge blue eyes silently saying, Why are you making me leave you? I'm afraid.

124

It was in that instant I finally understood the depth of love one human can feel for another. Perhaps even what it feels like to be a mother. I wanted to grab the caboose, pull the train back into the station, and squeeze her in my arms. But I had to let her go.

We survived the first day apart. After that, while she had days here and there that she couldn't manage to get to school, by the middle of February she was pretty much back to her regular routine. The commute took a toll, but she seemed to adjust. I was doing writing consultancies for the UN so I could work from home. This was a solution for our money woes, but I was working on issues I'd promised myself I'd never again touch. I was back in the system, even if from a distance. Feeling like my life goals were, yet again, put on hold.

Rather than comforting each other, Jean-Robert and I grew more distant. I don't believe it ever occurred to him that it was hard on me. We fell into a pattern. I'd go to bed around ten o'clock and read until I dozed off, and he'd stay up all night using the computer. He'd come to bed around five in the morning; I'd be up a half hour later to get Charlotte off to school. So our time together was limited and tense, at best. I never questioned what he did online. With all of the difficulties of helping Charlotte through this transition and the abuse case she was filing against her brother, I didn't have to confront the reality that I was in a sexless, loveless marriage. And that was a relief.

One morning, however, I couldn't ignore it any longer. After returning home from dropping Charlotte at the station, I settled on the couch with a cup of coffee. While checking my email on my laptop, the only computer we had, I was suddenly paralyzed with disgust at the sight of some pictures I had not downloaded. I'm not particularly squeamish, nor am I a prude. But when a photo of a glassy-eyed, naked woman, bound and gagged, with the snout of an apparently live pig being shoved up her ass popped up on the screen, I lost it.

I broke into a cold sweat. My head started to spin. That horrifying nauseating image is forever imprinted in my brain. I immediately deleted it, and searched all Jean-Robert's files. I found hundreds of similar images in the thumbnails. I trashed every one.

His friend Marc had sexually abused the girl now in our care. What if she were to find these images on our computer, in this safe haven? She would feel betrayed and in danger again. My first thoughts were for her. My next thoughts were for me. What kind of monster had I married? I'd convinced myself he was just not very sexual.

Or that maybe the problem was me.

Maybe he was afraid of HIV and couldn't bring himself to discuss it. He'd mentioned, more than once, that he couldn't maintain an erection if he had to use a condom because it made him think too much about the act. I blamed myself for the fact that we'd need to use condoms to prevent transmission from me to him. I'd even imagined he might be gay. I could've handled that. Even an affair would have been better. I could comprehend being attracted to another breathing human being, but *this*?

The realization my husband preferred online porn to me, his wife—S&M and bestiality, no less—made me feel unlovable and broken. Up until that moment, I'd only known he simply did not desire me. Now I knew what he *did* desire and it filled me with confusion beyond belief.

Once he got up that day, I confronted him. "I've erased all of your files. Your disgusting photos."

He did not respond, but just stared at the computer sitting between us.

"How dare you download these when you know Charlotte uses this computer too. If you *ever* download another image to my computer, I will smash it and throw it in the trash."

Never mind that it was a brand-new Mac I'd purchased in the States just weeks before. I would have destroyed it to stop him.

"And how dare *you* mess with *my* files?" He, apparently, didn't comprehend the severity of what he'd done. "Anyway, you knew I liked pornos, what did you *think* I was doing at night? Playing games?"

I knew nothing of the sort.

He left the room for a shower. By the time he returned, he acted as if nothing had happened and asked if I wanted another cup of coffee.

None of my friends or family had any inkling as to what was going on between Jean-Robert and me. They knew about Charlotte, and assumed I was having a rip-roaring time with my boy toy. His mother even referred to our bedroom as "the playroom." I was too ashamed to tell anyone the truth. I went on living this lie, focused my attention on Charlotte, and escaped, whenever I could, into cooking, which made me feel whole. Producing nourishment made me feel I had a purpose, that I was able to at least contribute something to this otherwise unbearable nightmare.

After Charlotte had been back at school for a few weeks, I told her she'd have to do a few things around the house. She was not happy with this, but I stood my ground. I gave her a budget to do the grocery shopping once in a while, and taught her how to sort laundry and prepare a handful of simple recipes. I couldn't know what her future would hold. I wanted to be sure that, no matter what, she'd at least be able to take care of herself. She resisted at first but learned quickly, and even began to enjoy cooking. The kitchen was where we could get away from Jean-Robert and just be girls together.

On my birthday that year, my first as a married woman, she and I made cupcakes on that early April afternoon. Then we sat together and watched a movie. Jean-Robert was nowhere to be found. When I finally reached him on the phone about nine that evening, he seemed perplexed I'd expected him to take part in celebrating my birthday. Yet, in hindsight, it was one of the better birthdays I spent during my marriage.

By June, Charlotte was sixteen and had begun dating a boy from a nearby town. She'd met him on the train and a romance had blossomed. He was a few years older, worked full-time, and had a gentle manner.

On August 12th, the night of the Perseids meteor shower—the night each year with the most falling stars—she came home and sat in the chaise longue next to me on our massive terrace and told me, in the darkness and silence of the ever-rolling stars, that she'd just had sex for the first time.

I'd never told her about my diagnosis, however, and Charlotte had no idea how complicated sex was for me. In fact, Jean-Robert had suggested early on I no longer tell anyone I had HIV unless they needed to know, like my doctors. He said he felt it had been too much of a burden on me to be so open, and perhaps I should live my life more discreetly and keep my status a secret to our friends and family in Belgium. Indeed, I was happy to silence that part of my story for a while.

This role was new to me, having never been the confidant in such a situation before. Nor was I prepared for raising a teenager. I stopped breathing for a moment, my eyes fixed on a slow-moving satellite, and listened. She ended with, "Are you mad?"

"No, I just hope you're really ready for this. Sex is an amazing thing, Charlotte, and I hope you'll always enjoy it. But you also have to understand there are consequences. Promise me you'll always be safe."

"I will, Mama Bear, I promise."

A few months before, I'd asked my gynecologist about local resources for teens where my foster-daughter could learn about safer sex and STD/HIV prevention. Fully aware of my own history and health conditions, the doctor looked up coldly and said, "Why? This is Belgium. We don't worry about such things here. Just put her on the pill, she'll be fine."

I was shocked, and decided to take her prevention and awareness training into my hands. This was, after all, my profession. Charlotte had no idea that I was living with HIV—and wouldn't for years—but by the time I was done teaching her about condoms, she knew she didn't want to become pregnant, that much she understood. She said she just wanted to be loved and feel close to someone nice who was not going to hurt her.

On that warm, unusually clear summer night, she told me how her boyfriend had put candles around his room, and given her a massage, gently caressing every inch of her youthful skin. How they eventually melted into one another. Of course, she had no idea how much I wanted such an experience myself. During the entire time she lived with us, she observed that things were strained between Jean-Robert and me. But she could have had no idea of the growing schism that kept us on distant emotional shores.

In the fall we enrolled Charlotte in a school where she could live on campus during the week. Sort of a boarding school, but it felt to her more like a penitentiary. She spent every weekend crying and begging us not to send her back. My heart shattered every time we went through this. On one hand I thought it was best so she wouldn't have the awful commute and could make some new friends. I also needed space to get my own life back together a bit. On the other hand, I wouldn't have wanted to be there, either, so I felt her pain. A no-win situation. Eventually, following many phone calls and in-person visits, Charlotte decided she'd made amends enough with her birth mother to move back with her.

By early October, Charlotte had left the boarding school, returned to her old high school, and moved back in with her mother. My life was, at last, again my own. Jean-Robert and I still had issues to deal with. His refusal of sex had shifted from simply not seeking it to actively telling me he didn't want it.

"You should exercise. You're getting fat and it doesn't look good on you." He didn't desire me. He began to blame me for why we'd never once had sex. "Why don't you take care of yourself? I used to think you were attractive."

After months of this, I began to believe him. My mother had told me the same sorts of things, after all, so it must have been true.

"You're not ugly," she'd say, "but you're not pretty either."

In a perverted twist of fate, I'd fallen back into the destructive patterns of withheld love that echoed my childhood. Only this time, I'd chosen the path, not been born into it.

One Down, Eight to Go

Antananarivo

Madagascar: An island off the continent of Africa
Population: 26.9 million
Capital: Antananarivo

Broke and needing distance from my marriage, in the early summer of 2000 I reluctantly went back to consulting in public health. I'd promised myself I'd never do this, because it took such a toll on my health and well-being. But my responsible side kicked in and before I knew it, I'd gone from being a freelance artist to writing papers for the UN. That led to trips to Geneva, which led to work for international public health NGOs, and more for the UN. So it was a new chapter in my unexpected career began. By October, I was preparing to get on a plane headed for Madagascar.

On one hand, I was angry with myself for going back to work I thought I'd put behind me. On the other, I was happy for the chance to escape my unhappy "real" life and slip back into a world I'd so deeply inhabited for years. The comfort of the devil you know, I suppose.

The circle of global public health workers is, in the end, not that big. Once that network's activated, it's easy to tap back in. Through my former colleagues, I was soon offered a consultancy on HIV counseling and prevention.

I told my husband. "Jean-Robert, listen, I've been offered a short-term assignment, but it involves travel. Are you okay with that?"

"Does it involve being paid?" he queried dryly.

"Of course."

"Then I don't even know why you ask me. You have to make money for us. Do your share, you know."

I bit my lip and let this slide. I was the only one in the family who worked. I'd been supporting us both since we'd met two years prior, and later Charlotte as well. But his personality was volatile, so I always asked, as if seeking permission, to mollify his giant ego. Even though I knew he'd want me to make money and that I'd do it regardless. In fact, I couldn't wait to leave and was a little too happy to accept and book my travel.

"I think the...distance will be good, for both of us. I know I need some. It's been a crazy year with Charlotte and everything," I said.

"Where is it? Geneva?" he asked.

"Madagascar."

"Madagascar?" He looked at me in surprise. "Wow, when you said *distance* you weren't kidding."

Following an early morning two-hour drive to Brussels from our little town, then a one-hour flight to Paris followed by a nearly twelve hour flight south to Madagascar, I finally arrived on the red island. It was the longest journey I'd made to date without crossing more than two time zones. Landing in Antananarivo around two in the morning, I'd spent nearly twenty-four hours in transit. Despite the hour, my friend Patrick—whom I'd known for years and whom I'd stayed with in Delhi years before—picked me up. He'd been working there for a couple of years and he and his wife, Mei, again extended their hospitality, inviting me to stay with them. Patrick gave me a hug and immediately teased me. "I hope those shoes weren't expensive."

"No. Why? Just my casual kicks." I looked down at my white sneakers to see that they were now the hue of tandoori chicken. In just the short walk from the terminal to the parking lot, they'd become covered in dirt. "Oh, shit."

"They don't call it the red island for nothing!" Patrick said, as we climbed into the vehicle for the ride to their home.

I slept late the first morning and awoke to the sound of hip-hop. Their children, Sophie and Benjamin, were taking dance classes with some of the neighborhood kids. I stumbled sleepily into the living room to see what was going on and was tapped on the shoulder by a small, beautiful, Malagasy woman who quietly asked me "massage?" I thought I was still dreaming, rubbed my eyes like a toddler and said, "Me? Moi? Massage? Oh oui oui ouiiii!"

She escorted me to an oversized closet which doubled as storage and craft-central for the kids. When the craft table was properly swathed in towels, it became a massage room. As she lit a candle and some amber incense, she explained that she came to the Brenny/Zegers house each Saturday and Mei had suggested I might also like a massage. Once I settled in on the table, she dug her small strong hands into my jetlagged, pretzeled muscles. I was back to sleep in seconds. At some point she woke me enough to have me roll off the table and go back to bed. Next thing I remember was waking for dinner; spaghetti, I believe.

The following day, Mei and Sophie took me for a drive into town. Antananarivo, or Tana, as the locals call it, is stunning. One is constantly climbing and descending the dramatic landscape and the contrast of the lush purple flowers on the jacaranda trees overhanging the deep green Lake Anosy, in the center of town, with the red hills in the background was a combination I'd never before seen in nature. There was a mixture of colonial wooden architecture and modern glass structures. The cars seemed to be held together with spit and good wishes but miraculously always managed to ascend these impossible hills. It was not uncommon to get into a taxi that had a jerry can by the passenger seat with a hose feeding fuel to the engine, set next to a spare battery juicing the radio and meter. It's actually a good thing that it's such a beautiful place, because the scenery distracts you from the haphazard finagling of day-to-day life.

The work I'd contracted for involved designing a training package for primary health care workers and their clients—mostly sex workers—to do peer education and counseling. The ultimate goal was to introduce the female condom, a polyurethane alternative to the male condom, and develop a base of informed users, thus providing them more options. My first trip was a sort of fact-finding mission—and a great chance to reconnect with old friends. Ultimately, I'd make four trips to Madagascar. I'd gladly sign up for a fifth.

By my second trip, it was clear that the level of knowledge around HIV was extremely low. Peer education was a mystery. Counseling, a completely unknown foreign concept. What was strong and vibrant were the stigma and discrimination that surrounded the pandemic, along with a list of myths and misconceptions that perpetuated the spread of the virus through ignorance and fear.

With this in mind, I suggested to an acquaintance who worked for the US government that I would be willing to speak at their internal, informal brown-bag lunch scheduled for World AIDS Day, which falls each year on December 1.

"You know, Wendy, I've been reading the paper here every morning, and I have to say I'm shocked by the way HIV is presented. I mean, really, the language is appalling! It feels like I'm reading stuff from a decade ago."

She shook her head, her dark cropped hair barely moving, as she rubbed her hands together. She pushed her glasses up on top of her head, rubbed her eyes, and simply said, "Oh I know. Man, do I know."

I blurted out a few of the examples that keep popping up and raising my heart rate. "'AIDS carriers' and, oh, my favorite, 'contaminated people,' for example. Do they not understand there are individuals at the end of every statistic?"

She blew out a long breath. "You don't have to tell me, Martina. I deal with this every day. I think it's one of the challenges particular to an island nation. They're a bit more cut off and see themselves as different from everyone else. Which, in a way, they are. But they're still not immune and I don't know how to get the messages out. The *right* messages, that is. Nobody will talk about it."

"Hasn't anyone living with HIV come forward to share their experiences? Publicly? On TV or the radio? I mean, it's a new century, and it's not exactly a new issue."

"Oh no, not a soul. And I don't think anyone will. I wish we could at least get someone to speak to my staff. They're clearly not the general public, but even those of us working on the issue are not well informed. It's a challenge, to put it mildly."

I thought about this as we continued discussing the politics of US government work and how it would change now that George W. Bush had been elected. Everyone was expecting major cuts to public health work, or at the very least, a change in the core mandate.

"Aren't you doing a World AIDS Day event next Friday?" I asked. "A small internal thing for staff, no?"

"Yes. It's just a lunch thing with our little team in-house. Nothing fancy but to at least remind people why we're at work every day! Did you want to join us?"

I was thinking, *Hell no!* I hate World AIDS Day. I live it 24/7 and the last thing I want to do is focus more attention on the worst part of my life. But I thought I could help by speaking privately to her staff. Then they'd have met at least one person living with HIV.

"Well, I was thinking. If you want, I could speak to your group."

She nodded. "Um, sure. You mean about the female condom?"

"No, about myself, actually."

She looked baffled. "Yourself?"

"Yeah, you know, I'm HIV positive—have been for, gosh, almost nine years."

Silence for a moment. Then, "Oh, wow. I had no idea," she said. "Well, that would be amazing! I'm sure the staff really will appreciate it! I think you'd be the first person most of them have met who would *admit* to living with HIV. Even though they work on the issue and probably interact with HIV-positive people all the time."

We smiled at one another. But then she frowned. "You're sure about this?"

"I've done it a million times. Bringing a real person into the room changes everything. Puts a face to the epidemic, you know, all that stuff. I'm happy to do it. It's been a while, but since it's a small internal event, it'll be fine."

"Wow. Thanks so much, Martina. This is brilliant!" She hugged me before we got back to work.

That morning, I rushed to finish up that day's tasks so I could find a taxi and make it over to the Mission for the luncheon. A bit frazzled, sweating in the heat of the Southern Hemisphere summer, I settled into the back seat of the taxi and laughed at the unlikely choice of music. Don McLean was singing "American Pie." I sang quietly along to the lyrics: *...that'll be the day that I die. Bye, bye...* The fragrant purple trumpet blossoms of the

134

jacaranda along the lake reminded me to relax and take in the beauty as we drove uptown, and uphill, from the hospital where I was based.

A less memorable pop tune followed as we got stalled in traffic. In Madagascar, people often only work half a day on Fridays, so traffic jams up early. Soon I was feeling antsy (I hate being late) and checked my watch to see if we'd still arrive on time. The news came on the radio. About three stories in, my heart began racing as an announcement came over the radio.

"Today, at the US Mission, for the first time ever, an AIDS victim will tell of her tragedy in public in Madagascar. We'll be covering this live event so don't miss out on hearing the story of how this woman became contaminated, and tries to face life with this scourge."

Shhhhhhhhhhhhhhhhhhhiiiiiiiiiiiiiiit. I think I only thought that, but I might've said it out loud.

This was bad. In the days since I'd seen Wendy, it had gone from an internal brown-bag lunch to a major public event. With media in tow. I was not prepared to go public in this way in Madagascar. Not that I really cared who knew about me, I'd been the poster child in the UN for years. But I knew it would do more damage than good, here, at this point.

The people I was trying to work with—the sex workers and clinicians—would view me differently now. They'd have a harder time seeing me as a professional. I'd seen that happen a hundred times. The moment I disclosed my status, I went from being a public health specialist to a side-show act with zero credibility.

But more important, the prevailing attitude on the island was that HIV was a foreigner's disease. The people knew that many goods and services must be brought on to the island, and viruses are no exception. So they blamed the foreigners for bringing it, deeming it *their* fault and also *their* problem. So the Malagasy were having a hard time realizing it didn't matter how it got there, only that it was spreading rapidly among the population.

No, if I was the first to go public here—a blue-eyed, blond foreigner—it would confirm the suspicions and give weight to the myths. The public health workers would be set back. They'd lose years trying to convince the population that it was, indeed, their issue to tackle.

Once at the venue, I flagged Wendy. Too late. She was at the podium preparing to announce me. The back of the room was full of TV cameras and furry mics on booms for the local stations. It would be too hard to get through. So I found one of her assistants and handed her a scrawl I'd penned in the taxi over:

I'm so sorry, but I can't speak. I will explain later. Trust me on this, please.

She took the note up and slipped it to Wendy. Who glanced down, furrowed her brow, and took a deep breath.

"I'm so sorry to tell you all that, due to unforeseen circumstances, our guest speaker will not be able to join us today. So let's continue with the rest of the panel. Kathleen, do you want to take the mic? Thank you."

Following the event, once the media had cleared out, Wendy and I discussed my staying silent. Although she didn't enjoy the awkward moment at the podium, she agreed with my decision not to speak. First impressions are powerful, after all.

Had I just spoken informally to a small group of Wendy's staff, that would have been fine. But being broadcast live into the homes of all Malagasy, would set the national response back years, if not decades. It was best that they waited until a Malagasy was ready and continue their behind-the-scenes advocacy in the meantime. We said our goodbyes and headed to our respective homes for the weekend.

Far too early for my taste on the following Monday morning, I made my way from the neighborhood guesthouse where I'd started staying, over to my friend Patrick's place across the street. He gave me a ride to work each morning, as many of the international organizations were based in the same part of town.

The bonus of a ride with my former UNAIDS colleague was that, assuming I could get my nocturnal self up in time, a hot bowl of oatmeal and a cup of freshly brewed coffee would be waiting for me. No conversation expected, because we'd be listening to the BBC News on the little gray radio that lived atop the fridge. I could slip into the house, take my seat at the table, and only be expected act human post-feeding.

By seven, we were always in his huge US-government issued SUV, a perk for being head of his mission. His driver opened the gate, drove the car into the street, and jumped out to shut the gate behind us. Then we were on our way down the potholed red roads of Antananarivo, into town.

I watched for my favorite pack of dogs who ran wild in the neighborhood. Centuries back, a French colonist had brought along a few *bichon frisé* as pets. They'd escaped and proceeded to breed. So it was now common to see packs of these cotton-ball dogs all over the country. But, instead of a fluffy, well-groomed white, they were often a rusty shade of orange, from the red earth so famous on the island. They were still adorable, and still very yappy.

As per our daily routine, once we were on the road Patrick and I looked through his stack of local and international newspapers that were delivered each morning. He handed me half the stack and kept the local rags. "Let's see what Madagascar has to say about the World AIDS Day events last Friday. Not much probably. But maybe I'll be happily proven wrong."

I was looking at the *International Herald Tribune*, probably at the funnies, when he let out a snort. "Martina, here's a good one. You should read this, halfway down the left side."

Indeed, there in the left column was a short article about the event I'd backed out of three days prior. They listed those who *had* spoken and a few key messages taken away from their coverage of the luncheon. Toward the end was the line that warranted the snort.

Unfortunately, the key speaker—the victim with AIDS—was unable to join the panel because she died.

I sucked in my breath, then burst out laughing. Patrick was watching me in the rearview mirror. Without skipping a beat, he said, "Well, my dear, all things considered, you look fantastic for a dead woman! How *do* you do it?"

I've had some strange words written about me, and been called plenty of things, but this was a first. Although, clearly it won't be the last. News of my demise had been greatly exaggerated, to paraphrase Mark Twain. I could only hope that next notice would be many decades away. I suspect I'm a little bit feline and will have nine lives.

One down, eight to go!

When I returned to Belgium, after that long, long journey, Jean-Robert picked me up at the airport. "I need to stop in Liège on the way back," he said. "It'll just take a minute."

I was too exhausted to protest. We stopped at the office where he was volunteering on some project he'd never finish. We were there for nearly two hours. By the time I finally got him to leave, I was close to tears.

At that point he grew angry. "You are so impatient. You're so selfish," he said. "Why can't you let me do *my* work sometimes? It's always about you, *n'est ce pas?*"

I tried to explain that a full day journey was enough reason to want to be home, but he just got more annoyed. In the car, as we were exiting the lot, he cut off another driver. Rather than politely excuse himself, he braked violently, got out and started screaming at the other guy. The other driver jumped out and came after my husband with a crowbar. I shrank as small as possible into the passenger seat and held my breath until my husband got back in the car and we sped away.

When we finally got home that day, I found the house a disaster. Crusted dishes piled eight high in the sink, laundry all over the floor of the bedroom, the sheets on the unmade bed stained with sweat. I wanted nothing more than to go directly back to the airport and head back to Madagascar. I should have.

Cats, Catsup, and finally, Calm

Spa, Belgium

My consulting concluded, dishes washed, and the house cleaned, I was home, yet looking for the next position. The next chance to escape.

"*Putain, merde!*" The stream of my husband's pee stopped abruptly as my cat, Ruby, screeched at him, breaking the all-too-short stretch of silence I'd so desperately needed to concentrate on my job search.

I hit *save* on my laptop at the dining table in our common room and took a deep breath, noticing our younger cat, Saphir, high up on the exposed beam above my head, watching the doorway and shrinking back as if terrified.

Tugging at the zipper on his gray Levi's with one hand as he brushed unkempt, long brown hair from his flushed face with the other, Jean-Robert yelled, "Your fucking shit of a cat! He wants always to dominate me!"

I bit my lower lip, squeezed my eyes shut, and pulled my chin in to my sternum. If only I could disappear, or hide in the rafters like Saphir.

"Can you fucking believe him? I'm trying to pee at my own fucking house, and he has to come in and harass me to shit," Jean-Robert ranted.

"Why don't you close the door?" I responded calmly, trying to pull a veil of peace back over the room. "You can't really be mad with a cat who trained himself to use the toilet. Usually people think that's his best quality—he's self-toilet-trained," I added lightly, trying to inject some levity.

"Yeah, well, *il m'emmerde.* He always bugs the shit out of me, like it's *his* toilet, not mine."

His toilet? He'd never cleaned it once that I knew of. In the background rose a gentle tinkling as Ruby relieved himself.

When we'd lived in Geneva, Ruby had used to watch me like a surveillance satellite, orbiting my existence. Amazingly, he taught himself to use the toilet. On that modern Swiss model he could even flush. Here, without thumbs, he of course couldn't grasp the dangling chain in our centuries-old house. In both abodes, I'd been delighted to be relieved of the scooping and shoveling of poo and acrid, clumped-up pee. My husband couldn't see it that way. When Ruby began scratching the tank I knew I needed to go flush for him.

That made my husband that much angrier. "Why don't you wipe his fucking cat ass? *Putain,* fucking cat, always wants to show who is the 'big man' in your stupid life."

Yes, my eight-pound cat enraged and intimidated my two hundred-pound husband. They hated each other, and always had. I should have trusted Ruby's instincts. My cat had always been the smarter of the two and, ultimately, won all their battles.

On the way back to my computer, I stopped in the kitchen to check on dinner. I was cooking Pad Thai again, from scratch. A real production to make it in our rural town. Finding the ingredients was an all-day adventure in Liège, an hour away, but it reminded me of visits to Thailand. I didn't really mind the hassle, but because I didn't know my way around Liège, I generally end up going with Jean-Robert, who seemed increasingly annoyed by everything. Especially me.

After putting the angel hair noodles to soak, and pressing the water out of the tofu, I checked on the curry paste I'd made up that morning. I sneaked a little dried shrimp—my favorite part—but then felt guilty because it'd taken searching three stores to find them. This package came from the basement of a poorly lit Chinese shop near the street with the prostitutes displayed slowly dancing in neon-lit windows at the edge of the city center. Just off the parking lot where we leave my car—my red VW convertible that Jean-Robert had long ago commandeered.

Standing in the kitchen, I reviewed the recipe in a dog-eared cookbook purchased a few years back in the Bangkok airport with leftover baht. Oh shit, I thought. I forgot to buy limes. I needed the limes, but more than anything, I needed to get out of the house. It was bad enough my husband constantly fought about ridiculous things, but when he involved my cat, over *urinating* for God's sake…I needed to clear my head to make sense of the situation.

His incessant verbal jabs felt like someone working a skewer through my ribs to bleed my soul. No one thing was unbearable. But it never let up. The constant stress and anxiety felt physical, like bronchitis—sharp pains in my chest that at times made it hard to breathe.

"Jean-Robert?"

"*What?*" he snapped back from behind the folding divider he'd built to surround his monstrous desk, which took up an entire corner of our common room.

"Have to go to the store, I forgot something for dinner."

"Fine, can you pick me some choco milk? And, *ouai*, I'm stressed—get me some frites, eh?"

"Thank you. You're welcome!" I muttered to myself, irked that he'd asked for fries when he knew I was cooking dinner. Anyhow, he laughed whenever I said thank you. He considered any expression of gratitude a waste of breath. I could count on one hand the number of times he'd said it to me with sincerity.

I pulled on my old ski jacket, the warmest thing I owned, plus a wool hat and a pair of gloves. I'd learned to keep my jacket upstairs, so it stayed warm. Downstairs was too cold in February. My office had no heat, so I tended to hover near the kitchen, which was always warm.

I left the common room and stopped in our bedroom for my purse. It was on top of the old dark-blue trunk I used as a dresser—the kind once portered aboard steamers for glamorous voyages across the Atlantic. I found a twenty-euro note and slid it into my pocket. I pulled out my cell phone, then stuffed it deep into my sock drawer. I didn't want to be reached.

Ruby was asleep on the end of the bed. He looked up with huge green-grape eyes, the shade stark against his black fur. The little white patch on his neck had always reminded me of a priest's collar. He squeezed his eyes in a gesture I've always taken to mean "I love you Mom, I always will." He purred and stretched a paw out as I passed. I touched his silky black fur, and lingered on his neck as he rubbed his head into my hand. My first and likely only dose of affection for the day. I hoped to pet him again later; he and Saphir were all the companionship I had.

In the nearly two years we'd lived in Spa, I'd never managed to make a friend. I knew a few of Jean-Robert's buddies, but we weren't close. Locals no doubt saw me as a transient. Even the ones I encountered each day at the newsstand refused to acknowledge my greetings. We were (both) known as The Americans, oddly enough, since Jean-Robert was Belgian. Apparently, we were not to be spoken to. I felt very alone in town, though even more so at home.

Despite asking him to stop, my husband still spent his nights on the computer feeding an addiction to porn. He'd come to bed at five or six in the morning, just as I was waking up. I sensed he'd been with a hundred women online and felt disgusted by the smells of his solitary cyber-sex; a sweat he'd worked up all alone.

I descended the black-veined white marble steps down to the front entry of our centuries-old carriage house. Even if it wasn't a happy home, I loved its depth of years.

I dislodged my bicycle from the jumble of still packed boxes in the entryway. After unlatching the heavy oak door with the small paned windows, I guided my bicycle out in front of the house. I could smell that the mailman had peed against the house again. What was it with men marking territory in this country? I sometimes felt like they were part dog, lording their power over each over, and especially women. It drove me crazy. I've had to hold my pee for hours in some unlikely places, yet they could urinate in public, on a whim. So not fair.

I walked the bike past my car. Once Jean-Robert had stopped my car dead on the freeway, in the fast lane, due to road rage. Then sped up again, forcing another vehicle off onto the shoulder. It was the same car he'd driven to pick me up from the airport when I returned from Madagascar, when he'd picked a fight with the driver who'd come after him with the crowbar. It was the car I was now afraid to ride in, even if I was driving, because it felt cursed by his demons. It reminded me of moments with him at the wheel when I'd feared for my life. I pulled my hat down over my ears, zipped my jacket up around my chin, and mounted my bicycle.

I hoped they'd have limes. To my Californian self, they were basic rations. In Belgium in winter it might not be so simple. I opted for the Match down past the park. It was generally better stocked but most important, farther away than the GB Super, in walking distance. The Delhaize was even farther away, but the sky looked silver with pending snow. So I compromised to avoid riding to the outskirts of town. I had Dutch saddlebags on the bike, so no need to worry about carrying things—as long as my legs could pedal, I was good to go. Twelve liters of water plus a bag or two of groceries on each handlebar and a small cake in my front basket was the most I'd ever managed. But I have the thighs of a ballerina and was never in a hurry to get home.

I felt safe inside the store; invisible, normal. I wandered up and down the aisles looking at things I didn't need, just to revel in the mundaneness. I found the limes and carefully selected half a dozen, inspecting each carefully even though they all looked the same. Maybe that's what *buying time* really meant: lingering over purchases to avoid returning to reality. I took more of it collecting the other items on my list, then silently endured checkout. Lifting the shopping bags, I headed back into the cold, feeling better for the brief visit.

Groceries secured, I pedaled back rattling toward our house along the cobblestone streets, stopping at a tiny dark shop that sold fries and meatballs. It always smelled like stale grease. I always felt as if I'd been coated in Vaseline by the time I left. The thing that makes Belgian frites so tasty is that they're double fried. Twice the grease, twice the flavor. Twice the blocked arteries, no doubt.

The young clerk asked, "Do you want mayonnaise for your fries?"

"Oui." For a moment I chose to believe they were *my* fries. Unlike most Americans, I prefer mayonnaise, not ketchup. Perhaps it's my maternal grandmother's Belgian roots coming through. As she slathered on the white stuff, I snapped back into the reality that they were for Jean-Robert, and blurted out, "Oh, and ketchup, too?"

"That'll cost extra. Ten centimes!"

"Fine. Yes, sorry, ketchup, *s'il vous plait.*" She added it along the other side, folded up the grease-stained butcher paper cone, and handed it over.

I took the oozing mess outside and did my best to eat only the fries doused in a maximum quantity of mayonnaise to hide my slip-up. I used one last fry to scoop off the remaining mayo into a trash can. With just a trace, I could always blame the shop girl. I had to hide my mistake or I'd hear about it for days. I felt nauseated, and stopped again for a mineral water, hoping it might calm my stomach.

Once when my sister Adrian and her husband had come to visit, Jean-Robert had shown them around town. They stopped at a water spigot that smelled of sulfur.

"This water is so good for the humans," he explained, "you should try it. It really is so good—it comes from the, uh, how do you say? Sewers!"

Adrian and Don were first struck speechless, then awkwardly declined. We all laughed when we later discovered he had been trying to say from *the source*—meaning the spring.

I stuffed the fries into the front of my jacket, as I'd once done with a tiny kitten rescued from the back of a restaurant. The bundle warmed my chest as I rode back home. Spa was postcard-perfect that evening. Tree-lined streets and garlands of lights strung over the crossings to make it feel like it was always Christmas.

A long black wrought-iron arcade to my left served as the shelter for a flea market the last Sunday of every month, my favorite thing to do in town. It reminded me of the splendor of Spa's history; of a time when kings and queens and ridiculously wealthy aristocrats had strolled through that park each morning after taking the waters as part of their "cure."

Hooded kids on skateboards morphed, in my mind, into elegant women with feathered hats and men in spats with walking sticks.

As I neared the entry to our park—as I explained earlier, le Parc de Quatre Heures, transformed in the early 1900s into a cul-de-sac of private homes—my reverie faltered, then vanished. I remembered I was headed back upstairs to the hornet's nest that was my real life.

On any given day, I could return to find Jean-Robert in a good mood enjoying a delightful moment of whimsy. It was equally possible I would have to walk on eggshells to avoid screaming daggers of anger. Or a full-on assault for some fault I'd never understand. Fists never hit me, but furniture got tossed across the room. Being in my husband's presence was always a volatile mystery. The deepening circles under my eyes and my hypersensitive flinching at a creak from the floor above the entryway reminded me I lived in a self-imposed prison.

My mother's voice rose in my head, yelling down from the bed she nearly never left—where she read Louis L'Amour frontier adventures and countless romance novels as she ate cookies and chocolates directly from a large paper grocery bag she kept next to her bed.

"You're so cold and unlovable," she used to say. "No boy is ever going to want to hold you." She was half right. Plenty of boys had, in fact, wanted to hold me; they just hadn't wanted to love me.

I walked slowly up the stairs and into the main part of the house, carrying the shopping bags and his fries. I dropped the bags on the kitchen counter, pulled the fries from my jacket and delivered them to his desk, where he was deep in a computer search.

"They're cold," he snapped. "And why is there mayonnnnnnnnnnnnaise? *Merde*, you know I only like ketchup. Pffffffff."

"Sorry, the shopgirl didn't... sorry," I replied with a *you know how they are* shrug and a jut of the chin. Then I backed out of his space toward my safety zone, the kitchen.

Half an hour later we sat down together for our meal—a regular event that always surprised me, as a family dinner was something that never happened in my childhood. This regular togetherness, like so many things, confused me. Our life was so tense, yet we always ate together when both were home.

We vocalized our respective rituals. "Bon appétit," I said.

"Cheese!" he replied.

I'd never been kind enough to explain that it was actually *Cheers.* Instead I'd been letting him say that, to the delight of Anglophones, for ages.

As we ate, I mentioned I might be up for a monthlong consultancy in Eritrea, worried he'd be upset I might be gone for so long.

"It's interesting work, and closer than Madagascar. I'm a little afraid to keep doing these consultancies, though. I fear getting sucked back into the bureaucratic nightmare and ending up again at the UN, when that I worked so hard to leave. That environment nearly killed…"

"*What?*" He pushed his half-full plate toward me, spilling the Pad Thai. He shoved his chair back, thick untoned arms braced against the long wooden table. His left hand rested on a stain: magenta dye, from when I'd used to paint. "How *dare* you! How dare you even consider to *not* taking a job. You can make so much monies. That will pay our bills for months so I can stay here and work on my projects."

What projects? I thought. A thesis on computer porn?

"Not to take it. *It kills me,*" he said, mocking my voice by saying the last words an octave higher. "*Merde alors*, you are so fucking selfish," he continued. "And also, this Chinese-Japanese fucking thing you make for the dinner is just showing off, like everything you do. I'm going out for some meat. Some real food."

The chair tipped over as he leapt up in a fury. He grabbed his coat and keys, stormed outside, and sped away in my car.

I stared at the chair lying on the floor like a dead body, and breathed a deep sigh of relief. I'd have at least a few hours of peace.

Without a sound, our young cat dropped from the joist onto the table to eat the spilled food. As snow began to fall outside on the adjoining terrace, the barely audible rasps of her pink tongue, were, blissfully, the only sound in the finally-quiet room.

Up for a Challenge

Asmara

Eritrea: Horn of (East) Africa
Population: 3.5 million
Capital: Asmara

"Princess! How are you?"

"Hello there, Stephen! I'm well. And how is my favorite bodyguard today?" I smiled back at this former soldier. He held his six-foot frame proudly. His wide-set eyes were smiling. We'd first met in Uganda, his home country, and crossed paths periodically here and there around the world.

We hugged in the too-quiet lobby of the Asmara InterContinental hotel. Built during the recently ended Eritrean-Ethiopian war, its only civilian guests were me and another consultant, a woman from Germany. The rest of the rooms were used by UN peacekeepers, battalions of Italians. He clearly didn't think I was safe in their presence, though I doubt it was their firearms he was worried about.

Stephen scanned the room over my shoulder. "Are these Italians behaving themselves?"

"Yes, my dear, they are. Even if I might secretly wish they weren't. And anyway, you're here to protect me."

"It's for your own good. I don't trust these guys, you know."

"I'm the Princess of Madagascar! I'll be just fine."

"But that is exactly *why* I need to protect you—you are the Princess! Anyone can see that!"

We burst into laughter and headed to the café for a snack. Just prior to coming to Eritrea, I'd been working in Madagascar off and on for six months. For reasons unknown, Stephen had started calling me the Princess of Madagascar. Not sure how it evolved, but it stuck.

Stephen was in Eritrea with the United Nations Department of Peacekeeping Operations (DPKO), rolling out the first-ever HIV training for uniformed troops. The world of international HIV work is a very small one, and those of us in it living with HIV seem to find each other like spies on a bench in Gorky Park.

After our break, Stephen headed back to a weeklong workshop for journalists on how to write and report about HIV. I would join him for a panel in a few days. I made my way over to the office where my colleague Astrid was working—my contact person in Eritrea.

Eritrea has a distinct Italian flavor, following sixty years of colonization from the 1880s through the 1940s. Many of the old-timers speak Italian rather than English, if they have a second or third language after Tigrinya. If it wasn't for the arid heat and khaki-colored landscape, one could be in a suburb of Milan.

With the Eritrean-Ethiopian war freshly finished only a year before, Asmara, the capital of this tiny troubled country, was quiet and felt very empty much of the time. Despite the vacant city, office space was in short supply.

Several narrow windy roads and countless bouncy hills later, the taxi driver left me at the entrance to an industrial warehouse-looking building. A seemingly *vacant* industrial warehouse-looking building. Empty except, that is, for Astrid—an effervescent Canadian in her fifties with cropped blond hair and a smile wide as her country. She was waiting for me outside this lonely structure and immediately saw the surprise on my face.

"Oh, don't worry, *this* isn't the office," she said. "It's just where I meet people so I can escort you personally to my oasis in the sky."

She gave me an impish grin, one I'd quickly come to adore. Astrid had a wicked sense of gallows humor, which drew me to her even more. I followed her upstairs, down hallways, and along windowless corridors and up and over and finally to a door that led us out on to the roof.

The roof? Where the hell was she taking me?

"Ah, we're almost here! Watch out for the wind vent, it'll wreak havoc with your hairdo."

I instinctively smoothed a hand over my head, then laughed, remembering my hairdo was a ponytail. Not much to mess with. Atop this huge building was a corrugated-metal add-on structure that held four makeshift offices. In subsequent meetings, we'd mostly avoid it in favor of working in cafes, my hotel lobby or Astrid's wacky apartment that had stickers of food all over the exteriors of the toilet and bathtub. Blissfully, she had air conditioning—whenever the city's power was on, which was *most* of the time. Several days a week, anyway. Too many hours in that oven of an office would've left us shrink-wrapped in our clothes. But on that day, without AC, ten floors up under the blazing sun on the horn of Africa, we attempted to set out a plan for my time in Eritrea.

"So, you'll be working with two gentlemen, both ex-military. Everyone here, of course, is ex-military, following the conflict," she said. "They'll arrive in an hour, but I wanted to brief you on our overall goals."

"Sounds good. My understanding is that you—they—want to set up a network of people living with HIV. Is that right?"

"Exactly."

"And what do they have so far? Have they held any sort of meetings yet?"

"So far, they have an office and a lot of good intentions and energy," she stated, suppressing a giggle.

"So we're starting from scratch."

"Yes. I hope you've packed your magic wand because this is not going to be easy. Their budget is next to nothing but the need is enormous. They're counting on you, and from your résumé I think you're the woman for the job. Oh, and by the way, between you and me, please mention *women* every chance you get. During the war, men and women fought side-by-side, but now those same women have been put back in traditional garb, covered up, and sent back home to be quiet and serve their men. We may have another war brewing in the kitchens!"

"Okay, then." I smiled at her, wondering what I was getting myself into. My consultancy in Madagascar had gone well, but I'd had a team to work with. Here I would basically be on my own, so I had to be on my game. Intellectually, I knew I could do this job in my sleep. Emotionally, I was still broken down from my years at UNAIDS. I hoped I wouldn't fail them, or myself.

148

Just then we heard a light slam of the door across the way, then footsteps crunching across the gravely roof toward us.

"Oh, that'll be our boys. Seems they're early. Here goes, Miss Martina!" In 2001, no Eritreans were public about their status, so names were sometimes 'edited'. In this vein of respecting privacy, I'll call these two fellows Wedi and Ato.

After introductions, I started nervously chattering about the networks I'd been involved with and how I was sure I could help them out. I tended to go overboard trying to prove my qualifications, my worth, in hopes people I'd just met would believe I was competent. A few paragraphs into my monologue, I realized these two tall, thin, chisel-faced, men were staring at me with furrowed brows. Only Wedi spoke English well. Ato understood a few words; he mostly looked at me like I was a cuckoo clock he wished he could silence.

"Wow. I'm sorry, let's slow down and start again. How do *you* want to proceed?" I finally asked, pretending to tidy my ponytail so I could wipe my sweating hands without them noticing.

"Well, we thought that you could come to see our office. That's a good place for starting, no?" Wedi said.

"Of course. Let's do that."

I said goodbye to Astrid and followed the two lanky guys back down the long path to their white four-wheel-drive vehicle. They drove me to a seemingly-abandoned house on the edge of town. I'd been in the country for only a day or two, and there I was, either being abducted or about to embark on a great adventure.

I sucked up a dose of blind faith and prayed for the latter.

Inside were a desk and a few chairs, blank walls, and a bookcase. I made a beeline toward the single computer, shiny and new, plastic wrap still covering the keyboard and around the cables. The power plug was tightly wrapped with a twist-tie tucked on top of the CPU.

Ato tried the light switch, but no lights came on. I guessed then we'd be doing our work longhand.

"Wonderful, isn't it?!" beamed Wedi, the taller of my colleagues, Ato, the smaller, quieter one glowed with pride behind him.

"Yes. Wow. Absolutely. This is, uh, a great space. A bit far from town, but lots of room! So then, let's get to work." We'd stopped on the way for sodas at roadside vender who sat on an ice chest, patiently waiting for customers. We placed our respective thick glass Coke bottles on the desks. "Okay. Good. So tell me, what is your plan so far?" I asked.

Wedi and Ato darted eyes at each other.

"Uh, have you got a mission statement?" I continued.

They looked at me with furrowed brows.

"Have you got a timeline?"

We all smiled. For a moment, nobody spoke.

I tried a more general approach. "What do you hope to have accomplished by the time I leave?"

"A strong, thriving network of all HIV positives in Eritrea," Wedi responded emphatically, as Ato continued to smile.

"Of course. And how many people do you have so far?"

"Well, there is another guy. And, then, us." They glanced at each other as if for confirmation of the math, before continuing. "So, three. Yes, we are three."

I nodded. We were clearly still at square one even if, in their minds, they were already selling T-shirts and baseball caps at fundraising rallies.

"Alrighty then. So, let's do this. Let's pick a date, maybe six months in the future, for the first national meeting of people with HIV in Eritrea and work backward from there. Does that make sense?" I searched their faces for understanding while they translated and spoke to one another.

Finally Wedi said, "Six months is much time from now. Why so long?"

"A coordinated event takes time to plan. Time to book a room, send out invitations, decide on speakers, organize logistics, all of that. Longer than you'd expect. And, of course, since we're talking about folks living with HIV, we have to make sure at every step along the way that things are safe for them."

They sat back in their chairs, confused.

"Not *physically* safe in the sense of needing weapons. Most of you are trained as soldiers, so I know you can hold your own. I mean emotionally safe. Prepared for the consequences of being known as HIV-positive. This is a first, so getting people to come to a meeting will not be easy. A few, yes, but most will want to hide. We have to make it worth their while. Assure them they won't be outed by attending."

These two warriors were so determined, it hadn't occurred to them that not everyone would be ready to step forward. I'd been there myself, early on, not fully grasping the fact that most people are extremely reluctant to be involved in anything labeled HIV.

And rightfully so. Even in San Francisco, where services abounded, the stigma and discrimination was ever present. Here, in a country ravaged by war, raw with pain and suffering and families broken over an imposed border with the country that used to be their own, anything that made you different was amplified. Something that made you different *and* a public health risk would probably feel insurmountable.

Ato pulled out a lined pad and we set to work. A few hours later we'd a drafted a mission statement and a rough timeline. We then started thinking about the specific tasks needed to accomplish our goal of uniting the HIV-positive population.

The name of the network would be Bidho, a Tigrinya word that means "challenge." Well chosen, as we had a daunting road ahead. But I felt sure their enthusiasm would carry us through, and it looked like I was the right fit for the job. I felt proud every time I made a suggestion and realized it was just what was needed. For the first time in years, I truly felt useful.

The Eritrean consultancy was a dream. Along with my work for Bidho, I did a few trainings for other local organizations and also sat in with Stephen for the DPKO training with local journalists. I was again astonished by their choice of language. 'AIDS sufferers', 'contaminated patients', 'vectors of disease'—there was still so much work to do to counter the disgrace and prejudice.

I started my collaboration with DPKO through a staff member there, a Kenyan named Michael Munywoki, and developed a new understanding and respect for the missions they undertook. They often went far beyond the horrific stories we hear about in the news. Indeed, they were also engaged in extensive training, intended to increase capacity of their local counterparts on various subjects.

During the month I spent working with Wedi and Ato, we met with many local leaders—religious, social and political. When possible, we'd invite Stephen to join us.

One meeting we held was with a mufti—the head of the Muslim faith in Eritrea. We met in a small office adjacent to the great mosque of Asmara. Despite the small space, the chairs seemed enormous. There was no table, so it felt like a cramped living room. The mufti was happy to talk with us but said there was no one with HIV in Eritrea, so why were we there? Then I said something about my having HIV, and then Stephen said something. The mufti look stunned but remained resolute, since we weren't Eritrean. When Wedi and Ato spoke up, however, he nearly had a heart attack. He immediately agreed to do his best to bring around the religious leaders he worked with and guided.

The Coptic bishops we met in a more typical conference room, at their headquarters, were, to our surprise, not so welcoming. They basically dismissed us. I'd expected the opposite. I felt ashamed of my own presumptions.

In between work with Wedi and Ato, I agreed to speak to other groups on behalf of Bidho and in my own right. I spoke at the local medical school. The students were astonished to see a woman—a white woman—so boldly speaking about HIV. They assured me the virus wasn't an issue in Eritrea, despite my arguments to the contrary, but I believe they still benefited from having someone to ask frank questions of.

Another afternoon, I had a heated discussion with Dr. Jim Yong Kim, a public health doctor I'd met years before in Geneva. He had visions of opening a clinic for people with HIV and talked about how he'd make it so everyone would know where to go.

"The words *HIV Clinic* will be boldly signposted so nobody will mistake it for something else," he said.

"But nobody will come," I replied. "It will terrify them. Humiliate them."

Again, I was reminded of the importance of having people living with HIV involved in decisionmaking. After a long argument he finally began to see that a sign so attention-getting would scare people away. His intentions were good, but he hadn't considered the perspective of the client. I hope he took our conversation to heart, as later, much later, he would become the head of The World Bank.

In mid-May of 2001, toward the end of my month in Eritrea, there was a knock at my hotel door. I nearly jumped out of my skin. Nobody except Astrid knew which room I was in, and she would've called before coming up to see me. I hadn't ordered room service and it was too late in the day for housekeeping, so I was surprised when I opened my door to a group of female staff huddled around the entrance. Tall, short, thin, round, brown-skinned in hues ranging from light to dark, this dozen or so women were still in their housekeeping uniforms. The olive green of their boxy shirts with names embroidered on a front pocket set off their beautiful dark eyes.

"Ma'am, we're sorry to bother you, but could we come in?" one asked.

"Sure," I answered. "But I don't need anything."

"No, but you see, we do. Please."

"Of course." I moved to let them enter.

A couple of them walked over to the desk where I had my papers stacked. One picked up a flyer and waved it at me. They'd clearly been in my room before, probably each day during my stay, and seemed remarkably comfortable.

"This," a short, plump, older one said. "We see you know about HIV and, well, we were wondering if you could teach us?"

I smiled. "Of course!"

A day or two later the group, which seemed to have expanded, came up to my room after their work hours. I explained the basics of HIV and did condom demonstrations to rounds of giggles and short bursts of applause. We spent an hour together, with them asking questions and me giving answers and as much information as they wanted.

The next day when I came back to the hotel after work, I found a small gift, wrapped but with no note, just *Thanks* written on the floral-patterned paper. Inside was a fridge magnet in the shape of Eritrea.

For Bidho, we organized a number of meetings and workshops. One was with about thirty positive women from around Asmara. They told me harrowing stories of their time on the front lines of the war with

Ethiopia. They'd fought side-by-side with male soldiers. They'd been trained, armed, and sent to defend their country. Now they were frustrated to have been thrust back into the roles of wife and mother. They often weren't allowed to work. Sometimes, were barely allowed to leave their homes.

The war for Eritrean independence might have been over, but a gender war was brewing. I understood why Astrid had asked me to speak up specifically about women at every chance. In the end, following my insistence and workshops with these former fighters, women as well as men were appointed to the board of Bidho. I was certain they would stand their ground. I was also certain I'd learned more from them than they ever could have from me. They were the some of the fiercest women I'd ever met. It gave me new courage to face my own demons.

By the time I was ready to leave, we had a plan in place. Their network would endure. Years later, during another visit there, I would find a picture of myself, with those two soldiers I'd first met, Wedi and Ato, on their office wall. They said they called me "the patron saint of Bidho."

Everything Changes

Spa

Soon after returning to Belgium from Eritrea, Jean-Robert announced, "We should get divorced."

I remember watching him from across the large common room, knowing he was right.

Following a long stretch of silence, he added, "I mean, I don't *really* want this."

I felt a momentary pang. Did he actually want to stay married?

He continued, "For me, especially, being divorced sucks. I'm too young for this bullshit. For this stain on my life."

Nah. He was still an asshole.

I looked at him, shrugged, and simply replied, "Okay."

I was, at least, relieved he'd been the one to initiate ending our marriage.

Oddly, once in agreement divorce was the way to move forward, we started getting along better. I did more consulting, he did more nothing. We continued to coexist as roommates, watching a lot of American TV on rented DVDs. We were plowing through *Sex and the City* when I got an email from the head of human resources for UNAIDS in Geneva. It read something like this:

Dear Martina,

I trust all is well with you and your family. I wanted to let you know your dream job is finally ready. UNICEF is creating a P4-level position in New York on HIV in the UN workplace. I hope you don't mind, but I have already sent them your curriculum vitae.

Warmest regards,

Johanne

She'd actually applied on my behalf. I responded immediately, thanking her before even asking for more information. Perhaps it was the nightly doses of Manhattan with Carrie Bradshaw and the girls, but I could see myself in New York having brunch with female friends, like in the show.

A few weeks later, I had a phone interview with a woman from UNICEF in New York. I sat on my terrace as the sun dipped to dusk and bats flew low in the sky. She asked how I would approach the work, what kinds of skills I could bring to the job, how good my French was, and so on. The easiest interview I'd ever had because I knew without a doubt I was the right person for the job.

Days later, I was offered a month-long consultancy in Malawi. I was to do an assessment of the whole UN system there and develop a plan to implement an HIV in the Workplace program for UN personnel in that country. It was kind of perfect, because in the years since I'd left UNAIDS, I'd asked former colleagues at every turn if they'd started educating the staff yet. I still felt strongly that this needed to happen in order for the UN to maintain credibility as a leader in the fight.

I asked the woman in New York if she thought I should skip the consultancy, in case she was considering hiring me. "You should take it," she said. "It will be an excellent experience. That said, you probably shouldn't plan to stay longer than mid-December."

She didn't need to say more than that. I understood. Although she wasn't making a firm offer, I was high on her list of candidates.

The Warm Heart of Africa

Lilongwe

Malawi: Southeastern Africa
Population: 18.6 million
Capital: Lilongwe

It was my second trip to Malawi, a country I would best describe as red, whether bone-dry or flooded. Also, maybe a few steps shy of boring, as it's notoriously quiet. When I was first there, in 1996, I was struck by the beauty of the stark countryside and the gentleness of the people. The AIDS epidemic was in full force, and rows of coffins for sale, stacked liked shoe boxes, lined the dusty roads leading in and out of towns. That sight had been heartbreaking, but it now seemed the country was taking action and people living with HIV were at the core of the response.

On my first trip I'd been on an evaluation team with an international group of doctors and social workers looking at the efficiency of the National AIDS Program. I remembered that assignment fondly. Working with Moses from Zambia, and Jens from Belgium, in particular, had been great experiences. They were all a part of my extended FuhKaWee tribe.

Now, six years later, I was overwhelmed by how much worse the stigma and intolerance had grown. Before there'd been hints of mistreatment, but now the vitriol was palpable. Whenever I mentioned HIV or AIDS to my colleagues during interviews, eyes glazed over. Responses were cool, and as dry as the landscape that surrounded us.

Although the UN is fairly conservative as a whole, I could not comprehend the hostility I now encountered at every turn. Some staff acted embarrassed to reveal their lack of knowledge. But many were simply arrogant, making it clear through comments or expressions that they felt they were above anyone living with HIV. I suppose it was a sort of coping mechanism, but really it was just denial.

In my optimism, I'd imagined those working for the United Nations would be more open-minded, more accepting. And yet, the case there was the opposite. My colleagues were often shut down and adamant that this was not *their* issue, but someone else's problem. It was as if the clock had spun backward, and they were erasing the chapter of AIDS in their country. Trying to design a program that would last and be embraced by those it was meant to help would require every brain cell my skull encased.

I had to keep reminding myself that Malawi, like so many countries in Africa, still had laws against homosexuals—their sexuality, their relationships, their very existence—a community so unfairly associated with the spread of the virus. People forget that well over eighty percent of infections occur in *heterosexuals*, yet a tiny part of the population and their perceived "immoral behavior" continue to be blamed. Meanwhile the country, including the United Nations family, was very hard hit: Staff and their loved ones were falling ill. UN staff receive excellent benefits and should be accessing health care, and yet they kept quiet and the virus spread.

In later years, we would learn that in Malawi, as in several other countries, the rates of infection were actually higher among UN personnel than in the general population. The only reasons we could find for this was that they were simply too embarrassed to go for testing or treatment.

Just the week before, I'd coordinated basic training for the staff, and we'd invited a few people from a local NGO to speak about their experiences. There were about fifty people crammed into the stuffy conference room at the UNDP building. Sitting on folding chairs, the UN personnel listened politely. Following the testimonies, I thanked the speakers. Adding, "Let's now open it to questions."

Without asking to be recognized, one man in a dark-blue suit blurted out, "How were you so careless as to get it?"

Another man with no jacket and his sleeves rolled up, asked our speakers, "Have you prayed to God to find a better path?"

Frustrated, I stood and publicly shared, (for the first time since I'd returned to Malawi), that I was living with HIV.

None of these people had met me before. They gaped as if I'd just removed my left arm to reveal a long green alien limb.

"Your comments, with all due respect, are not appropriate here," I said. "These people have come to share their experiences so you can learn. They are not here to be interrogated. And, let us remember, this is the United Nations. Comments about religion should be left at home. Now, if you'd like to ask any questions more along the lines of understanding what life with HIV is like, then please do. Ask them. Ask me. Ask any of us."

"Was it true that the medications had to be refrigerated?" asked a petite woman in a green dress.

"Was it hard to remember to take the pills at the same time every day?" another woman asked.

"How do you juggle doctors' visits with work?" a tall man standing in the back wanted to know.

Questions quickly and easily answered.

"Yes, some of the meds do need to be kept cold," one of the NGO speakers replied. Another adding, "at times, the scheduling of taking the pills was a pain, but easy enough to sort out."

"My boss knows I have HIV so he lets me start late if I have a doctor's appointment. He's very supportive," explained our third guest.

And on it went. Our time was nearly finished, but I threw another question out to the audience, since they seemed more engaged now. "I'm sure many of you are supporting loved ones living with HIV," I said matter-of-factly, knowing the rate of infection was very high and had been for some time. "Does being a caregiver ever affect your work?"

Nobody responded until finally, the same guy who'd asked our guest if he'd been saved by religion raised a hand. "You know, none of us are really dealing with this. I mean, in our program work—yes, of course—but not in our own lives. This is really a problem of the poor."

His arrogance and ignorance slammed into me like lead bookends. I stood up straighter, gathered my composure and stepped over to draw my favorite diagram on a flip chart.

"Okay. This is a triangle, or, really a pyramid." Next, I drew a horizontal line to separate a small portion on the top. And then, another about halfway down.

"This, the top part of the pyramid," I said, tapping it, "is where HIV starts in every community. Always. It begins in the elite. Among people who have access to money and entertainment and travel and other opportunities most never get. People who are invited to work receptions and cocktail parties and maybe get tempted to have a drink—or two—they might otherwise not be offered. People who are often away from their families, feeling lonely and with money in their pockets. Sound familiar? *People like us.* This is where HIV starts. *Always.*"

I glanced back. The crowd was rapt, staring at me. I continued, drawing downward-pointing arrows in the middle section of the pyramid.

"Once the epidemic starts in the elite few, the virus spreads. It has its worst impact on the poor, these folks at the bottom of the pyramid." I colored in the bottom section with a purple marker.

"HIV is *not* a disease of poverty," I added. "It simply has the worst impact on the poor because they don't enjoy access to health care or education, and so don't know how to avoid infection in the first place."

Now a lot of eyes were staring back at me with an even blend of *aha* and *oh no.*

"So why don't you ever hear about rich people with HIV?" one woman asked.

"Good question. First, let's imagine the scenario of an unwanted pregnancy and, for a moment, put aside your personal beliefs on how those should be dealt with. Two young girls become pregnant, a rich one and a poor one. The girl from the poor family probably has no option but to have the baby. So, whether she wants or not, some months down the line, everyone will know. Keeping that pregnancy—that sexual experience—to herself is implausible.

"Now imagine the rich girl. She can abort, if that is feasible where she lives, because she or her family has the money. Or she can make an extended visit to a distant family member, go off and have the baby, give it up for adoption, and nobody is the wiser when she returns. She has options. She *can* keep a secret."

The crowd was now on the edge of their seats, riveted by my tales of sex and secrets.

"So, clearly, HIV isn't visible like a pregnancy. But the options still depend on your economic standing. If you're poor, your only option, most likely, is the public clinic—the one everyone in town knows is the place for people who have HIV."

Collective nods crossed the room, though a few gazes fell. I suspected they are all envisioning the entrance to the clinic in Lilongwe, not far from where we were sitting.

"But if you have money, like we who work for the UN, you can go to a private clinic. You can even visit a doctor in another country. You can keep it a secret. And because of the stigma, people with options often do keep very quiet. They feel it's not safe to speak out, so they deal with the virus privately."

"That makes sense, actually," one woman said. "I believe there are probably many rich HIV-positive people in Malawi. They just won't admit it. So what can we do—as UN staff? What can we do to help?"

"Well, the first and most important thing you can do is to get tested for HIV and know your own status," I said.

She watched me intently; for a moment our gazes locked.

"And if you find that you're positive, consider sharing that information, at least with your closest loved ones," I added. "The more who speak out, the more the stigma will break down. Even just going for a test is a start, because that helps others find the courage to do the same. *Testing is key.*"

We'd gone over our time. The managers were getting antsy. Or maybe the discussions were hitting too close to home. The Resident Coordinator, a regal woman from Ethiopia who held the most senior UN position in country, gave me hand signals to wind up.

"Okay, we're out of time, but I want to thank you all for your participation and great questions. I know this is a hard topic to discuss, but it's critical that UN personnel practice what we preach. We should all know our own status. Please, if you never do another thing about HIV, go for a test. You owe it to yourself to know the truth."

As people rose and collected their things, the guy who'd asked about religious salvation stood and addressed me. "On behalf of everyone here, I'd like to thank you for this powerful session. I think we've all learned a lot. I wish you the best. I'll pray for your soul."

As I shook my head in disbelief, the crowd dispersed, I hoped most of them would do something more proactive than pray for me, but I'd done my best. The rest was in their hands.

Navigating the COVID-19 pandemic has brought these same notions of inequity again to the surface. All one needs to do is consider the difference in treatment received by those in power—financial or political— versus those without access to the same services. The health gap has, yet again, reared its ugly head, this time consuming the lives of millions from marginalized communities. History, tragically, continues to repeat.

Those sessions, while the most important part of my work, were exhausting. I was looking forward to a weekend to sleep and reflect on what I wanted for the future. Quiet time alone was a luxury, and in this landlocked agrarian country, I was feeling lucky to be getting quite a bit of it. Malawi is a sleepy place and I fit right in.

One of my first weekends there, I'd been invited to dinner at the home of the local head of UNICEF, Catherine Mbengue, originally from Cameroon. Despite being in an Anglophone country, we spent our evening conversing in French. She asked me a lot of questions, and just before dessert, it dawned on me that this casual dinner was actually a clandestine second interview for the job in New York. Catherine was verifying my fluency in French. We were well onto laughing and sharing more wine by then, so I assumed everything had gone well.

Saturday and Sunday, I slept, and then slept some more. On Monday I felt revitalized and was ready to start another week's work.

As the sky shimmered from deep cobalt to soft lavender, the waking southern sun pushed through a line of fire-streaked magenta. That seemed to be the signal for a nearby rooster to cock-a-doodle-doo his good morning to the neighborhood.

I loved this sound, so rural, so part of this earth. Yet, even in Malawi, deep in the warm heart of Africa, the rooster's call seemed more urgent on a Monday morning. I felt compelled to rise. Rubbing sleepy eyes, I heard the approaching flip-flop steps of the guesthouse server bringing my clanking tray of coffee, juice, and fresh fruit. Confirming it was, indeed, time to get up.

This was the height of mango season, so I always anticipated the familiar orange knob on my plate resembling a tropical hedgehog escaped from an African fantasy land, forging his way through a field of bananas and pineapple but never making it past my fork. I slurped up the last of the succulent fruit, scraping the inverted peel against my teeth, letting the juices drip onto my chin. I dropped the naked skin into the trash and peeked out the window at the bright, lush green landscape, then sent my hide to the shower.

At twenty past seven in the morning, right on time, the crunch of tires on the gravel announced Winston pulling up in the white four-by-four with the large UNAIDS logo on the doors. We'd been in this routine for three weeks, with three more to go. My gentle Malawian driver knew to hover, and I'd be out in a minute. I exited my room, locked my door. I hauled my heavy bag laden with reports and laptop up onto the passenger seat. The handrail at the top of the doorframe was the best way to hoist my short self up behind it.

"Morning, ma'am," Winston said quietly without looking over at me.

"Good morning, Winston. How are you? How was your weekend?" I asked as I settled in next to him as he sat, hands at the ready on the wheel, in the driver's seat.

"I am blessed, ma'am. I've had a good rest and a lovely weekend. Thank you for asking."

I smiled at him as he reached under my bag and pulled out a large white envelope with the UNICEF logo and a date stamp from New York. "This came for you, ma'am, over the weekend. Found it in the mail pouch this morning when I stopped in on my way here. Thought you might like to see it before we got to the office."

My eyes widened as if I'd been offered the golden ticket to visit Willy Wonka in his chocolate factory. By the thickness of the envelope, I just might have been awarded the prize. I slit open the envelope with a key and slid out a thick stack of documents enclosed in a blue and white folder.

Clipped to the top of the stack was a letter.

Dear Ms. Clark,

I am pleased to offer you the two-year position of Human Resources Officer for HIV in the Workplace, based at headquarters in New York....

I couldn't read further, as my eyes filled with tears. I'd been desperate for a drastic change and that job was the perfect next step. It was the one job I'd vowed to take, the one I truly wanted because it mattered. After my consultancies, I was enthused again, and ready for a new challenge. A new purpose. The work and the move would definitely meet all those needs. Most important, it was a way to leave my marriage with head held high, confidently moving forward. It was my ticket to a new life.

"Oh, thank you, Winston. Thank you so much. You have no idea how long I've been waiting for this!"

"Oh, yes, ma'am. The UN can be slow sometimes; looks like it took more than ten days to reach Lilongwe from New York. I hope it is good news."

"Oh, it is, it is." I didn't tell him that in many ways, I'd been waiting years for that letter. For that chance to tackle the system from within and hold it accountable. "Yes, yes, it's very good news! Winston, they want me to go work in New York and coordinate their new program on HIV in the workplace! To help staff cope better with HIV and AIDS—basically what I am doing here, but—for all of UNICEF, globally! I'm so excited. I hope I'll be able to concentrate on work today!"

He smiled back at me, perfect white teeth cutting a crescent moon across his skin. "You'll be fine, ma'am, today *and* in New York. I know it is so. You will be fine. God will look after you."

I tried to compose myself, clutching the papers to my chest like a nerdy six-year-old with her first set of longed-for schoolbooks.

As soon as we reached the office, I signed the acceptance and faxed it to New York, confirming with an email to the HR officer (who now felt more like my savior than my new employer) that I could start at the beginning of 2003. Just one month away. I'd have a huge amount of organizing to do to coordinate an international move and start a new life in a place I'd often visited but only for short stays. But I was up to the task.

Later that day I called the local UN medical services to arrange the required physical. They invited me to stop by that day to start the paperwork.

"Good afternoon, sister, how are you today?" I said to the middle-aged nurse with graying hair neatly tucked in a bun.

"I am well," the nurse replied, "it seems we have some very important business today. For *you*, for a change!"

I'd visited their office many times, but it had always been to figure out how I could help *them*. This time, they were going to help me secure my new job.

"Yes, I've been offered a position in New York with UNICEF!"

"Well, let's just see if we can't collect some of your blood and get those tests done, so you can be off to that very big city!"

She organized everything for me, including a chest X-ray at the local hospital I'd visited many times to learn about their services for people living with HIV.

Being a patient, even if only for a routine physical, suddenly made these services seem that much more real. I understood at deeper level how rudimentary things were for those who don't have access to private clinics. Inside the public hospital, the machines were rusty and cold, the painted concrete floor rough and chilly to my pampered pink feet. It felt a million degrees outside, but I was shivering for the first time in weeks, feeling utterly exposed with my naked chest against the X-ray machine.

Having spent most of my Monday running errands and organizing things, I called Winston to come pick me up and return me to the office. Back at my desk, I sat and reflected. How privileged I'd been. Not just because I'd had access to education and came from a rich country. But because I'd been exposed to so much; so many cultures, and lifestyles, and realities—good and bad, around the world. I could never say I'd walked in anyone else's shoes, but at least I'd gotten a glimpse at the path. To me, that is the greatest wealth one can attain: meaningful interactions with people in other countries, on their terms.

My life as a consultant had been chaotic, and I'd allowed a bad marriage to drag on far too long. Finally, while working in this sleepy, small, sub-Saharan country with red dirt roads, enormous lakes and miles of poverty, I'd hit the jackpot.

Like that early-rising rooster, I had something to shout about.

Back in Spa, I had ten days to organize my move. Jean-Robert and I were still in agreement we would get divorced. But he wanted us to stay married long enough—another two years—for me to get Belgian citizenship.

"I don't trust your government," he said, "and no matter what, I want to be sure that you can always see the doctor. Even if you have to come back here. I just don't trust your country to care for you."

I was touched and knew that despite our complicated, sexless marriage, on some level he did truly care.

Christmas 2002 was my last in Belgium. Before the calendar turned over, I was starting over—alone—in New York City.

CHAPTER 7

UNICEF

Repatriation to the United States
of George W. Bush's America

New York

New York City: Center of the Universe
(Ask any New Yorker)
Population: 8.4 million

Following seven years as an expat, I found myself maneuvering a mountain of suitcases through the arrivals hall at JFK airport. I was thoroughly exhausted after six weeks in Malawi and then less than two weeks in Belgium to pack. I'd been suppressing my emotions for years. As I set foot back on American soil, they began surfacing. I felt as if I'd been released from captivity, though I'd been my own captor. I now needed to become my own heroine.

Leaning on the wobbly cart, with tears streaming down my face after clearing immigration and customs, I exited into the arrivals terminal. Home at last. I'd visited the US many times during my time living overseas, but never for more than a week or two.

There in the terminal, I saw my friend Carole waiting for me. We'd met while living and working in Geneva some years back. She was British, but had been based in New York for decades. "Martina! Martina? Where are you? You're so tiny behind all this baggage!" she said, hugging me.

"Yeah, most of it's emotional," I replied.

We heaved my stuff into a taxi for a maddening death chase—weaving in and out of traffic at high speed as light snow dampened the roads—to a cheap hotel I'd booked near chaotic Times Square. A tiny, windowless box with a leaky toilet. The chains of the elevator clanged inside the wall at the head of my bed. Reality was beginning to hit: You live here now—get ready, kiddo, this is going to be one hell of a ride.

It might've been less daunting to return to my home state of California, after seven years abroad. This was New York, post-9/11. George W. Bush's America. I had much to learn.

That same day, I went with Carole to look at apartments. Being told I was HIV-positive had been hard, but apartment hunting in Manhattan as winter unfolds pulled a close second. When I was diagnosed, I thought my life was over. After the first tour of apartments in my price range, I *wanted* my life to be over. I'd imagined finding a nice two-bedroom around Union Square for $2,000 or less. The foolishness of hope! By the end of my first afternoon I was questioning my sanity and my decision to move here at all. I had to reevaluate my financial situation—and my tolerance for living in a shoebox.

Two days later, my eldest sister, Alexandria, and her wonderful daughters, Genevieve and Spencer, joined me for New Year's Eve. They had a much nicer suite at a hotel down near Wall Street, so I spent an evening with them. I needed to be surrounded by people I knew and loved. We rode the ferry to Staten Island and back, then walked along the waterfront to their hotel as fireworks lit up the sky.

From the warmth of their room, as we watched the ball drop in Times Square on TV, it struck me that I really was starting fresh. The events hosted by Dick Clark weren't happening an ocean away, they were just uptown. It was the first moment since accepting the job I'd allowed myself to relax. Thinking about how monumental this move was, I was afraid and nervous, elated, and overjoyed, and confused all at once. In crumpled clothes, and stiff from sleeping on a couch, I was awakened by my two young nieces. "Auntie M, get up! Let's go eat pancakes! Hurry!" Genevieve pleaded. 2003: a new year in a new city with an entirely new life about to start.

On the first Monday of the new year I reported to UNICEF at 633 Third Avenue. The forty-one floor building, constructed in the 1960s, was a mix of offices and condos, as well as the New York City offices for the governor. I threw myself into work, meeting with counterparts from other organizations. Researching background documents. Speaking with colleagues about developing training materials.

My task was to set up an internal HIV in the Workplace program to educate all 20,000 UNICEF personnel on HIV awareness and prevention. To encourage testing and, for those who were positive, provide options to access adequate care and treatment in safe and discreet ways. Between contractors, consultants, staff and their dependents, this program would serve approximately 100,000 individuals across 165 countries. No biggie.

At the end of the day, even an international machine as monstrous as the UN was made up of individuals. The possibility of having even the smallest influence on how my peers thought about and made decisions was intoxicating. If our staff could firmly grasp the issues, surely we would deliver much better programs to the world.

During my first week, while filling out piles of paperwork to get back into the system, I met a bear of a man named Mark Stirling. A teddy bear, that is.

I wasn't feeling too well, but perked up when I met this tall, graying, charismatic Australian who welcomed me on board as if I were his long-lost cousin. He was in charge of the HIV program section of UNICEF, the part that supported the work with beneficiaries, primarily women and children, mitigating the pandemic. My desk would be in Human Resources, since I was there to support staff internally, but he would be my mentor and second supervisor. In fact, during the initial two years, my post was financed through his budget.

He gave me a list of all the people in the organization working on HIV. I was delighted to see the name of the Zambian doctor I'd met on my first trip to Malawi.

Mark's brow furrowed. "You know Moses?"

"I do! We did a program evaluation together years ago. He's lovely, such a brilliant man. UNICEF is lucky to have him. How's he doing?"

"Bit tired, I'd say. Works too hard, but don't we all?"

The joke was that in any country you could always find the UNICEF offices because ours was the one with the lights on at night. There was also a joke that might have explained our need to work 24/7: The World Health Organization knows everything but does nothing. UNDP knows nothing and does nothing. UNICEF knows nothing but does everything.

It's partially true. We're always on the front lines but, at times, without having fully thought through the best course of action. As a result, our staff fought hard for the rights of children and women, but not necessarily in the most efficient ways. Working too hard was seen as not only commonplace but admirable and expected. Staff well-being was, and largely remains, considered unwarranted for the United Nations system. When your mandate is to take care of the most vulnerable populations on the planet, it's easy to overlook the welfare of your own staff. Just as one can't drive a vehicle far with a faulty engine, however, staff can only give so much before needing to recharge. Humanitarian workers get so bogged down in emergency response mode, we forget to take care of our own.

"Well, that's great," Mark continued, "Moses and the rest will all be here in a few weeks for our annual meeting of the regional chiefs. You'll be there."

"Sure, I'd love to. I'll put it on my calendar."

"Sorry, that wasn't a question. You *will* be there!"

I smiled at his piercing blue eyes. He was teasing me while showing how determined he was that my work be a success.

Mark had actually been instrumental in the organization's first efforts to support staff living with HIV. When he was head of the country office in Zambia in the mid-1990s, he'd set up a program called Caring for Us. And that was what it was: the staff taking care of one another. On their own time, and at their own expense, personnel would send food baskets if someone was home sick. They visited coworkers who might need extra help. They raised money to cover funeral costs when a colleague or dependent died.

But soon the financial and emotional burden became too much for the staff on their own. The organization had to step up. Now, many years later, I was tasked with making sure the larger organization—not individual staff—looked after the workforce. Mark expected a lot from me, which was fine. I was a woman on a mission, conveniently the same one as his.

My personal priority was still finding a place to live. I would be earning a nice salary and given a relocation grant to cover temporary accommodations and moving costs. Being $15,000 in debt, I didn't want to spend another penny on a hotel. I was determined to find an apartment no matter how rundown I felt. The human resources officer, Judy, told me I was actually eligible for a rental subsidy because of my international contract.

With this knowledge I signed for an outrageously overpriced but supremely gorgeous two-bedroom garden apartment—the ground floor of a brownstone, with a tiny backyard near Union Square. A little statue of a cherub stood in the middle of the yard. Slightly below street level, the apartment had little natural light, and I started referring to it as my bat cave. It felt safe and secluded, a place to hide out while I attempted to reconstruct my life. I signed the lease to take possession mid-month, but the real estate agent took pity and gave me the keys at signing. I moved in the next day, two short weeks after arriving in Manhattan—a record by most standards. An eternity, according to my exhausted feet.

Early that morning, I went to Bed Bath & Beyond and bought an inflatable mattress, a set of dishes and flatware, a teakettle, bedding, and a few towels. I arranged for them to be delivered that afternoon. The prior week I'd shifted to a hotel closer to Union Square, my new neighborhood. After the shopping spree, I went back there, checked out, and in three trips wheeled my suitcases eight blocks to the new apartment. *Anything* to save money.

By the time I rolled the last bag in my new place, I was spent. Vomiting, then crying as I collapsed into a heap on the creaky old hardwood floor. The heat felt blissful. Falling snow silenced the world outside as the temperature dropped to match my waning mood.

171

My friend Carole, who lived just a few blocks away, came to meet me for brunch the next day, though I couldn't imagine eating. My stomach was roiled like a corner puddle on a busy road, constantly sloshing about.

"You knooooooow, I was thinking, Martina," she stretched out in her lovely—albeit fading—English accent, "we could go to one of those posh garden stores down in SoHo and get you sorted out with some outdoor furniture."

"Carole, are you serious? I know you like the garden and all, but it is *snowing.*"

"No, no, I know," she said, "but exactly. Garden stuff will all be on *sale* so you can buy it for next to nothing right now. Use it in the house, and then when your shipment arrives from Belgium, you're ready to pop it out back!"

"Clever!" That evoked my first laughter in weeks. "Let's do it. Let's eat some greasy breakfast and go buy some lawn chairs!"

In the end I had only ginger ale and rye toast, but for a moment I felt better. Later that afternoon we hit up a few more stores for their after-Christmas sales. I bought an overstuffed chaise longue I lovingly called my "princess" chair, a sofa and a desk, as well as a few lamps.

I lived like this for five months until my things arrived from Belgium. I'd foolishly left the shipping to my husband, who had apparently sent everything by dog sled. Although I'd designated each item to be sent with a post-it, and even selected the shipping company, my things still didn't arrive until June.

But somehow, it all felt right. I needed my life to be stripped to the bone so I could slowly layer it back together. I'd brought some items with me, of course, in my voluminous valises—pretty things, like my favorite essential-oil burner, candlesticks, and a statue of the Virgin Mary I'd received as a child during a visit to the Trappist monastery where my uncle was a monk. I'd flown back with a few books, my dream catcher, my guitar and tap shoes. It didn't exactly look like home, but it looked like me—sparse, eclectic, and in need of nurturing.

As the days passed and winter progressed, it was becoming difficult to walk, and I couldn't seem to keep food down. Each twenty-four hours felt like a week. I assumed it was just exhaustion and the bitter cold, but I couldn't seem to warm up. Ever. Anything I ingested soon came flying back out from a variety of orifices. I was severely dehydrated, debilitated by muscle cramps. After a visit to medical services and then a tropical-diseases specialist, I was diagnosed with giardia—or as my friend Maryanne calls it, spray-paint expulsion.

"Well, you could have picked it up here—parasites are everywhere—but I'd put my money on Malawi, I'm afraid," said the slightly-hunch-backed, elderly doctor. "Where did you stay while you were there?"

"A guesthouse. My own self-contained unit on a compound. You know, like a little studio. Well, compared to New York, a massive one-bedroom!"

He smiled. "So you had your own kitchen. You prepared all your own food?"

"Ah, no. Not really. I ate out often for dinner, or ate snacks I prepared, but breakfast was always brought to me."

"Fresh fruit?" he asked without looking up, as he listened to my breathing with a stethoscope.

"Guilty as charged."

"Giardia. Those little guys are all over the place, particularly if people don't know to wash their hands when preparing food. Assuming they have clean water and…well. You know the drill."

"All too well. I feel like an idiot. I know to only eat fruit I peel myself, but the mango was just too delicious to resist. Guess I'm paying for it now."

"Don't worry. I'll give you a course of Cipro—antibiotics—and you'll be better in no time. Get this filled and promise you'll be more careful in future."

I thanked him and left, stopping in the ladies' room on the way out. My cast-iron stomach had busted a seam.

It took only a few days for the antibiotics to make a difference. I was no longer spending half my workday waddling to and from the toilets. I was still dehydrated, but was on the mend. And finally had an appetite again.

One painfully long day at a time, I began to function in the huge, loud, crowded city. I got lost in the shuffle of eight million neighbors and was happy for the anonymity. I felt that winter more deeply than any I'd experienced in years. At times I was ecstatic. At others gray and moody and only morosely reassured to be back in the world of saving the world. Maybe some of that do-gooding would be applicable to my personal crisis. I was only one woman, not a displaced community, but felt like a refugee. Mostly, though, I was just happy to have the privilege to redefine who I was, and what I wanted.

In February, we had the meeting of the regional chiefs and, as promised, Moses was there. He seemed smaller than I'd remembered, relying more heavily on his reading glasses, and a bit withdrawn. I tried several times to chat, but he acted distant. Perhaps he didn't remember me as well I remembered him.

Meanwhile, the giardia was mostly resolved, but I still wasn't feeling energetic. The move, the new job, winter and the chaos of the city took their toll.

Around the middle of February, I started to feel a painful tingle I'd experienced once before. I tried to dismiss it, but the needle-like jabs on the left side of my torso, just under my breast, were too strong to ignore. In less than twenty-four hours, my skin was blistering. I'd developed shingles again.

I'd had them early on in my diagnosis, possibly as a result of stress and exposure to a child with chicken pox. The virus lives on in anyone who's had the disease, and under stress, it erupts like volcanos on one's skin. The infection runs along the nerves, which is what makes it so much more painful than a normal rash or hives. It feels like burning magma is welling up from within, charring the skin every inch of the way.

Accompanied by Carole, I went to the emergency room. The doctors immediately knew what was wrong and put me on a massive dose of acyclovir. It was the weekend, so on Monday I was able to see a private doctor—an HIV specialist—who yelped like a puppy when I lifted my shirt and he saw my skin.

"In my twenty-some-odd years of working in New York City, I have never, but never, seen a case of shingles like this. You poor thing. You must have an incredible tolerance for pain. My God."

"Well, at least I'm not a hypochondriac!" Never comfortable with doctor appointments, I fell to making stupid jokes.

Dr. Fontana smiled, took my hand and said, "I'm so glad we're here to help you. You'll be better in no time. Meanwhile, I'm sending you home to sleep for a few days. This is a reaction to stress. I don't know what's been going on in your life, but honestly, just riding the subway is enough to trigger this in some people."

"Ha!" I was happy to hear him respond with equally stupid jokes. "Yes, life's been in a bit of upheaval, but it's all good. I'm sure I'll be fine."

"Want to share?" he asked, as he proceeded to clean up the rash and bandage my weeping skin.

"Well, I just moved here—to New York I mean—and started a new full-time job. I left my ex-husband in Belgium and had to find an apartment."

"And you don't call that major? Jeez. Finding an apartment in New York is no small thing, missy!" He winked and squeezed my shoulder. "What a trouper. You're going to be just fine. Take the rest of the week off and come see me in ten days, or if anything changes. Welcome to Manhattan!"

I thanked him and called in my sick leave. Feeling guilty that already twice in under six weeks at my new job, I'd been ill enough to stay home on doctor's orders. I was afraid they'd regret hiring a positive person, even though neither of my illnesses were directly related to HIV.

Since time heals wounds, within a few weeks I was beginning to make headway at work. My colleagues and supervisors were supportive, and I felt I was finally in the right place. We'd tried to organize a regional meeting, again in Malawi, but at the last minute, Moses—who was by then UNICEF's regional AIDS director for East and Southern Africa—suggested we postpone. He felt it was too much, too soon, and perhaps I should focus on the policy end of things at headquarters. I followed his advice and began working closely with other colleagues around the system.

Although many people had contributed to laying the groundwork for initiating our workplace programming, a core team in New York was leading it. Among them were Laurie Newell from UNFPA, Roxaneh Bazergan from DPKO, Dr. Sudershan Narula of UN medical services, my friend Nick Fucile from the UN, and Alan Silverman, on loan from UNICEF to design and rollout training materials. We all had different strengths, and while we occasionally butted heads, we made a wonderful team.

Another person I worked with closely in those early years was Christine Bendel, a Swiss-German who was tough as nails on the outside and Silly Putty within. Christine had been hired at about the same time as I had for another organization, UNFPA, to do essentially the same work. I quickly grew to adore her. I was the creative out-of-the-box ideas person. She was the teacher's aide who put all the crayons neatly back into the box and made order out of chaos. Between us we'd come up with some great products—a guide for office managers, and a self-help book for staff, for example—that pulled the best of what had been done among the various UN entities, to create our new program.

In late June we organized a weeklong meeting and invited two individuals who were key to designing a how-to implementation guide for running an HIV in the Workplace program in any given office. We called it our *tool kit*. One was Kirk, an operations officer and office manager for Zambia. Kirk was a clean-cut fortyish Canadian who'd grown up in Africa thanks to missionary parents. He was all about checklists and clear, concise instructions.

"Leave no room for interpretation," Kirk said. "Step 1, step 2. step 3, etc. Make sure an idiot can follow the plan and you'll be fine."

The other was Jane, a quiet Kenyan in her thirties. Jane was the kind of person who would smile and agree and speak only when she had something to say. When she did, it was always worth hearing. Like Nick, she'd started her career with the UN in an unrelated area of work, but her passion and dedication to working on HIV in her own life quickly catapulted her into working on it for us. We were lucky to have her gentle, intuitive wisdom.

"We need to have people go for HIV testing," Jane said. "Condoms are great, but if they don't know their status, they'll just carry them in their bag or pocket and think it's enough. Only when a person knows, *really* knows, do they take it seriously."

We all agreed, and managed to draft a document that personnel at any level, from support staff to management, could use to implement in-house activities within a given UN office, anywhere in the world.

We also had a bright intern with us for the summer, Brian Goldman, who began work that would guide our efforts for years to come. He read through the Annual Country Program Reports for each country where we had personnel. He mapped out what in-house awareness activities for staff on HIV were being implemented—if any—and with what kind of budget. It gave us a snapshot of what was happening (sadly, not much), and that exercise was repeated for many years. Brian was with us only that summer, but his work was important, as was that of the many interns who followed him. Brainstorming with these great young minds was one of my absolute favorite parts of the job.

On the morning of our last day together, Mark Stirling came in to say a few words of closing and thanks for the hard work we'd put in. "Sadly, I'd like us to start with a moment of silence."

I whimpered and covered my mouth. I'd heard rumors I'd refused to believe, but now knew were true.

"Moses died earlier today. In his last hours he finally acknowledged that he has been living with HIV—with AIDS—for some time. He was so proud and sure that, as a doctor, he could manage it himself, that he never told anyone. He was embarrassed and ashamed."

I struggled to remain calm as the silent crowd listened in shock.

"We all have blood on our hands, as I see it," Mark continued. "Moses' death is unforgivable. We have all let him down. I have, the system has, we all have. We need to make this right so that no more staff die unnecessarily. Let's learn from this and dedicate our work to his legacy. He changed the way governments responded to the epidemic in sub-Saharan Africa. Let's now change the way the UN responds to HIV in-house."

We sat together in silence. My stomach twisted into a pretzel. I felt light-headed. This beautiful man who'd so impressed me years before was gone. I felt more determined than ever to make our interventions a success. Not just for Moses, but for all the other people living with HIV who didn't have the courage to speak up before it was too late. I had a chance to give voice to a population who feared to speak.

By August we had officially launched within UNICEF and UNFPA (in under eight months, a record turnaround time from inception to implementation, by UN standards). Every office would be held accountable for implementation of the HIV in the Workplace program. It was too late for Moses, but just in time for so many others.

In November that year, I traveled extensively. First to Kenya, where I was welcomed with cries of *"karibu"*—Swahili for welcome—and a warm hug from Jane, who'd been with us in our June meeting. I did my first trainings for staff in country offices and, after what felt like an eternity, was at long last doing the job I felt I'd been hired for. It was there, another six months later in Nairobi, that I met Woody.

Meeting Woody

Nairobi

Kenya: East Africa
Population: 52.6 million
Capital: Nairobi

I was staying at the Holiday Inn in Parklands, a lovely, albeit rustic, complex with little waterways running through the tropical grounds. Low wooden bridges linked the palm-lined walkways between the blocks of rooms. Giant frogs serenaded guests at night. Some people complained about these frogs, who seemed loud enough to swallow up a room per *ribbit*, but I found them soothing. A reminder life continues even while I slumber.

The UN complex in Nairobi, called 'Gigiri' for the neighborhood where it's located, is next to the Karura Forest. It was too far from the hotel to walk, but a quick taxi ride away. The sprawling campus, hosting most of the UN organizations based in Kenya, is adorned with a combination of national flags and native trees. Meru oaks, tamarind, and parasol trees. It was common to see monkeys swinging among the branches or peering through office windows at staff as we worked. Due to the high altitude,

Nairobi gets more rain than many other parts of the country and is, seemingly, always green. As the compound is self-contained, with a bank and cafeterias, I never ventured downtown.

During my first week there, I was ready to do an awareness session with the staff of one of our local offices when realized I didn't have a penis model for condom demonstrations. I asked colleagues in medical services, but they didn't have one to lend. No one in our HIV program section had one either.

There I was, on the continent with the highest rates of infection, where mitigating the spread of the virus was a priority. Yet nobody, it seemed, had the tools to do the basic job of education. Frustrated, but not deterred, I grabbed a banana from the cafeteria at lunchtime, and went off to my training session. I'd used a banana for my stand-in model the day before. While not ideal, it does the trick, even if the banana goes soft after the deed is done.

In a windowless conference room that served as a training center, set up like a classroom, twenty staffers were seated at individual desks. Standing at the front, I was about to introduce myself and begin when a short white middle-aged woman I'd met earlier that week, with glasses and spiky hair, flew through the door, nearly knocking me over with her enthusiasm. "Wait, wait. Martina, wait!" she yelled.

I looked around. Forty bemused eyes stared up at us. I said, "I'm just about to start my session."

"I know, but this is important," she insisted. "I have something for you."

"Now? Can't it wait?"

"No, really. Now."

"Okay, uh, hang on, folks, I'll be right back," I said. "This won't take but a minute. Meanwhile, pass this quiz around. Don't worry, just do your best. I promise the only hard part about it is knowing that it's double-sided."

The group laughed and turned their papers over in unison, then got down to the task of ticking off true-false boxes. At the beginning of each session, I always had the group complete a quiz on the basic facts. This allowed me to assess what they knew versus what they did not. Then I understood where to focus.

"What's so urgent? Everyone okay?" I said to my excited colleague.

She turned her back to the group and ushered me over to a corner. "I have *this* for you." She removed something wrapped in a brightly-colored scarf from her shoulder bag.

"Oh. Okay. What *is* it?" I asked, intrigued.

"It is a, um, a, you know, a *model*."

I frowned. "Model?"

She leaned into my ear and whispered, "penissssss model." Then giggled and handed it over, scarf and all.

I unwrapped the package to find a wooden penis swaddled inside. "Oh, wow. Excellent! Can I hold on to this for a while? I have a lot of trainings in the next few weeks."

"Oh, I don't want *that* back. It's yours. Someone said you'd been looking for, uh, one of *those*. I had it left over from an event we did last World AIDS Day. Good luck!"

"Thank you so much! This is brilliant. And look, it matches my hair! The wood, it's blond!" I beamed as I held it up against my shoulder-length locks.

She smiled awkwardly and began backing out.

"Thanks again," I called after her, enjoying her silly unease. "I'm going to call him Woody!"

Woody became my faithful travel companion. I would carry him with me on work trips for years to come.

I laughed to myself that someone who worked full-time in the United Nations could be so embarrassed by something so harmless. And yet, I knew she was in the majority. If everyone were comfortable with sex, sexuality, even basic anatomy—which was apparently embarrassing even when represented by wooden models—we'd have a lot less educating to do. It's a shame we don't teach this stuff clearly and matter-of-factly to children everywhere. That would save us all a lifetime of hassles.

I finished the training and headed back to the hotel for a quick rest before dinner. Trainings always exhaust me, particularly in high-prevalence places where the choice of every word I uttered was critical. I was quickly learning that UN personnel were far less educated about HIV than I ever could've imagined. What I *was* beginning to understand, now that I was focused entirely on that population, was how embarrassed they often were to simply seek information.

Employees seemed to feel that, because they worked for a renowned international organization, they were supposed to already know everything. Also, when the issue was something so controversial yet personal as HIV, they shut down and held on to false beliefs and half-truths. It was as if they thought that, if they hadn't learned before joining the UN, it was now too late to find out. Best not to embarrass themselves by asking questions.

Creating a safe space for asking those very questions was going to be an urgent challenge.

Back in my room, with cricket song alerting me to the setting of the sun, I dropped my bag on the spare bed, the one nearest the window. I always sleep in the bed closest to the door, in case I need to make a quick escape. From what, I don't know, but I've always felt like that.

The top of my black canvas bag fell open, and my new friend rolled off onto the floor. I was going to have to find him a case—can't have my new travel mate rocking about naked in my luggage! I pulled out all of my training gear in hopes of finding some inspiration for this problem of people not asking questions. Then I looked for my other anatomical model.

That one, a vagina, was wrapped in plastic, square and ever so slightly squishy. Although I didn't use it as often, I always carried it, just in case. I was amazed at how many people—including women—had no knowledge of the female anatomy. More than one woman had told me they were afraid to use a condom, because if it came off during sex, it would end up inside of their bodies. As in, deep inside, floating around in their rib cage.

This is not possible, of course. There is no way a condom can get past a woman's cervix. Sperm, yes. Viruses, yes. Condoms, no. So whenever that issue came up, I brought out my silicone model and passed it around. Then people could see just how a woman's reproductive organs are situated and shaped.

I was now realizing that model needed a name, too. I decided to call her Sil. Silcone Sil.

Sil was given to me by a delightful man, Mitchell Warren, who used to work for the Female Health Company, a British firm that manufactures and sells female condoms. He ran its educational nonprofit arm, and I'd worked with him a few times over the years prior to joining UNICEF. Before he left his job as the "female-condom guy" (a title he absolutely loved), I'd called and asked him to send me a model, since I'd left the last one he'd sent me with clients on a consultancy.

"Mitchell, how are you, my friend? I can't believe you're leaving the female condom for work on vaccines!"

"I'm great," he replied, "and, I know, it's a change. But I really believe in the research, and, you know, it's time for something new."

"I hear ya. I'm all in favor of a vaccine. I mean, if we could find one for HIV and get people to use it, it would certainly improve *my* sex life!"

We both laughed and caught up. Then he asked, "So, what can I do for you, Martina?"

"Ah, you know me well!"

"Yes, the famously phone-phobic Martina calls and immediately I know you want something!"

"So true. And yes, I do. I was wondering if you could send me a new vagina model. I left my last one in Burundi."

He paused and I could almost hear him smile. "You know, of all the great parts of the job, this is the one I'm going to miss most. Having women ask *me* for a spare vagina! I'll have one in the mail tonight."

"Thanks a million, Mitchell. I don't know who I'll turn to next time I'm in need."

Incidentally, after leaving the Female Health Company, Mitchell went on to work for AVAC, the AIDS Vaccine Advocacy Coalition. He's now lending support to the work on COVID-19, while keeping HIV on the agenda, particularly as it relates to this new global pandemic. Like many who worked on HIV early on—doctors Anthony Fauci, Carlos del Rio, and Seth Berkley, to name a few—Mitchell's knowledge is invaluable as we navigate this new crisis.

Remembering this conversation, I set my models on my bed and played with them for a moment like a child with Barbie dolls.

"Woody, meet Sil. Sil, meet Woody."

"Well, hello there, Sil. You sure are purdy," I said in a hee-haw voice.

"Why, thank you, Woody. You're not so bad yourself." I gave Sil a more sultry, Mae West type of affectation. "And I'll tell you, I'm glad to have the company. It gets lonely in her luggage. Maybe we can get to know each other better. I'd ask you to peel me some grapes, but . . . come up and see me sometime!"

"I'd like that, Sil. I've been a bit lonely myself, trapped in the cold metal bottom drawer of that anxious little UN lady's desk. Sure would like to warm up next to you, you silicone sexpot!"

I nearly choked on a fit of giggles. Then put them back into my bag. In doing so, I caught my finger on a stack of construction paper cards cut into quarters for people to use during training sessions. I took one out and started a list for myself.

1.) Find a case for Woody and Sil.

2.) Confirm onward flights.

3.) Training—how to get everyone to ask questions.

Wait. That's it!

If I gave everyone a card at the beginning of the sessions and asked them to write down a question, then I'd be able to get them talking without anyone having to expose their lack of knowledge. Eliminating the possibility of shame would allow personnel to save face.

At my session the next day, I handed out the cards. "I want everyone to write something down. You can even write 'I don't have a question,' but put *something* down. When you're done, I'll collect the cards. I promise to answer everything as best I can before we leave today."

Reluctantly, people started writing. After a few minutes I collected the cards. While the group completed a quiz, I sorted and grouped them by types of questions. *Magic.* It had worked. I'd received twenty solid questions from that group of thirty, and they could stay anonymous.

When I returned to my hotel and packed my bags for my early morning flight the next day, I tucked Woody and Sil beneath my folded jeans, smiling at the good week I'd had.

Downtime

New York

Traveling internationally for work quickly became a large part of my life. And I loved it. When I was home, I hosted jam sessions at my apartment where friends would come and play. In stark contrast to my life in Spa, I again had friends. These "salons" took on a life of their own: musicians were soon joined by storytellers and singers. It felt reminiscent of something Gertrude Stein might've done in Paris in the 1920s. There, in a poorly lit, overpriced garden apartment in Manhattan, I had begun to reconstruct my life.

One primarily focused on work, to be sure. But thanks to the abundance of, well, *everything* in Manhattan, my days also included creativity. I took a beginning pottery class and even a jewelry-making class. I took writing courses, too, and generally tried to fill up as many hours of my day as possible. I'd arrived feeling empty and spent. New York was a perfect place to feast on cultural riches.

I'd also started working out regularly, to build strength. Through a friend, I'd been introduced to a bear of a man who became my personal trainer, Ludlow. He became one of my closest friends and talked me down from my stress over many a workout, coffee, or beer.

The city never really felt like home, but it was a good place to have landed.

Contact with Jean-Robert was infrequent, but we stayed in touch. He'd moved on, and in, with a new woman. While I was working on reinventing a new and improved version of myself: Martina, Manhattan Edition.

I began to enjoy my own company and was happy to stay single. I needed the time to be on my own. As my fortieth birthday rolled around, I felt good. Uncharacteristically, I decided to treat myself to a relaxing, luxurious birthday weekend during an extended work trip.

CHAPTER 8

middle age, a marvelous milestone

Turning 40 on Zanzibar (Part 1)

Stone Town

Tanzania: East Africa
Population: 59.7 million
Capital: Dar es Salaam

ero-four, zero-four, zero-four: That's the day I turned four-zero. If I was going to turn forty, Sunday, April 4, 2004, was a hell of a good day to do it. To mark the occasion, I decided to treat myself to a jaunt to Zanzibar. Not the schmoozy New York City bar in Hell's Kitchen but the archipelago in the Indian Ocean. I was already scheduled for a work trip in the region, so I added this to my itinerary.

To me, the name Zanzibar, like Timbuktu or Kathmandu, evokes the exotic allure of ultimate adventure. Those three syllables sound at once enticing, like the smell of cinnamon and cloves on a cold day, yet foreboding, like a silent glance from an informant warning you to be careful and not get lost in the labyrinth of unmarked streets. I've always been drawn to architecture influenced by Islam. I suspected Zanzibar would be both a beautiful and fascinating place because of the spice trade and its links to the Arabian Peninsula and Africa. Besides, even if the actual day totally sucked, I'd always be able to casually toss off "my fortieth birthday, in Zanzibar." That alone brought a smile.

I arrived the day before my birthday, after a flight from Dar-Es-Salaam, and went directly to my hotel. Emerson and Green, now known by its street address of 236 Hurumzi Street—*Huru-muuze* meaning "set them free." An old transformed house that, legend has it, is where in the 1880s the British paid the Arabs to liberate their slaves.

My sleeping quarters, The South Room, were reached by crossing a creaky footbridge from the top-floor veranda to a small open courtyard enclosed only by a wooden gate. To which, I trusted, I and the innkeepers alone had a key. From the gate I'd advance six steps to my right and make a U-turn to enter the front of my 'room'—a word that hardly seems appropriate since half the space was open to the sky. There was a toilet in a cool tiled room ventilated by open decorative spaces at the tops and bottoms of the walls, behind the hinged barroom doors at the end of my room. Directly across from the gate, behind the wall, of course, was the sink and vanity. Immediately to the right of that was a magical-looking teal-green stone bathtub, half under the roof, half under the sky.

On the eve of my birthday, I treated myself to a four-course meal at the rooftop restaurant of the hotel. Sitting barefoot on the Persian-carpeted floor, I ate freshly grilled fish and spiced rice at a low wooden table. Supported by an endless quantity of fluffy colorful pillows, I also enjoyed several fruity cocktails and enjoyed the live entertainment, African dance and drumming. Afterward, I teetered down from the restaurant and across the passage to my room.

Drunk on the glorious dining experience, I could gaze out above the rooftops to the moonlit ocean. I had a panoramic view of Stone Town, the historic section of Zanzibar City. I decided to indulge in an outdoor bath. The moon was full and bright, but between the wooden latticework and the vines and bougainvillea hanging above, I would be hidden from view during my long soak to transition the last evening of my thirties into the first hours of being forty. From the cool smooth tub I could open wooden arched shutters to survey endless rows of rusted corrugated roofs, jutting mosque towers, and precarious satellite dishes, all interspersed with lush green trees.

I slowly rose from the deep tub. Still damp, I padded across the smooth broad terracotta-tiled patio to the bedroom, dropped my towel, slipped into pj's and snuggled into my queen-sized bed with the cobalt blue linen sheets. Their intricate embroidered flowers complemented crisp white pillowcases. I tucked the mesh mosquito net around the corners of my bed and left the turn-down-service frangipani next to me on the other pillow. I ate the requisite chocolate, then let the smell of the tropics—jasmine, ginger, sandalwood—waft through my dreams until the lavender tones of dawn alerted the roosters and religious alike that the day was due to begin.

As I began to stir that early April morning, the wailing call to prayers at daybreak was followed by an automated recording of clanging bells at the nearly-forgotten Catholic church, dwarfed by the shadows of mosques. The sounds filled my mind before my eyes had begun to hesitantly pry open and focus. I lay in my princess bed and reflected, first on the previous days, then back on the past four decades.

Two days before, I'd been in Addis Ababa, where my colleagues surprised me during the last hours of my visit with a birthday cake and gifts. Another colleague, not even knowing it was my birthday, bestowed on me two stunning scarves, one crisp white linen with blue satin trim and the other a silky deep olive green. Ethiopians are as generous as they are beautiful, and somehow I'd deeply touched this woman. She'd called me into her office and said, "My dear, I want you to have these, and to never forget us. You help so many others confront their fears. I want to make sure you know that we are always with you."

For most of my life, I'd convinced myself I'd never be older than thirty-six. Why, I have absolutely no clue, but I was sure that was all the time I'd have. My diagnosis at twenty-eight just seemed to reinforce this notion, when the doctor told me I probably had a good five years to live.

My thirtieth had come and gone and I didn't get sick. Thirty-three came and went—the dreaded five-year mark—and I wanted to bitch-slap that San Francisco doctor. Even thirty-six came and went, although I'd had some bumps along the road.

And now here it was: forty. I'd never thought, having HIV, I'd live for twelve more years—and without the need for treatment, no less. When people made casual jokes about the alleged awfulness of turning forty, I always replied, "Well, it's certainly better to turn forty than *not*."

I was far from upset about this milestone. Mostly I felt amazed. I've always loved birthdays, the one day we're entitled to indulge ourselves. I always take the day off, referring to it as "International Me Day," my own personal holiday. Particularly since testing positive, I treasure every year my self-designated holiday arrives—another year that I've beaten the odds.

As I lingered in my warm bed, sun rays crept in through the slatted windows to play tic-tac-toe on my torso. I thought back to a recent phone call with my father. A happy man in his late seventies, he'd chuckled and said, "Another couple o' weeks and you'll be middle-aged!"

"Excuse *me*?" I shouted into the phone. "I'd hardly call forty middle-aged!"

"Well, kiddo, just how old are you planning to be? Sounds like pretty darn near the middle to me!" I could all but hear him grinning, trying not to laugh at my relative youth. This memory made me smile as I admired the tooled mahogany woodworking throughout the room. Fragrant spices—clove, nutmeg, and cardamum—wafted up from the market below and mixed with the salt scent of the Indian Ocean just blocks away.

After an ample breakfast of eggs and beef sausage, toast and coffee and a glass of fresh passionfruit juice, I joined a colleague who was also staying in the hotel. We took a half-day tour of Unguja, the island incorrectly but widely referred to as Zanzibar. Heading out of Stone Town, past the tall, carved wooden doors on huge old tabby buildings. Women covered from head to toe in head scarves and full length dresses with long sleeves walked through the narrow streets about their morning errands. We passed areas thick with vegetation—fruit-bearing trees, palms, and, of course, spice plants—and ended up at a stunning beachfront resort where I rushed out to dip a toe in the warm ocean. I make it a ritual to do this in every natural body of water I meet. A storm was brewing miles offshore. It made the sky an amazing hammered-steel color, rising to meet the blue above it and dropping to the touch the clear, nearly green water that lapped up on white sand so pale it matched my untanned skin.

Following endless driving in our tour guide's rickety van, we made a visit to a spice farm and a most welcome stop for locally-brewed ginger beer. After returning to the hotel, we planned to go for a late lunch next door at the understated Kidude Restaurant before heading to the tiny airport to fly back to Dar es Salaam.

Just as we stepped out of the lobby onto Hurumzi Street, the skies opened. A downpour worthy of an Indian monsoon let loose. After months of drought, the locals were giddy with relief. Some ran inside to get shampoo and soap then showered in the street. Sheets of water slammed down. Children squealed and flip-flops slapped as everyone scurried in and out of the long-awaited rain.

Clean water is vital to survival. Far too many people around the globe lack this basic need. The result is drought, illness, diminished access to work or school, and even starvation.

The scenario that sticks most prominently in my mind goes something like this:

A family member in a rural village gets sick with diarrhea. The mother or wife has to go to the river to get water to wash the sick person, his soiled clothes and sheets. The water isn't clean either, contaminated with bacteria, viruses, or parasites. So the problem persists. The caregiver spends even more time collecting water, so she has to keep her daughter home from school to handle the cleaning and cooking while she nurses and cleans up after the sick person. The cycle continues and, due to a lack of clean water, another girl child misses out on an education.

I've learned to honor and respect water, so I took this downpour as an auspicious sign on my most special day.

Birthday Cake (40th Birthday, Part 2)

Dar es Salaam

After our short flight back to the mainland, we arrived at the check-in desk at our modern well-appointed hotel with views overlooking the Indian Ocean.

"*Jambo*! Welcome! Passports, please," the clerk said.

"You'd better give me a nice room—today is my birthday!" I said.

The clerk flashed a *Yeah, right, lady, sure it is* smile and took my documents to confirm my reservation. "Oh, it really *is* your birthday! And a fine one at that, on this Sunday! Happy birthday, miss!"

I can't say the room was spectacular, particularly after the magical space I'd just left in Zanzibar, but it was spacious, had a comfortable bed, and a view of the ocean. After yet another birthday dinner that night with my colleagues from the Dar office, I returned upstairs to find a cake sitting on the coffee table. It was from the hotel staff, decorated with "Happy Birthday 40th Miss" in red lettering on white icing with chocolate shavings around the edge and a spray of bougainvillea gently placed above the writing. Next to the cake stood four roses—two white, two pink—in a tall glass vase. Never before had such a kind gesture been waiting for me on my birthday.

I brought the cake into the office the next morning. "I can't eat this all alone," I said. But there was a weird vibe and my offer was essentially rejected.

During my training session, someone asked a question about nutrition and suggested maybe it was best for people with HIV to stay a little bit fat, in case they got sick.

"*That* is a lovely idea, particularly today, when I have birthday cake to eat," I said. "But, sadly, it's not the case."

The group leaned closer. This was clearly not the answer they were expecting.

"You see, HIV is a very tricky virus, and it fools the body in many ways. So, if she"—I pointed randomly to a woman in the front row—"and I get stranded on a deserted island and run out of food, our bodies will react very differently."

"Why is that?" asked a small bald man toward the back.

"Well, let's assume I am HIV-positive, and she is negative. Her body will do the normal thing and eat the fat first and save the muscle for last. So she'll become lean but still be able to function. Assuming, of course, she can keep hydrated. Water is key, don't forget."

The group nodded, looking keen to hear the rest.

"My body, however, because the virus has done some nasty rewiring, will eat muscle first and leave fat for last. This is what makes it so hard for people with wasting syndrome to function. They lose all their strength."

"Wow, I never knew that," said one of the participants.

"Yes," said another. She was a doctor and nutritionist specializing in HIV. "It's strange but true. So it is key that people with HIV eat well and stay as fit as possible. We all need to stay in shape, of course. But it's even more critical for them. It can keep them healthier longer."

"That said," I continued, "we can always allow ourselves a little indulgence now and then. And actually, I brought in some cake this morning, so maybe we can share. I think we're done with our session for today, so thank you, everyone, let's enjoy a bit of unhealthy cake!"

I turned to my colleague from the local office. She smiled widely, and as the doors to the conference room opened, the group plus some others started singing "Happy Birthday" and wheeled in a small table balancing a large pink box.

Much to my surprise, that office had *also* organized a cake—a *huge* three-foot sheet confection slathered in rich yellow icing—and had invited all staff to join in the festivities. Turns out the heads of our Ethiopian and Tanzanian offices had a rivalry that dated back years; one was not to be outdone by the other. So I benefited from their competition as we celebrated, for the fourth time, my fortieth birthday, in gracious African style.

CHAPTER 9

taking care of our own

The Smoke That Thunders

Livingstone and Lusaka

Zambia: Southern Africa
Population: 18.3 million
Capital: Lusaka

A s we approached the small airport at Livingstone at the border with Zimbabwe, on the hop from Johannesburg, I feared I was in for bad weather. My fourth country in three weeks, the second since turning forty four days before. The sky looked overcast; the air misty. Only after I was in the rickety taxi and on my way to the hotel did I realize the skies were clear. What we'd flown through was not gathering clouds but the mist from Victoria Falls. The smoke that thunders, as the locals say.

I arrived on the second or third day of a weeklong retreat for the UNICEF office in Zambia. As this was one of our hardest-hit countries, I was invited to meet with my colleagues to get a more in-depth view of what they were dealing with, as well as to encourage them to get tested and know their status. A task that sounds simple but was actually the most challenging part of my work.

At times I even have to remind myself that it's better to know you have HIV than not. In twelve years with it, I'd never been sick, and felt almost guilty I'd told so many people, putting them through the stress of worrying about my future. I, too, sometimes fantasized that ignorance might be bliss. Then I remembered this was exactly how any pandemic (COVID is no different) spreads—through ignorance and fear. So I continued my personal mission to educate and open minds. To tell my story, and lead by example.

Every time I shared, it took something out of me, because I again exposed myself to the reactions of others, which I could rarely anticipate. Sometimes I felt replenished by the prospect of helping; rewarded, fulfilled. At others I felt battered, exploited, empty. After several weeks on the road, I was getting tired, and prayed that this retreat would revitalize me. That it was being held at one of the most spectacular locations on the planet was definitely a bonus.

The baboon that lingered each day on the balcony of my hotel room, though? Not so much. The woman a few doors down had settled in for an afternoon nap one day and woke to find a primate in her room stealing sugar packets from the coffee service tray. They were equally surprised to see one another. Luckily, the baboon had what he'd come for and quickly departed.

They're cheeky creatures, and my guy was more flirt than thief. He liked to lounge about, seductively eyeing me through the sliding glass door. He'd run long arms over the railing, shifting from one side of the balcony to the other, striking various poses. Not unlike a few men I'd seen tipsy in bars. Sometimes I'd try to ignore him, but as my room looked toward the mist above glorious falls and endless rainbows, I wasn't about to close the curtains. Other times I'd catch him pleasuring himself as he watched me. That's when I usually left for a walk. I'd put up with a lot of harassment living in New York, but this was too much.

The week before I'd been in Mombasa, Kenya, at a beach resort for Easter. There I'd been harassed by a pack of rhesus monkeys who'd smelled my bag of peanuts and tried to mug me. First, they'd circled me, looking cute and tiny. But as they jumped and lurched at my snacks, relentless as mosquitoes at dusk, I made a dash for my room with a trail of tiny simians chasing me. Safari in reverse. I'd vowed to never walk the streets of Mombasa again with nuts exposed.

The retreat was already under way, so I took advantage of a gap in the schedule and hiked to see the famous falls. I'd heard of Victoria Falls, but am not easily impressed with "things you must see in life." But I thought, Well, I'm here. I might as well go see what all the fuss is about. I walked down to the well-maintained path adjacent to the hotel and followed the signs. The trees became increasingly dense as I headed toward the falls.

As did the vendors. When the first merchant tried to rent or sell me a rain jacket, I shrugged him off as a con artist preying on unsuspecting tourists. After the fourth, fifth and sixth, I started to think perhaps they were there for a better reason.

I was already becoming damp from the mist and hadn't even seen the falls yet. I walked down a soggy portion of the trail in squeaking, squishing sneakers. I was now under an entire canopy of vegetation. Just as I turned another heavily-wooded bend, a roar unfolded as if I'd put my head under water in a rapidly-filling bathtub. The intensity of the sound was palpable. Within seconds I was drenched from head to toe.

I stopped to watch rainbow after rainbow dancing across the mile-wide vaporous chutes as the water fell more than three hundred and fifty feet. I'd seen waterfalls before, of course, but nothing like this had come remotely close to the magnitude of this natural splendor. Victoria Falls is the largest sheet of falling water in the world.

Already soaked, I ventured closer and was overwhelmed by a sense of vulnerability. Insignificance. My heart pounded as I realized I could be washed away in an instant, like a leaf on a creek, and nobody would even know I'd ever been there. I hiked to a higher spot overlooking the falls where local kids played fearlessly in the water pooled from the mist.

One young woman asked me to take a picture of her with her young daughter and sons. I thought this was odd since it would be on my camera, and I'd have no way to get the photo to them.

She insisted it didn't matter.

"Ma," she said, "I have seen this great wet smoke. It is in my mind's eye forever. I simply wish you to catch this moment in your machine so you may keep it for me. Would you kindly do that?"

"Of course." I smiled and snapped away.

After the falls, I went back to the conference room and found my colleagues. When my session came up, I had them pair off and talk to each other about their fear of being tested for the virus. A ten-minute exercise. Having an odd number of participants, I sat on the floor with a flirtatious, handsome young Zambian.

"Chanda, I'm afraid to be tested for HIV," I said. "Could you support me to go for a test?"

He smiled so beguilingly I melted into his warmth, feeling my face flush. Was he even listening, or just flirting? "Of course. I should probably go for a test myself, but...but it is so bloody scary." His voice dropped an octave as the smile slipped away. "I know I *need* to know, but I don't *want* to know. I don't want to be the next person in the coffin heading into the ground."

How could I answer that?

"I know what you mean," I replied at last. "But they have amazing medicines now that really help people live longer. As long as you know what you're dealing with, there is so much you can do to live a long, full life."

He held my gaze a moment too long, then forced the seductive grin back as if to lighten the mood. "True. Suppose I need to know in case I want to get into a relationship. But it's still so frightening." He took my hand. "I'm glad we can do this together. I'm afraid I'll not test if I have to go it alone."

I wasn't sure which part was the role play, which for real.

Despite a common reluctance to be tested, and even with alarming stigmas, individuals from high-prevalence countries seem far less perturbed by the notion of entering into a sexual relationship with a person with HIV. I suppose it's because they've heard about it for so long. Everyone's topped up with information.

In Europe or North America, however, heterosexual men are woefully uneducated about it. They see it as someone else's problem. Nobody targets *them* with information, so it's not entirely their fault. They're simply unprepared to deal with an HIV-positive partner.

Each of these scenarios serves as reminders of the complexity of the human condition.

The fear around HIV in Zambia is beyond description. With a prevalence of over fifteen percent, and more than twenty-five percent in some urban areas, everyone's lost a family member. Yet they often remain unable to confront it personally.

Between sessions, one of our international staffers—a Scandinavian woman—said, "It's good you're here, these people are all so touched by this disease. Not like us. We're lucky; it's really not our issue."

"Excuse me?" I stared at her.

"Well, you know, HIV is rampant here, so we have to keep educating them. Luckily for people like us, from rich countries, we don't really have to worry."

"I see. I didn't realize the virus cared about border or wealth, but that's an interesting perspective." I continued to my seat, shaking my head and rolling my eyes.

Clearly she hadn't heard the part of my introduction when I revealed I was living with HIV.

At the coffee break that afternoon, a woman named Angie started chatting with me. "Martina, I don't know what to do anymore. My sisters and brothers have all passed from this terrible thing, and I'm so tired. I have twelve little ones—my nieces and nephews—at home to raise. Plus my mother, my sick auntie, my own four children, and my husband. My kids are angry because they know they won't be able to go to college after all, since I have to pay for everything for everyone else. My husband and I worked so hard to put everything in order so our children could have a better life. We've been faithful, God-loving, and hardworking. I don't have HIV, but everyone else in my life has been touched. I just can't do it anymore. I never have a moment alone to even think."

She explained that by the start of April she'd already spent most of her projected annual salary on funerals for extended family. She had nothing left and didn't know how she was going to get through the rest of the year. Hers was a stark, harsh reality I'd never fully comprehended before.

I took her hand. "I can't begin to have the answers. But I'll try to think of something." I feebly suggested she drive around the block twice before heading home. So that, at the very least, she could have a few solitary moments to herself in the quiet of her car.

She hugged me. "Thank you for listening, Martina. It means a great deal just to know someone cares. I know you'll try to help us; that's a lot."

Angie's story shook me to the core. Yet I knew my colleagues were still in much better shape than some I'd met elsewhere.

The retreat ended on Friday morning. Rather than put me on the bus directly back to Lusaka with the other staff, our country director arranged a ride back for me with two of our water and sanitation engineers, so I could visit some of our field projects.

I sat in the back seat of the four-by-four truck with Clement, a quiet Zambian junior engineer. Our chief engineer, a rotund Indian with lilting flowery English, teased Clement about his apparently very pregnant wife. "Now you must get serious about being a father for the first time."

Clement struck me as a *very* serious young man. And a shy one. He seemed unnerved to be seated next to me, a senior colleague from headquarters. So I quickly realized that these two had a rapport and the older man was trying to soften up the atmosphere. Clement seemed more at ease after this banter. He relaxed and told me about their work.

"The people we support through the water projects actually spend a lot of time with us because building a well is slow business," Clement said. "So while we are together, we teach them about how important it is to have clean drinking water so as to avoid diarrhea. But they just don't want information about HIV. They don't want to be tested, or walk for a day just to reach the clinic to receive what they expect will be bad news."

The people he worked with were much more focused on building a new well than learning about an elusive virus that seemed destined to attack them all, no matter what they did.

"So what do you do?" I asked. "To try to reach them."

"Well, we just do it anyway. Teach them about the links between lack of water and poor sanitation to disease. We show a lot of pictures and explain that if everyone doesn't get sick from the tainted water, then they won't have to walk to the river so often to collect more to clean up after ailing relatives. Things like that."

"Does it help?"

"I don't know, but we have to try. Our country is dying." His voice trailed off as he stared bleakly out the window for a moment at the passing green countryside.

Turning back, gazing with sad eyes, he added, "We always tell them the best bet would be to just use condoms, but they don't get that. They go blank whenever we talk about prevention."

Water was immediate—thirst they understood—but HIV too tiny and distant to comprehend. These messages are hard to transmit even in industrialized countries, which have the benefit of every possible medium of communication. In remote, rural settings it's nearly impossible to explain how something you can't see, touch, or smell can still kill you.

The COVID-19 pandemic has forced us to relive many these same issues with the anti-maskers. Denial is a dangerous drug.

Disease is often mistaken for witchcraft—a spell cast upon the sick one for doing something wrong, rather than exposure to a pathogen. When I'm in places like Zambia, I understand why. People work so hard merely to get by on a daily basis, and despite their hardest efforts some mysterious force is punishing them with no rhyme or reason. Even though I understand the science and the spread of the disease, I still find it hard to comprehend the depth of pain people endure.

Similarly, with COVID, the inequity of access to quality health care has resulted in certain populations being harder hit than others. In the US, for example, some families only see the statistics on the nightly news, but don't know anyone affected. While others have lost multiple family members, and entire communities are decimated by the pandemic.

The beauty of Victoria Falls was rapidly fading from my mind. I was no longer in the luxurious setting of Livingstone where rich tourists fly in to "experience Africa," then escape before they get bitten by mosquitoes or scratched by a thornbush. I was now visiting people in quite different circumstances: abject poverty.

In one village there were no adults left alive. No one over the age of fourteen. I met a girl, the eldest there and by default in charge, who'd turned to sex work so she could feed the other children.

A colleague translated quietly into my ear as she softly spoke. "I go to the village nearby for food but I don't have enough money," she said. "So I let the men have me for some maize and a few coins. Sometimes I get very sick since my baby came. The sister at the clinic says I have the HIV, but I don't have time to worry about that. Since my parents died I have to look after these little ones."

A pair of thin dusty boys, maybe six and eight years old, tossed a cricket back and forth as a game. One stuffed it into a ripped pocket when he realized we were watching. He smiled up, revealing a few missing front teeth, and put out his other hand. "*Kwacha*? Dollar?"

I gathered these orphaned kids had become a bit of a freak show and were accustomed to being visited by curious *mzungu*—white foreigners.

My colleague whispered, "Don't give him money. He'll never go to school that way," as our driver handed over a box of food and some blankets. Battling this war of survival alone, these children had more strength and fight in them than any hardened soldier I'd ever met.

The stunning landscapes we passed on the long stretches of road between villages now paled. The view could not banish the heaviness in my heart for the work I could never complete. I had just been reminded that, no matter how much we did, it would never be enough. Like the falls, the task was just too large. It dwarfed me. I could barely begin to scratch the surface of the issues our staff were dealing with.

By that point I'd been living with HIV for more than a decade, but only now understood I knew nothing of the realities of this epidemic. I was still asymptomatic, partly because I had good insurance, lived in a country with excellent health care, and had access to clean water and healthy food every day. And partly because I was just damned lucky.

I'd never yet been sick. Never had to give my own money to bury a family member. I didn't live with the fear everyone I knew was going to be dead in ten years. I'd lost at least a hundred people in my life over the years, but that didn't come close to the numbing statistics they dealt with in sub-Saharan Africa. I'd once told a Zambian friend, back in

New York, that early on—in 1993—I'd quit counting when the number of deaths hit fifty.

She'd sighed. "Me too. But that was just in my family."

I found Zambians to be the most gentle and wonderful people on the planet. I sometimes referred to them as "lamb people," for they were soft and quiet and infinitely huggable. Some of them told me that is exactly *the* problem, "We're too gentle. We don't stand up and fight and take on insurmountable challenges."

I'm not Zambian, so I don't know if this is always true. But it breaks my heart that, in one of the most beautiful places on Earth, a virulent thing that cannot be seen with the naked eye can wreak such havoc. These people do not deserve this, I thought. Nobody does.

I remained powerless to fix the pandemic, there or anywhere. But I felt rejuvenated knowing that, because of my visit and our pointed discussions at the retreat, at least twenty-four of my hundred or so colleagues in this small country had already gone for a test. They told me so. Before I left on Tuesday, just four days after the end or our retreat, entire teams of workers had visited the local clinic, together, for testing. That was success.

I caught these fleeting moments and stored them in my personal-experience well to draw upon when I felt used up. I smile in reflection as I write these words now—for really, these instances are all that any of us ever truly have.

When I returned to New York, I relayed these stories to my colleagues in human resources during a weekly management team meeting.

One of the legal advisors, a petite Spanish woman who was chairing that day, asked if anyone had any further business before we adjourned.

I raised my hand. "There's a serious epidemic in-house," I said. "We have got to increase our efforts because our staff are under tremendous strain."

I was met with a silent indifference from my half dozen colleagues. But I was allowed to continue. As the sun was setting, the other managers listened politely while they gathered their notes and belongings. The chairwoman said, "Martina, go on, but please make it quick. It's late in the day."

"Because our staff are considered the rich ones, they're usually expected to care for everyone in their extended families," I explained. "Often taking in the orphaned children of all their siblings or relatives who have died of AIDS. How do they decide which children to put on their insurance, for example? If they can claim only six but have ten living under one roof, what do they do? Remove their own children to cover the orphaned ones who have HIV? It is an impossible scenario."

"Well, Martina," the legal advisor said. "If you worked more closely with our HIV program people, we wouldn't have this problem, would we? We're UNICEF. We take care of children; that's what we do. Maybe *you* are the one who needs to increase efforts."

Livid, I bit my tongue. I had to be in another meeting immediately following, so I took a few deep breaths, tabled my issue for the moment, and left. As I walked to my next meeting with an HIV program colleague, I told him what had happened.

"Who said this to you?" he asked. I told him and he said, "Well, that explains it. She's one of the ones who's climbed the ladder entirely from within."

"What do you mean?"

"A policy person who's never worked in the field. In fact, I don't think she's ever even visited one of our country offices. She only knows what is at the end of her nose. She doesn't get the bigger picture."

Soon after that, with the help of Mark Sterling, I found my way onto the agenda of our senior management team. I could not neglect the problems I had seen. "Our staff are not, and cannot be, covered by our program work, because funders do not donate money to support staff," I reminded these decisionmakers. "Children in the care of UN personnel are the lucky ones. Our program money must, by virtue of our mandate, go to the child-headed villages and the worst-case-scenario settings. Not to UNICEF staff."

That said, I added that it was the ethical responsibility of each UN entity to invest the money necessary to keep our staff healthy and provide support so they could continue to be productive and manage their lives.

That presentation would be one of countless to follow with managers in all parts of UNICEF and beyond. A plea I made repeatedly, yet which often fell on deaf—or at least closed—ears. Amid our often remarkable efforts to stem the AIDS pandemic in the world, we were overlooking the needs within our own family.

In Manhattan, our small team of colleagues from the different agencies worked more and more closely together. We were struggling to have our messages heard, so we relied on one another to strategize and, above all, not give up. UNAIDS had by then funded a full-time staff member, Alan Silverman, to develop learning materials, and we were collaborating at every level.

The UNDP, The World Bank, and The World Food Programme, among other organizations, had also developed in-house training programs and were borrowing ideas and resources from us. The time was ripe to shift from agency-specific programs and institute a system-wide HIV in the Workplace program for the entire UN.

Working together informally was simple. Creating an official mechanism to serve all staff world-wide was going to be another story. We had the people and the tools, but as yet not the approval of the very top management. When a meeting with these senior leaders was secured, it was unanimously agreed upon, among our small working group, that I would lead the briefing for the most senior management of the United Nations, including then—Secretary-General Kofi Annan.

Next Slide, Please

New York

"Next slide, please," I said, as I stood on the thirty-eighth floor of the United Nations Secretariat, casually trying to tug my dark gray pinstriped skirt back into place. I'd lost weight, and it kept inching around. In the private, wood-paneled, windowless conference room of the Secretary-General, I was addressing His Excellency, Kofi Annan. He was slight in stature, and his signature goatee—now white with age—was a stark contrast against his dark skin. He was joined by his most senior staff from the Secretariat, as well as the heads of several agencies. Wardrobe malfunction was not what I needed at that moment.

Fortunately, individuals who cared more about trying to save the world than about fashion surrounded me. Nobody seemed perturbed by some shimmying fabric. At least I didn't aim the laser pointer in anyone's eye. All in all, it was going well.

"As you see here," I said, pointing to the presentation, "and as I'm sure you already well know, our personnel policy states we never test for HIV as a part of recruitment or periodic medical exams. We simply verify that the individual is fit for work."

I craned my neck to the left to see if the head of the UN Atomic Energy Agency had heard me. His Oz-sized head hovered above us on a video screen patching him in from Vienna. He was probably nibbling a piece of Linzer torte when we weren't looking. At last I saw his delayed smile of acknowledgment and turned back to the requisite death-by-PowerPoint routine.

I could have done this presentation in my sleep. But now I was on my best behavior, trying to engage a dozen world leaders in the short fifteen minutes I'd been allotted. I assessed the room. I stood at the far end of the heavy conference table. I'd been allocated a small, separate table.

Mr. Annan was seated diagonally to my left, at the middle far side of the table where, he could surveil the door. And anyone who passed through it. The others were in what I assumed were their usual spots for this weekly meeting. The IT tech sat quietly in the corner to my right, controlling all the knobs and switches.

Following months of negotiations, we'd been granted a slot on the agenda of the weekly senior management meeting. We—our small interagency, self-appointed, task force—needed their buy-in so we could shift our plans into action. This would become the first interagency hands-on training on any topic ever mandated for all UN personnel. No small sell! If we succeeded, we'd be making history.

Brushing a wisp of hair from my eyes, I continued. "And, of course, that's a good thing. The UN certainly doesn't want to be seen discriminating against people living with HIV, or those who've developed AIDS."

I chose my words carefully in hopes precise language would clarify the huge difference between the two.

Smiling, the Secretary-General nodded in encouragement. I pressed on, but as my next words bubbled up, a ruddy fist slammed on the table. All eyes turned to the silver-haired, ready-to-retire head of the Department of Peacekeeping Operations.

"Zis is crazy. We *should* test ev-e-rrrry-one! Why not? Why in the world do we let zose people run around for the UN without knowing zey have the HIV?"

My smile slid off somewhere into my jacket as I bit the inside of my mouth—*zose people*. I wasn't going to let that pass.

As wheels cranked in my brain, the cheery Indian lilt of Dr. Sudershan Narula, head of Medical Services, jumped in. She adjusted her cardigan, pulling it closed. "Oh, but Jean-Marie, you must know that we can tell if people are fit for service. It would be not proper to test them—it's not our business. Not proper at all."

Then the Great and digital Oz head piped in from Vienna. "But why not? We do zem big favor to test, no?"

These—I assume—usually well-mannered diplomats were talking over one another so rapidly; I could barely follow who said what. With each intervention, advocating for or against, tensions flared. Voices raised, including mine.

"*Excuse me!* Wait. May I *please* explain?" I said.

The room fell silent. The clearly amused-looking Secretary-General raised his hand. "Please! Please, everybody. We've invited our specialist here, let's give her a chance to clarify."

"Thank you," I said, loose skirt now fully askew. I moved closer to the heavy dark wood table. "With all due respect, in a perfect world, what you're suggesting would be wonderful. If we could just test everyone on the planet for HIV, we could solve a lot of problems. But we can't. That's not reality."

I took a deep breath and plunged on. "Do you understand how rampant the discrimination against people with HIV still is? Even here in the UN. Until the day arrives we've solved *that* problem, we cannot and must not test our staff mandatorily."

"But of course. I know zis, but we are not just ze world," spewed the senior-most peacekeeper, Jean-Marie Guéhenno. "We are ze UN, and should be ze first!"

"No, sir. We should not. And here is why." I could feel the shoulders of the IT guy crouched beside me, next to the videoconferencing controls, tense. He seemed afraid to breathe.

"We cannot, because we cannot control what happens on the other end of that test. The peacekeepers always ultimately belong to their countries—not to us. N'est ce pas, monsieur? If we test one of your troops from a country with discriminatory laws, then maybe he gets kicked out of his unit. Then what? How does he support his family? Who feeds his children? Us? You? I don't think so!" Exasperated, I straightened until I'm sure I grew a half an inch in my high-heeled boots.

"Our primary function is to protect people, not ruin their lives." I raised my eyebrows, feeling my neck and face heat with a flush as I morphed from a well-behaved underling into a woman with a mission. I'd already addressed the General Assembly, and President Clinton at the White House. No point in holding back now. "Mandatorily test a staff member, soldier, or civilian, and discover they have HIV? If that information gets out, they may lose everything. It's our job to educate them so they will go for testing of their own volition. It is *not* our place to force them to. We simply cannot do that. It would be unethical."

Dr. Narula, winked at me as she tucked her slippery sari back under her cardigan.

"Thank you. Perhaps we can continue?" said the Secretary-General.

I'd reached my final slide. The IT tech turned off the projector and I shared a few anecdotes from my extensive visits to our country offices. By then I was calm again.

Throughout my talk, though, these senior UN officials had been listening with only half an ear. Except, of course, during the brawl over testing, at which point they'd all jumped in and slung a few verbal jabs.

"Reversing the impact of the AIDS pandemic is a key priority area of work for the United Nations," I added. "We need to start at home."

As they clicked away on their BlackBerrys, I glimpsed eyes rolling and papers being straightened.

"People like me need to know they can count on you. In nearly ten years with the UN, I have repeatedly faced insensitivity and ignorance regarding HIV."

A few eyes glanced my way, looking dismayed.

"We must have an educated staff if we're going to actually help others, help governments, and deliver on our mandate. You'd be surprised," I continued, "how many of your people have unprotected sex while serving in emergencies around the globe, for example."

I heard a few nervous giggles. I'd hit a sensitive spot there. They'd all served in humanitarian emergencies, and many in conflict zones. They had to know I was right.

"Our staff are extremely vulnerable. We need to make every effort to educate them—to keep them alive. And for those who already have HIV, we must keep them healthy.

"I've had HIV for thirteen years. I'm lucky because I've never been sick, never needed treatment. Yet. But I hope that the day I do, I'll be able to count on the UN as my employer to support me, so I can continue to serve."

Heads shot up, giving me confused looks. Brows furrowed in silence as they searched each other's reactions. I let them ponder that as I collected my documents and concluded my presentation, thanking them all for their time.

I wasn't really worried about myself; I'd said it for dramatic effect. I love shattering stereotypes. I felt sure getting sick wasn't going to be my personal path with this virus; I had other roles to play. I'd said it for all those who didn't have access to people like the Secretary-General. At moments like this, I often recalled the words of a favorite professor I'd had in college.

"Martina, you are a white woman with a soul," Febe Portillo once told me in her resolute voice. "You need to always speak up for those who cannot. Not everyone will be able to go the places you go. Do not forget them. Speak not just for yourself but for *all* people. Then you will be heard."

"Thank you, Ms. Clark, for this lively and informative session," said the Secretary-General. "You can count on my support of this important work." His words were an implied endorsement that we had his approval to move forward—and then, with the grace of his gentle smile, the group moved on to the next agenda item.

The head of human resources for the United Nations, Rosemary McCreery, who'd negotiated the presentation on our behalf, caught my eye. She gave me an enormous grin and two thumbs up. She clearly believed I'd won them over. They would not forget this presentation, and our work could move forward.

As I was leaving the room, when I passed his seat, the head of peacekeeping, Mr. Guéhenno, called my name, then took my hand. "Zank you. Really, zank you. I'm sorry if I was not so sensitive," he said. He meant it. I could feel it in the warmth of his words and the strength of his grip.

A few days later I received an e-mail from the IT guy. He told me that in all the years he'd organized video conferences for the Secretary-General he'd never seen a meeting like that: *Absolute chaos*, he wrote. *Brilliant!*

I knew this had been a critical moment for our work, and for our team. I also knew that the next time I traveled out into the world to educate our staff and their dependents about the impact HIV and AIDS were having within the UN family, the Secretary-General had my back.

What Am I Doing Here?

Khartoum and Nyala,
Juba and Rumbek

Sudan: Northeastern Africa
Population: 43.1 million
Capital: Khartoum

South Sudan: East-Central Africa
Population: 11.2 million
Capital: Juba
World's youngest country, gained independence in 2011

In November of 2005, I made a whirlwind tour of Sudan and what is now known as South Sudan. Khartoum was my base, where I returned between trips. In only a week, I visited Nyala, Juba, and Rumbek. At the time, Sudan was the largest country on the continent. These were not neighboring locales. I flew on progressively smaller planes as the trip continued. My first excursion, to Nyala in the region of Darfur, was on a twenty-seat United Nations Humanitarian Air Service prop-plane. The flight was fine, but the landing haunts me to this day.

In the last remaining minutes of the flight from Khartoum, the guy in front of me had turned around to chat as we began our descent over the miles of refugee camps, giddy as a schoolboy. "Isn't it fantastic?" he said.

"Uh, what?" I asked, confused.

"Why, the runway, of course! It's amazing!"

"Yes, *amazing* is a word you could use. *Frightening* is another word that comes to mind." It was the first time I'd ever encountered an unpaved airstrip, and it seemed unsafe. Too malleable.

"No, no, it's definitely amazing. I'm the engineer who designed this runway, and it's the first time I'm getting to land on it. You should've seen it before. Now, *that* was scary." He beamed at himself, reflected in the airplane window as the sky disappeared.

I sucked in my breath, squeezed my eyes shut and grabbed the handrest as red dust billowed up, swallowing the plane, during our screeching touchdown. Once on the ground in Nyala, and as the dust settled, I exhaled.

His happiest moment had ranked as one of my scariest. I had nightmares for weeks.

My next jaunt was from Khartoum to Juba, in the south. By way of Nyala in Darfur. By the time I left Sudan, I'd landed on or taken off from that runway a half dozen times, but the last was as unnerving as the first.

After a full day of work in Juba, my colleague and host, Sheila—our program manager for southern Sudan—suggested we join the rest of the UNICEF team for dinner. Sheila was a thirty-something darkhaired American with the physique of a toned, thin yoga instructor. She was kind and soft spoken. She was also experienced at her job of helping local governments build up prevention programs, particularly ones supporting children and out-of-school youth.

At the compound where all international staff lived, we were invited to join in the festivities. It was Thanksgiving, ex-pat edition. Ten of us feasted that evening on what seemed to be marinated beef jerky over white rice, then we split a cooked tomato. I shared a warm beer with a colleague and savored it down to the disgusting dregs.

Every few minutes the TV would lurch back to life and a grainy newscaster would blurt out another repeat of the ongoing headlines from CNN, the only channel with a strong enough signal to connect.

"And in further news, yada yada yada shhhhhhhhhhhhhhhhhhhhhh..." And off they'd drift into a wash of white noise. It was frustrating when this tiny pipeline to the outside world got clogged.

We went back to drinking.

Somewhere around the last sip of beer, my friend Michael showed up. The same Michael I'd first met in Eritrea and with whom I'd since crossed paths in many places over the years. His white SUV was quickly identifiable by the enormous antenna on the front, jutting like a wayward finger flipping off oncoming traffic. Michael was career military from Kenya, and now worked fulltime for Peacekeeping. His job was to train the never-ending flow of new troops on the basics of HIV to make sure they kept themselves, and everyone they encountered, safe while keeping the peace.

"My sistaaaah," he said. "You are as beautiful as ever! *Karibu sana!*"

"Michael, what a nice welcome to find you here!" I said, as he hugged me a bit too tightly. "And you, my friend, you are as tipsy as ever! It's good you have a driver! How are you?"

"Ahhh, I am much better now that I have seen your precious face. What are you doing tomorrow morning?"

"Well, we did our sessions with staff—you know, the civilians— earlier today back in the office. Er…shipping container. Office container. Whatever. So I guess I'm free. Why? What kind of trouble are you going to get me into now?"

"Come educate the troops with me. We're doing a big training this week, and you know how much they like to have a woman come show them condoms!"

I could feel myself hotly blushing in the shadows of the compound, but agreed to be picked up at eight the next morning. I have a love-hate thing with the peacekeepers. I'm very much anti-military but I secretly adore working with them. Maybe it's the uniforms.

As soon as Michael left, I took my leave from the main house. Exhausted, I headed directly to sleep in the room I was sharing with Sheila.

My arm, serving as a pillow, was asleep under my sweaty skull. My hair was glued to my neck and forehead. Only the thwack of the wooden-framed screen door slapped me into consciousness. I popped one eye open and saw the slim shadow of Sheila, our UNICEF HIV Officer for South Sudan, crossing the porch outside, as she headed up to the compound's main house for breakfast.

My other eye was still in the dream—one repeated the past few nights—of landing on the red dirt runway in Darfur in a cloud of terracotta dust. I was relieved that I was no longer in that plane but on a rickety cot in the UNICEF guesthouse. It took me a moment to recall which one. Then I recalled Sheila having just left so it must have been Juba in South Sudan (then still a part of Sudan). My third country and sixth bed in two and half weeks.

It sometimes took several minutes to figure out where I was, mornings. This started happening about a decade prior, when I'd traveled extensively for UNAIDS. The feeling something is familiar, but you're not quite sure what it is or where you are. The worst case happened a few years ago when after several sleepy surreal moments, I recognized a painting on the wall.

Oh, I'd thought. I'm at home.

But on this day, I was still in Sudan. It was half past six, the sun was up but it was only about eighty degrees. If I stayed put, the heat and high humidity were tolerable. By nine, it'd jump twenty degrees and mere breathing would become a challenge. The air was still, not a breath of a breeze stirring. A rooster peered in at me from the porch where he'd been hovering after delivering his wake-up alarm at dawn.

Also, it was Friday. This I knew with certainty, though I wasn't always sure of what day of the week it is on the road. But the night before, we'd celebrated Thanksgiving, and that holiday is *always* on a Thursday.

I was now fully awake and remembering my conversation with Michael. I knew where I was and that I must be ready to go in about an hour and a half. What I couldn't quite recall was, What the hell am I doing here? I mean, I knew the reason on paper, but this was more an existential question. My tired brain just wanted to go home.

I could feel every coil of the creaky cot poking up through a mattress thin as a cotton makeup pad. It was so thin that I hurt all over after a sleepless, windless night. I slowly summoned the strength to roll each part of my body over onto its side, then grabbed the edge of the cot to balance myself as I extracted my numb arm and let it hang. As I flexed my fingers and squeezed my fist, pins and needles announced restored blood flow. I imagined an army of ants marching up my veins, dredging up feeling along the way. Soon I could now bend it enough to work out the stiffness in my elbow.

Why in the world *was* I sitting on a rusty cot in South Sudan, instead of at Adrian's in Northern California for the long weekend? Or at Alexandria's on Whidbey Island? I sat pondering the question but couldn't come up with a good answer.

I shook myself awake and got up, grabbing the towel I'd used to cover part of the bed, and headed to the bathroom. Pouring water from a bucket to wash the waste through the system worked to flush the toilet—mostly.

The shower was another story. I turned the handle and a spurt of fiery hot liquid blasted my chest. I was surprised that it was so hot, then realized why: it had been boiled by the sun. I also realized that was it. All my water. I soaped as best I could and coaxed out a few more drops, trying to somehow catch them in the curves of my body without letting anything on my face. The last thing I needed to do was swallow still water from the roof—Lord knows what'd been breeding in the cistern.

A proper shower would simply have to wait until that night, when I got to Rumbek. There, I'd been told—much to my surprise, since it was at the heart of the conflict zone—an entire camp was set up. I'd have my own tent with an individual shower and toilet. Pure luxury compared with this compound. And mine was the deluxe suite, the visitors' quarters. The rest of our colleagues were sleeping in shipping containers. If they were lucky, they had a small AC unit. If they were really lucky, the generator worked. If not, they had to sleep in a steel box that had baked in one hundred degree heat all day long.

I pulled my thick, heavy hair back into a ponytail, dried the drops still on my body and dusted myself in baby powder. After acquiring this ghostlike talcum glaze, I pulled on some clothes, squished swollen feet into sandals, and headed out to find Sheila.

I'd met her two weeks prior, in Yemen, at a weeklong workshop for program staff in the Middle East and North Africa. Sudan falls into this region. She'd arrived at lunchtime on the first day. Right away I noticed her obsession with the vegetable trays at the buffet. She stood back, admiring them the way one would paintings at the Louvre, or jewels at Tiffany's.

"Broccoli," she murmured longingly. "Oh yes, *broccoli*. And cauliflower. Oh my goodness, and carrots! Carrots! *Yesssss!*"

She continued speaking to her plate as she loaded it up with the fresh stuff, while the rest of us went for the pasta or chicken. For years following that, I'd assumed she was a strict vegetarian. Only to be corrected—amidst great laughter, I might add—when she told me she was just starved for healthy, fresh vegetables and salad after living for so long in South Sudan. The Thanksgiving free-for-all over a slice of boiled tomato should have tipped me off.

As I entered the main house, I could smell something akin to breakfast, my favorite meal. The dry scrambled eggs were a step up from the chewy mystery meat of the night before. But after dry toast and instant coffee with powdered milk, I won't lie, I was disappointed. The irony was that the locals we were there to help likely ate much better than we did because they knew how to work the land. The lush landscape of the south is most apparent when you fly from Khartoum and the earth shifts from tan to burnt umber to red and, suddenly, to deep hues of green. We foreign *mzungu* suffer because we can't afford to import the stuff we're used to eating. Our privilege is also our downfall.

"Don't you worry, Miss Martina!" Sheila sang as she sat down next to me. "Tomorrow you'll have more food than you'll know what to do with. The camp in Rumbek is a dream come true, and the Saturday morning buffet is heaven! It's also fun to watch the walk of shame of lonely hearts who hook up on Friday nights. Beer goggles keep us sex educators in business!"

"Ha! That's something to look forward to!" I said, feeling frustrated. "Really, though, I'm fine, I'm just wiped. This trip's getting old. Yemen was great—and the food was fabulous—but Cairo was a nightmare!"

"Why, what's wrong with Cairo?" she asked, sipping her tea.

"Oh, nothing's wrong with it, per se. The city's great, actually. Loud, but great. No, it was the meeting. Oh my God. *Horrible.*"

"What happened? Which meeting?"

I took a deep breath and answered, sucking in my anger. "It was billed as a meeting of human rights attorneys and advocates from around the Middle East. They were meant to draft a bill of rights for people living with HIV in the region."

She nodded. "Sounds interesting, no?"

"Oh, it was interesting, all right." I grimaced. "I was excited to be part of the deliberations and help with the recommendations, based on work we've done in other regions. But it all went very badly."

"Really. So what happened?" Sheila's eyes widened.

"In the end, these ever-so-wise protectors of the law decided that what they *actually* needed to write was a bill of rights to protect everyone *from* people with HIV."

"What?" Sheila spilled her tea as she gasped, "That's obscene!"

"Exactly. I was so disgusted. In the end, during my presentation, I didn't hold anything back. I told them I was embarrassed to be there. That they should be ashamed of themselves. Ashamed of calling themselves human rights lawyers."

I shook my head, staring down at my sad, dried-up eggs. "And the worst part is that the hotel staff came to us asking about how they should charge the extra meals."

"What extra meals?"

"Precisely. The ones ordered by the mistresses of the attorneys, while their wives went shopping. Plus, participants were hooking up in the evenings. One-night stands all over the place. Then they had the nerve to say people with HIV were immoral. That they're dangerous and should be locked up. Good grief! I need a new job."

"No. No, Martina, you need to keep calling the bastards out. That's exactly why you're so good at your job. You don't take any crap."

"I don't know… maybe I should quit venting in meetings. Maybe I should just shut up."

"The day you do, the day you stay quiet," Sheila said, "then *that's* the day you need a new job. Not a moment before. Promise?" She squeezed my hand.

She'd reminded me of exactly why I'd left UNAIDS years prior. And that though I was exhausted, there was still a lot of fight left in me. She was right: I wasn't yet ready to leave. I still had too much to do.

"Promise," I told her.

"Hey, Martina! Great session yesterday!" We turned to see Paul approaching, a young Canadian who'd been working as an emergency-response coordinator. He'd served in humanitarian crises around the world for years.

"Thanks! It was a bit ad hoc, what with the power cutting out and all that. Hope it was useful,"

"Absolutely. I'm always amazed at how little people know. I mean, like, it's 2005 and so many still don't know how you get it." He shook his head. "I thought your presentation on the basics, plus that excellent video with UN staffers talking about HIV themselves, were great. Once the internet comes back up, we'll look at the website on HIV in the UN Workplace, too."

"Oh, good. I created a lot of those materials! And the video, 100% my idea. I'm proud of that one. But, it's frustrating, too. I fly in, fly out, and sometimes never really know if anyone even cares or pays attention. So I appreciate your words, Paul. Means a lot."

"No problem, dude. All the documents on your little computer, with the DVD and your portable speakers. Right on! And the quote-unquote trrrraaaaaavel kit—looooooooooooove it!"

"Travel kit?" Sheila looked puzzled.

I explained. "An oversize baby-blue Hello Kitty pencil bag. I use it to carry a wooden penis, condoms, and model vagina. Always takes people by surprise because the bag looks so harmless and then, *ziiiiiiiiiiiiiiiiip*, out pops Mr. Penis! Well, actually, his name is Woody."

Our laughter was interrupted by the *beep beep* of the jeep arriving to take me out to the peacekeepers' base camp.

A half hour later, we were passing through heavy security after showing the guards my light blue Laissez Passer and special visitor's pass. Issued by the Sudanese People's Liberation Army, it allowed me to be in South Sudan, which was in the midst of fighting for independence from Khartoum. We pulled up to a large white tent, the sort you'd see at an outdoor wedding for the elderly and sun-shy. There we found about forty fit-looking soldiers in an array of earth-tone uniforms. My friend Michael was leading a discussion on modes of transmission. He and I have each given this speech a thousand times. He winked at me as he said "Risks of unprotected vaginal sex." Then went on to remind everyone, "Even though you're still paid by your national governments, you are now serving as UN peacekeepers. This implies special responsibilities."

As such, representatives are bound to Resolution 1308, which connects HIV prevalence rates to increased insecurity in conflict and post-conflict settings—an important but cumbersome document steeped in legalese. In short, if while on duty for the UN, one behaves badly and, in any way, increase the spread of the virus, that's making the world a less safe place—the polar opposite of our mandate to keep the peace and protect local populations.

After finishing up with a recap of our Code of Conduct and the punishments for sexual exploitation, he suggested a break. The group stood to stretch.

"My dear," Michael said, "we've been waiting for your lovely face to make our day brighter. And now you're here. Welcome to UNMIS!" That is, United Nations Mission in Sudan. "We are a very young operation, but a very proud one."

"Thanks, my dear. It's always a pleasure to work with you!" I said. "So, what can I do today to help?"

"Well." He grinned, "I was hoping you'd grace us with the condom demonstrations. We've saved the best for last. I know they'll be happy to hear you talk and have me shut my mouth for a while!"

"Condom demonstrations? You owe me a beer. Make that two. I'm assuming we're doing both male *and* female condoms?"

"Yes, my dear Martina, and I'll throw in a whiskey. Do you need models?"

I held up my famous travel kit and smiled. "Brought my own. You know me, always prepared for duty!"

I made the mistake of sitting down until the session started up again and Michael had had time to introduce me. The seats were metal and too hot for comfort. Plus, a perfect place for perspiration to pool. By the time I stood again, my soaked brown capris were molded to the back of my ass. Instead of trying to pretend I'd sat in spilled water, I whipped out my scarf and tied it around my waist. After weeks in the Muslim world I was still carrying it, even though here, in the Christian and Animist south, there was no religious requirement to cover my hair. A few villages over, I'd heard, they apparently didn't even wear clothes—which made sense in the brutal heat.

Arms free, I restated my name and job title to the eager crowd. "I've worked off and on with the peacekeepers for years. Although this is my first visit to Sudan, I'm delighted to be here supporting your important work."

As I bent forward to retrieve my demonstration goodies, the all-male, uniformed crowd also leaned forward, no doubt for a glimpse of cleavage. Well, why not? I gave it away; a freebie for these poor fools stuck in the heat far from homes and lovers.

Continuing through my presentation, however, I became increasingly aware the men were not paying very close attention. No nods of understanding, no furrowed brows of curiosity—just stares and smiles of appreciation for my D-cup rack. I tried moving my hands to one side. About half of the eyes followed my lead, to snap back into reality. The others were still lost in the glories of my bosom. I might not have taught them much, but they wouldn't forget me.

After the session finished, the head of the Pakistani contingent offered me a light blue baseball cap with the peacekeeper's logo, a souvenir. At that very moment, on a nearby table of training materials, I recognized the case for the DVD I used for my own training—the one Paul had referenced over breakfast—and realized that they'd already spent twenty minutes watching me on the video. So they already felt they knew me.

I'd been instrumental in creating the video, which featured testimonials of UN personnel living with or affected by HIV from around the world. There is nothing more powerful than a personal story. So, since we couldn't always get an individual to speak in the learning sessions, we'd made the DVD to fill in that far-too-frequent gap. It had become one of our most useful tools.

I'd never quite gotten used to being recognized in public. Arriving in a new country office (or mission tent) to find that the crowd already knew who I was, and felt a sort of familiarity with me, never stopped being weird. But if they remembered me enough to recognize me in person, perhaps they'd also remember the messages I'd tried to convey.

On another trip, a driver from UNDP who'd come to pick me up at my hotel had absolutely fawned over me. "Madame Clark," he'd announced in French, "it is such an honor to drive you. I feel so lucky to meet you personally."

"Thank you," I said, confused by the effusive tone. Halfway on our journey in to the office, I realized what had happened and corrected the error. "You know, my first name is Martina, and I work for UNICEF."

His eyes widened as he watched me in the rearview mirror. "Oh?"

"I think you're perhaps mistaking me for Helen Clark. She is a remarkable woman indeed, but I am not her."

After a moment of silence, we both laughed.

"I am still happy to have met you," he assured me. Even if I wasn't Helen Clark, the head of his organization and former prime minister of New Zealand.

At the end of the day in Juba, I was ready to haul my sweaty carcass into the SUV to return to the guesthouse. But the group swarmed me and begged for photos.

"Photos? You want pictures with me? Why?" I asked, although it was strangely flattering, in a pervy kind of way.

"Beeeee… Uh, because you are a great trainer and we've learned so much today!" one soldier said.

Uh-huh. The thought of these guys having my photo for who knew what reason creeped me out. I hesitated. Then again, if it would keep them from pursuing some Sudanese girl, what the hell, let them have a photo with a busty blond American. Young local girls—and some boys—desperate for money were constantly approaching these guys and hoping for a way out of their misery. So I swallowed my pride and let them snap away, hoping my pinup would distract them from a worse form of philandering.

On the drive back to UNICEF, I heard the familiar squawking of the radio but was surprised when the dispatcher announced that warring factions were active that day and headed in our direction. There were increasing clashes between the Dinka Bor and Mundari, often over cattle, about twenty kilometers away. Everyone had been told to prepare their "grab bag" so they could quickly be evacuated if necessary.

The driver smiled and looked over from the driver's seat. "Don't worry, we hear this about twice a week," he said. "We rarely get evacuated."

Rarely. Great. I was leaving later that afternoon anyway, and so wasn't as worried as I might have been otherwise. But still not feeling at ease in the million-degree heat, after posing for soft porn with clothes sticking to my sweaty behind. I wanted to hide in an air-conditioned corner, curl up into a ball and escape from the world.

All I could do was stare out the window at the passing landscape. What the fuck was I doing here, really? I began questioning my sanity, endlessly traveling around to world hotspots in hopes of teaching someone, anyone, how to use a condom and avoid getting or spreading HIV. When I'd first worked for the UN, traveling was considered safe. Our well-marked vehicles assured our safe passage. But that was changing. In fact, international personnel were increasingly the targets of kidnapping and torture. Wouldn't it be better to quit this ridiculous, sometimes risky work, go home, buy a little house somewhere pretty, get a simple job and just *live*?

My friend and former UNAIDS colleague Monica Wernette, who'd coined the term FuhKaWee tribe, used to share stories of moments like these. Moments we'd all had, when a vehicle got stuck on a muddy road or an armed crisis erupted, or the temperature hit one hundred and twenty. Moments when we were reminded that, as white foreigners, we probably had no business whatsoever trying to help others. We should have stayed home, become schoolteachers, and helped our own. I felt very much a part of the FuhKaWee tribe that day.

Just then, as we approached the edge of town, I saw a school in the distance. I'd earlier in the drive reached for my camera, only to remember it wasn't there. I'd been forbidden from carrying it while in Darfur, days before, where foreigners were not allowed to take photos in case of a security breach. Ultimately, it was fine that I couldn't snap a photo. As the woman at Victoria Falls had said, this image would be forever etched in my mind.

Along the right side of the pothole-riddled road trudged a line of schoolchildren, about thirty of them, ranging from probably seven to ten. All smiling and laughing loud enough that I could hear them inside the SUV, over the hum of the motor and the squeal of the radio warnings.

Each was wearing a UNICEF backpack. I knew these contained books, paper, and pencils. I felt proud. The people who helped these children were my colleagues. Every day those kids got an education was a good day. They were why I did what I did. *They* were why I was there.

At the end of that trip, on my last days back in Khartoum, I ran into Clement, the Zambian engineer I'd traveled with from Livingstone, at Victoria Falls, to Lusaka. He'd taken a short-term contract in Sudan to help build wells and share his extensive knowledge. A year or so later, I learned he'd been killed in a car accident just days after returning to Zambia to spend vacation with his family. I barely knew the man, but his passing hurt my heart. Through and through, he was the true embodiment of a humanitarian.

Things Come Together

New York

In 2006, back home between trips, I got a call from Jean-Robert. He'd had a child with his new partner and was trying to sort out his life. We'd been divorced for about a year by then and his call was unexpected.

"I've been diagnosed with borderline-personality disorder," he said. "I'm now on medication, which is helping."

I mostly let him speak, get everything off his chest, only commenting occasionally. "Oufti. I'm sorry to hear that, Jean-Robert. Truly. But I'm glad you're getting help." Inside, however, I felt an enormous burden lifting. Our problems had *not* all been my fault.

"As I am learning about my condition," he continued, "the more I understand what a nightmare my sickness must have been for you. I'm mean, my anger and insecurities would've been bad enough if we'd known my illness, but we didn't."

"Well, yeah. It was not an easy time. Not gonna lie."

"I'm sorry, Martina. I know my diagnosis in no way forgives my behavior. I do hope, however, that it might at least help you make sense of what happened, what I was dealing with."

He also shared that he'd run across a videotape of me addressing President Clinton at the White House. He'd watched it over and over, crying as he kept repeating to himself, "I was married to that woman and I pushed her away."

His calm demeanor and self-awareness were so incongruous from the man I'd married that I didn't entirely believe him. I muttered, "Oh. Huh. I forgot about that tape."

Continuing, he said that my traveling and working during our marriage was never the "running away" he'd accused me of but rather—he now understood—simply my attempts to keep us afloat. He told me he felt awful and knew that he'd never meet another woman like me, and for that, he was truly sad.

"Thank you for saying all of this, Jean-Robert. It means a lot," I said, and I meant it, even if I was still waiting for some cruelty to follow. It didn't. I believe, now, he was genuinely sorry.

"I hope you find happiness," I continued. "You deserve it, everyone does."

"You, too, Martina. Take care of yourself, please."

That was the last time we ever spoke.

Obviously, I survived Jean-Robert and am a better person for it, but I wouldn't wish those years on my worst enemy. I made my own share of mistakes in the relationship but living with an undiagnosed mentally ill person can leave one scarred and emotionally battered. I'd done it as a child with my mother and repeated the pattern with my husband. Although Mama was never diagnosed, in later years we realized she'd showed all the signs of narcissistic behavior. I suspect that no matter what she'd put her children through, she had endured far worse as a child. Even now, decades later, I am still triggered by narcissists. Their abusive manipulation, lying, and gaslighting, make it that much harder for me to maintain my own tenuous self-esteem. I remain forever traumatized.

In some ways, my attraction to Jean-Robert made sense; as awful as my mother's behavior was, it felt familiar. When I saw those traits in my ex-husband, it was appealing, even comforting for a time. I grew up thinking this was what love felt like: Pull me in, push me away. Butter me up, then scratch my psyche to shreds. A pattern I accepted because I didn't know any better. I thought that was all I deserved.

I could only hope that following his apology I'd finally be able to recognize the twisted wickedness of such personalities when I saw them. Then maintain enough clarity and self-worth to walk away and keep my spirit intact.

His call was one of the kindest gifts I'd ever received. I hadn't dated since I'd left him and still didn't know whether I was ready. But at least now I could close that chapter.

Later that year, I returned to Belgium. Charlotte and I had been in contact by email for several months prior and she'd encouraged me to visit. I spent a few days with her, and her then-boyfriend, and felt proud to see her managing her home as a grown woman. She'd returned to school and was winding up a program which would allow her to work as a social worker. She was strong and capable and confident. She too had been able to heal and was making remarkable strides in getting her life on track.

The following summer, she came to New York and stayed for a few weeks. We visited tourist attractions, spent time with my friends, and continued to build a relationship that was now completely voluntary.

While there is a twenty-year age gap between Charlotte and I, we are more like equals. Although she isn't my daughter, she filled a void in my childless life. She'd taught me what maternal love feels like, while I gave her refuge and a comforting shoulder. We've learned more from each other than I can describe, and for that I am eternally grateful.

With these relationships now both in a better place, I slowly began to live a life that resembled normality. I still traveled constantly, but now came home to a life I felt proud of because I knew beyond a doubt I was doing something meaningful.

In 2008 we officially launched UN Cares, the United Nations System-wide Workplace Programme on HIV. After years of preparation and negotiations and perseverance, I stood proudly with my colleagues at United Nations headquarters and listened to speech after speech, including one by Secretary-General Ban Ki-moon. It was now mandatory that all UN personnel worldwide were required to learn HIV awareness and prevention.

My friend Kate, whom I'd met in Mexico, was now also working with the UN, for UNAIDS. We stood together, smiling at each other, gratified by how far we'd come, both as individuals but also as part of the system.

We still needed to nurture our workplace program and had a massive training schedule ahead of us. But the work was under way; rooted deeply enough that it would not fall apart or rest solely on the shoulders of our small group. The UN was now, systematically, practicing what it preached.

Personally, I was happier than I'd been in years. I'd started dating occasionally but was still happy being on my own. That, in and of itself, was an accomplishment. I actually preferred solitude rather than being in poor company. I *liked* myself.

By that time I was putting fifty to sixty hours in at the office each week. More when I was on the road. I was clocking about one hundred and twenty days a year of not-very-glamorous international travel. In 2007, for example, I spent a few weeks in Kabul, Afghanistan, riding around in an armored vehicle. I wasn't allowed to leave my hotel unless escorted by a male guard, and even then, only to work. Or, if I insisted, to walk to the end of the block and back. I was probably never in any real danger, but the added stress was piled on top of my existing pressure. My body was starting to buckle under the strain.

That same year, I bought a three-unit apartment building in Brooklyn, and become a landlord. It made sense to invest in real estate and use the income toward my mortgage rather than continue to pay high rents in Manhattan. So on top of my extreme work schedule, I was managing the property where I lived, as well as two sets of tenants.

The developer I'd purchased from had converted the onetime commercial building into residential space. And as we—my renters, my cats, and I—were the first tenants, we were the first to discover his construction errors. Despite the impressive brick façade and curved corners, reminiscent of a castle's turret, the roof needed repair and the floors were uneven. When spring rains arrived, roof repair became a full replacement. So many friends and colleagues kept saying they admired me, how I was so strong and able to manage so much. They especially commended me on how brave it was to take so much on as a single woman. That, I must say, irritated me. The same comment would not have been made to a single man. But it *was* a lot to manage.

I'd recently lost a lot of weight, and knew it was more than I could afford to drop. Both emotionally and physically, I could feel burnout creeping up again. In June, I asked my new doctor (the first had rudely retired without my approval!) for some time off.

He dismissed me. "From what I read in your chart, I don't see anything that warrants it. I don't doubt you're tired, but I think you're being overdramatic. How 'bout I give you the rest of the week. That should be enough." It was already Thursday, but I took it.

My blood work was still good, although not as good in previous years. I *knew* something wasn't right. But I soldiered on, reluctantly following my doctor's advice that relaxing on weekends would be enough to restore my energy and good health.

CHAPTER 10

moments of truth

Things Fall Apart

By September of 2008, and only at the insistence of my friend and colleague Laurie Newell, I finally sought proper care. She could see what I couldn't. "Martina, my dear. You're not okay. You need a leave of absence," she said. "As your friend, I'm saying you're visibly not well."

As my eyes welled with tears, I not only knew she was right, I was relieved that, again—like Dr. Renold-Moynier a decade earlier—someone I trusted was giving me permission to take care of myself.

Over the preceding six months, my strength had been waning. I'd grown so exhausted I was barely functional at work. It hurt to walk. My hands shook, leaving my once-lovely handwriting scratchy and impossible to read. I also was having a harder and harder time with critical thinking and basic understanding of words or concepts. I'd gone from my normal weight of about 135 to below 110, less than I'd weighed in high school. On that day, on a corner near the Secretariat, standing with Laurie, I was a size 2—a size that had once fit preteen me for about a week in seventh grade.

She continued. "You're not coping, and your work's suffering. We—the world—can't afford to lose you, Martina. Please, take some time off. Rest. Get better, before it's too late."

I thought of my colleague, Moses, who'd died largely because he'd been afraid to ask for help. Had I learned nothing from his death? Laurie was right, I was killing myself.

I am forever grateful for her sensitive intuition and the strength she showed in speaking honestly to me.

By the time I'd finally found a new qualified HIV specialist, Dr. Bellman, I was severely anemic, with paper-thin nails. My hair was falling out by the handful. My lower back was in constant pain, and my hips and sacrum felt as if they were going to detach from my torso, fall to the sidewalk, as they scattered about my sneakers, like a discarded skeleton cutout from Halloween.

In the stark white room of what was probably once a floor-through apartment on University and East 12th Street, near Union Square, I sat in a metal chair next to the phlebotomist, two rooms down from my new doctor's own office.

"What's wrong, sweetheart? I see what's going on with those beautiful blue eyes," the technician said, as he tapped a vein to take my blood.

"I have to start treatment," I said.

"And?"

"I was never supposed to have to. I made it sixteen, nearly seventeen years without it. Why now?"

He laughed. "Damn, girl. You're lucky you got this far." Without gloves, he moved swiftly as he swapped one vial for the next, the blood bright against the pink palms of his dark hands. "Darlin', everybody I know is on treatment. We're the lucky ones. *You're* lucky."

"I don't feel lucky. I feel cheated. I used to be a survivor; now I'm just sick."

He shook his head and withdrew the needle, placed the half-dozen vials of blood into a plastic bag marked *Quest Diagnostics*, then took my hands. "Everything's going to be okay."

I had to acknowledge he knew the issues firsthand, but still felt annoyed by his attempt to smooth over what felt like well-earned anger.

Up until then, I'd convinced myself I was going to be what they called a long-term non-progressor: someone who never got sick or needed medical intervention. So being told I had to start treatment was like receiving that devastating diagnosis all over again. The difference was that back then the doctor hadn't known what to anticipate—nobody did—so any prognosis was vague at best.

By 2008, however, everyone knew much more. Since the numbers on my lab results had shifted dramatically, if I wanted to stay alive, I needed intervention. The truth was, I was losing the war against HIV. Which, after so many years of travel and personal and career stress, had finally launched a full-out attack on my immune system.

Although guidelines for when a person should start treatment are regularly being updated, most people start showing symptoms of disease progression after about five years. I definitely was an anomaly.

On the day of my first visit to Dr. Bellman, he ordered a slew of baselines to assess my overall health. And to confirm or negate his suspicions I was severely anemic. Then he kept testing. And testing. He sent me for tests, seemingly every day for weeks.

In checking for anemia, any result over about twenty-five is a bad indicator. My number was one hundred fifty-six. This wasn't a simple iron or B12 deficiency, nor was it genetic; this was systemic. He actually thought I might have cancer, which led to a bone marrow sampling at an oncologist's office at now-defunct St. Vincent's Hospital.

That was the most painful thing I'd ever experienced. I felt vulnerable and broken in new and unfamiliar ways, trying not to move as the doctor drilled into my aching body, while I leaned over the examination table clutching the edges with white-knuckled hands.

When the oncologist had finished the bone marrow extraction, he gently asked, "Would you like me to admit you? I can do that today, so you can at least rest a little. We'll feed you and the staff are *very* nice. I won't insist, but it might help."

I tugged at the too-big hospital gown. "No, that's okay. I have to go home and feed my cats. I'll be fine."

Once home, I wondered if he wasn't right. I'd never been as sick before, and I didn't know what to do or how to process what was happening.

When I returned to the specialist for the results a few days later, he was happy to report I did not have cancer. "But your rapid decline means your body's shutting down," he added.

He began talking about treatment, but I stopped him. "Can you give me a note for work, so I can get time off to think it all through?"

One of the greatest benefits of the UN was paid sick leave. Few people have this luxury in America. I would've been stupid not to have taken advantage. I might not even survive if I didn't.

The doctor stared at me for a moment, then said, "You've been at work this whole time? Wow. Of course, you *need* to take time off. Let's start with three months and see how it goes."

I was grateful for his concern. But hearing him say "three months," so quickly, made the severity of my situation pretty damned clear. I scheduled another appointment for the following week.

I left Bellman's office that day in the fall and made my way home to my cats, who cared about their crunchies more than my drama. I wanted to go to California and stay with my sister because I knew that with his note, the United Nations would put me on sick leave. But the doctor had also advised against traveling, worried he wouldn't be able to adequately monitor my health from a distance.

What I needed more than anything was true rest and recuperation like I'd had in Geneva. Which I could get with the help of my sister. But I followed the doctor's orders and spent what ended up being be a total of five months at home, mostly alone.

Not wanting to raise concerns, I told my friends—mostly colleagues I'd met at work and occasionally socialized with—I was okay and didn't need anything. Unfortunately, they took me at my word. They didn't know me well enough to understand that what I was really doing was isolating because I didn't want to be a burden. What I really did was push them away.

One friend insisted on visiting because she'd known me the longest and knew how stubborn I could be.

"Really, I'm fine, Maryanne," I told her on the phone.

"I'm sure you are, Martina, but I need to see you for my own sake. To make sure you have food in your fridge. And I need to give you a hug. This is me being selfish; please don't be mad."

I smiled and agreed. And indeed, it was a relief to have my friend sit with me in my kitchen for a few hours the next day. Maryanne brought an Italian apricot cake, some fine cheeses, and her wicked sense of humor. We drank tea and talked about our lives in Geneva, where we'd met years before. The visit helped. More than she could ever know.

"More cheese?" I asked at one point.

"No, thanks, I'm taking a parma-pause," she answered.

We both laughed, remembering a night when the two of us had driven in my red convertible to the top of the Salève, a mountain on the edge of Geneva. It was during the Perseids meteor shower. Creatures of comfort, we'd brought blankets and pillows and a picnic. We put the top down, reclined our seats, listened to Pink Floyd, drank red wine and ate cold cuts and cheese. It was that evening, between giggles and shooting stars, we coined the term "parma-pause" to indicate a moment of respite from eating the hard chunks of aged Parmesan we both loved.

Maryanne, also American, was ten years my senior and one of the first people I'd met when I moved to Geneva and started working for the United Nations. She was tall, with shoulder-length dark hair, perfect teeth and olive skin. We'd supported one another through surgeries, family and relationship traumas and dramas, and more boring work meetings than we could count. I'd made quite a few good lifelong friends in Geneva, but she was one of the few who also ended up in New York.

With rest and vitamins, iron pills and Ensure, I began to regain my strength and weight. But by that point the damage had been done. It would be irreversible without treatment.

In HIV, we measure two things: the viral load, or the concentration of virus in the blood, and the CD4, or fighter T-cell count—the system that fights off disease. Ideally, the viral load should be low (undetectable is best) and the CD4 should be high. My viral load, until the spring of 2008, had never been above 2,000 copies per milliliter, (c/ml) which was remarkable and considered healthy for someone who'd never had treatment. My CD4 count also had always been good, staying above 700 and often hovering around 1,000. The average healthy range is 700—1,200, so I was in good shape and had been for those first sixteen-plus years. But now everything had changed. My CD4 was down to 250 c/ml and my viral load had shot up into the hundreds of thousands.

I knew the math. I knew the science. What I didn't know was if I really even wanted to get better. Did I want to live if it meant taking pills several times a day, every day, for the rest of my life? The side effects they might cause included damage to my organs from possible toxicity. Also, lipodystrophy, where fat becomes redistributed and people start to look like spiders—fat bodies, hunched shoulders, thick necks, skinny arms and legs. And then there was the chance the treatment still might not work for me. So why bother? I felt I couldn't even discuss this with other people I knew with HIV, because they all seemed to be treatment advocates. I was on my own, in so many ways.

As I mulled over the decision, I found myself staring at my ongoing to-do list and the entry *Update will*. As a rule, I'm good at keeping up with the basics. I pay my bills on time, wash my dishes right after a meal, and make my bed each morning.

I couldn't, however, bring myself to update my will, even though I really needed to do it now, since I owned property. But some voice in the back of my brain said, if your will is updated and all your papers truly in order, you'll let yourself die. Because there would be nothing left I *had* to do. And the way I felt at that moment, physically and emotionally, I believed there was nothing left I *wanted* to do. So I left that one remaining task undone. Week after week, month after month, I read the list almost as a check-in to see if I was ready to give up.

I delayed the decision for the time being. But, at my doctor's suggestion, I saw a therapist he'd recommended. I had told him he could brief her on my case before I went.

"So, Dr. Bellman tells me you're having a hard time making decisions around starting treatment. Is that right? Is that why you're here today?" the therapist asked at our first meeting.

I sat in the high-backed upholstered chair of her mid-town office. "Yes,

I guess it is. I mean, I'm having a hard time, but really, it's about finding a reason to live. That's probably the bigger question."

She blinked and narrowed her eyes as if pulling me more closely into focus. She adjusted her papers on her lap. I appreciated her sense of style: elegant but simple. She was probably ten years older, but had beautiful olive skin and kind brown eyes.

"Do you think perhaps being ill is making it hard for you to think straight? That happens, you know. The physical can confuse the mental."

I shrugged. "Maybe."

"Is there anything else going on you'd like to talk about?"

"I don't know. I guess I'm just not coping. I'm so tired and can't work, which I feel guilty about. And I have the building I own, and I'm still dealing with finalizing the estate of a friend who died last year." I explained that my friend's family lived in Italy, so when she'd died unexpectedly, I'd agreed to help out for logistical reasons. Consequently, I'd never really been able to grieve because she felt more present to me in death than she even had been in life.

As the therapist took a few notes, she said, "Please, continue."

"And I'm alone. Really, I've already had a great life, so why bother? Why keep going?"

"What do you mean by 'alone'?" she asked, expression neutral.

"I'm single. I live alone. I have no family on the East Coast. You see, I travel all the time, so it's hard to make or maintain friendships. I know a lot of people, but few are close. I don't really have the energy, or even the desire, to see them anymore…So, you know… I'm alone."

"Martina, the fact you're here tells me you don't want to die," she said. "Something inside is pushing you to sort this out. Otherwise, you wouldn't have taken the time and effort to come see *me*. Our time for today is up, but let's figure out what that motivation is and focus on getting you to a better place. Then you can make the best decision possible."

I agreed to return the next week because what she'd said resonated. But as I was leaving I turned back to face her.

"Yes, something else?" she asked, eyebrows raised.

"Yes. My nieces and nephews and a few other young people I know…" I said.

"What about them?"

"I'm curious to know what they become in life."

She smiled and nodded ever so slightly. "Good. That's good. I'll see you next week."

Thanks to the healing powers of sleep, the help of the therapist and the optimism I felt on the election of Barack Obama, I reluctantly agreed to start treatment. I didn't care about much of anything in those days, but the hope in Obama's words, action, and demeanor was contagious. When I told Dr. Bellman I was finally ready to start treatment, he asked what had changed. "I guess I just needed a new president," I wisecracked.

The day before Christmas, I swallowed my first pills for a disease that was supposed to have killed me at least a decade earlier. Soon, feeling stronger and with a clearer mind, I began to see how very lucky I was. Lucky to be alive. Lucky to have experienced the extraordinary life I'd lived so far. Lucky to have a job, food on my table, a roof over my head. All of the clichés felt dramatically apt.

For the pills worked. I responded well. After an adjustment or two to my medications, I was on my way to recovery. So many people I'd met had not survived, but it seemed my time was not yet up. I used the rest of my leave to regain strength and think about where I wanted my next years to go. I wasn't quite ready to leave the United Nations, but the time would come. I'd need to have a plan in place.

After five months of sick leave I returned to UNICEF. I was healthier, but also had an entirely new understanding of what it meant to live with HIV.

I was incredibly fortunate that my colleagues and supervisors had remained supportive. Not a single person complained about how I hadn't been there. They welcomed me back with open arms. During my time away, I'd agreed to answer emails for any questions that might arise in my absence, but for the most part, everyone just left me alone to recuperate. They were practicing what we preached in facilitating my ability to get better and remain employed so I could come back and continue to contribute.

To my great relief, I saw upon my return that the work had continued without me. The program I'd labored so hard to help build was going strong. It would be fine with or without me. I took that as a measure of success.

At the end of 2009, I made my first work trip in more than a year—to Egypt, Jordan and Syria. I had the good fortune to travel to Jordan and Syria in the company of two younger Egyptian colleagues who could translate for me while I learned more about our programs and the challenges for staff in the region.

Working with younger people, whether on trips or in New York, was one of my greatest joys. At those moments I knew I was transferring experience and information to others who could continue on with our work. These inter-generational collaborations were an investment in our collective future.

On the Road Again: Vive L'Independence

Dakar

Senegal: West Africa
Population: 16.7 million
Capital: Dakar

I have a soft spot for Senegal. Its national holiday, marking its independence from France, falls on my birthday, April 4th. Having learned about our shared beginnings before I even knew where the country was, I'd always wanted to celebrate the day there. In 2010, Senegal had just turned 50—and I, 46—just two and a half weeks before my flight descended into Dakar. That year April 4th also happened to be Easter. On the phone from California, Adrian's son, Chris, kept wishing me a "very special happy *Beaster!*" I love that kid.

When I'd first visited some four years prior, I'd wanted to dress like a Senegalese. The traditional attire, made from Dutch-wax print material, known as a *boubou*, as well as the more fitted skirts with matching tops and coordinated head wraps, are works of art—individual flags flying the shape of each woman's physique. But such clothes are hard to carry off—and are the epitome of appropriation—when you're short, white, and blond.

Or, as one West African said to me, "Ha, with fine hair like that, you'd never be able to keep that t'ing upon your head. It fall flat on da floor!"

So I stick to my own boring outfits—Capri pants and button-up three-quarter-sleeve blouses with a simple tee underneath, for discretion, in conservative countries. Whenever I walk among the tall, lanky Senegalese, I imagine I'm a squat ladybug in a forest of mechanical ebony carvings, each more finely sculpted than the next. The trip was important for me. Symbolic of my regained freedom to travel. My freedom to choose the life I wanted to live. And that once again, I *wanted* to live.

It was my first extended journey since I'd gone on sick leave, a year and a half earlier. I'd taken shorter jaunts to easier places, like Europe. But in Africa, travel can be hard, and the work even harder. If I could make it through the coming four weeks, that would be proof I was back to my old self. I needed this trip. I needed it to be me again.

We touched down around half past four in the morning. The warm air caressed my face. And after a long, hard winter, it was like the soft touch of a lover's hand on my cheek. Welcome back to Africa, my darling.

I descended the stout steel deplaning stairs and boarded a little bus that would take us to the terminal. Once inside I headed for the diplomats' line at immigration—only to find nobody there. Seemed fitting. So I slid into the line for *étrangers* and waited my turn.

"*Bonjour*," I said to the immigration officer.

He responded with a stern glance, handed me my customs declaration and took my light blue UN passport. In his late twenties, he sat in a Plexiglas-enclosed booth. His dark-brown military-style uniform matched his skin.

"*Merçi, monsieur*," I said. His unyielding glance held for a moment, then wavered. He showed a hint of smile as he registered my date of birth.

Ka-chunk of the stamp. "Welcome to Dakar, Missus."

"*Merci bien, et bonne journée.*"

His lips parted, revealing a wide gap between his two front teeth as he softly replied, "You too, have ze good day."

Waiting at the baggage carousel, I was delighted to see very few airport staff around at that unforgiving hour. Arriving with three silicone vaginas and as many wooden penises can sometimes make entry a bit tricky. This time I was carrying spares to hand to my colleagues David and Salva, with whom I'd be working over the next several weeks.

The first time I flew to Senegal, a customs agent had gone through my bags and found a few hundred female condoms. After a rather in-depth discussion about what they were and why I had them, he made me give him twenty before he'd let me into the country. Clearly he saw the potential to monetize them, and I was happy to help him stimulate the personal protection market. Despite my travels, it was the first time I'd ever bribed a customs agent, much less with condoms.

Today, nobody cared. And thus, I went forth into Senegal, carrying multiple manufactured genitalia.

I'd come to Dakar for yet another long, boring regional meeting, but still was happy to be there because I'd get to see a lot of old friends. On my first day, I opened the curtains in my unremarkable room on the seventeenth floor of the beachfront hotel to check out the view. On a map of the continent, one will find Senegal at the edge of the curved bulge on the left, along the Atlantic. The foliage is rich and tropical, palm trees lining both beaches and wide boulevards alike. Although I'd never ventured beyond Dakar, by all accounts it is a beautiful country and I looked forward to my view.

My room overlooked the parking lot. The cars were, I'll admit, nicely parked, but it wasn't quite what I'd been hoping for.

On Monday morning, I entered the vast conference room on the first floor of my hotel and immediately ran into Erasmus. He'd been my boss when I was in Malawi on my last consultancy before I went fulltime at UNICEF. He'd been employed in the UN system for at least a decade, possibly two. He gave me excellent advice, contacts, and reassurance that I was making the right move to join UNICEF so many years prior.

I'd forgotten how gentle he looked—a broad smile gracing his handsome face. Recognizing me when our shoulders bumped, he took a step back, then slowly folded into me, resting his head in the arch of my neck, ever so slightly nuzzling my ear. Seeing him again so many years later was a reminder I'd made it out of the painful phase I'd been in when we'd met.

Soon I also ran into Salva and David. I'd be working with David—a diminutive, powerful Zambian whom I hadn't seen in nearly fifteen years—the following week in Liberia. And, just after that, I'd continue on to teach with Salva in Gabon.

I'd seen Salva periodically over the dozen or so years since we'd first met. But the last time I'd seen David was under a mango tree in Uganda, just two and a half years after I'd tested positive.

We'd met at a conference in Kampala. The site was riddled with bullet holes from years of civil war. Between sessions I'd walked around the building looking for patterns in the holes left from the battles. In a few places, light from inside oozed out in tiny streams, making the building seem fuzzy or out of focus.

The country had been at peace for a decade, but instability remained. The AIDS pandemic had stepped in where soldiers had left off, to wreak havoc on society. David, then in his early twenties, was a pioneer in establishing an African network of people living with HIV. I just barely knew him from that first meeting, though we shared a history of fierce activism. The current meeting in Dakar that brought us all back together was itself predictable and unremarkable. We all hugged. Then David, Salva, and I agreed to have dinner the night after next, to catch up and plan.

On Wednesday evening the three of us walked a few blocks from our hotel to a local restaurant. The savory scents of *thiéboudienne* and *poulet yassa* with ginger, sautéed garlic and onions, and freshly-ground peanuts welcomed us. We took a table in the back, away from the rumbling arctic-level AC unit so we could chat in peace. Before our sparkling and tonic waters were served, the electricity cut out. We laughed at ourselves for being stuck at the farthest possible table from the windows. But the darkness didn't stop us from catching up.

"The doctor gave me five years to live when I was diagnosed," I said. "Yet here I am—here *we* are—thinking about our pension funds. Cheers!"

We raised our glasses. Salva said, "You were lucky. My doctor gave *me* only two years."

"How old were you?"

"In my early thirties, with two small children and a dying wife. Right after I finished my master's, in fact."

We shook our heads in unison. Crazy.

"And you, David?"

"Me? Oh, I was told I had six months. I was nineteen. I'd just joined the seminary, and of course they kicked me out because I was shameful to them."

Our food arrived. We ate fish or, in my case chicken, cooked in spiced tomato-based sauces, pungent with ginger and served over fluffy white rice. We sweated in silence for some time, a heaviness punctuated by the hot stagnant air and flickering candles. The shuffling feet of the waiters, the clank of glasses and silverware from other diners finally brought us back to our conversation. We reflected on how much luckier we were than so many others.

"Back in those early days, things were so different," I said. "I became an activist because I didn't feel I had a future to look forward to."

"So true," Salva added. "So many, like my first wife, didn't make it. I've kept fighting for her. For our children who, blessedly, are healthy and thriving."

David said, "*This* has been so lovely. The food, of course, but the company. The reminder our work has not been in vain."

After dinner, as we walked back to our hotel that warm evening, faces flashed in my mind. People I knew I'd never see again. We three were definitely all people *living* with HIV, not *dying* of AIDS. It may seem like a small detail in syntax, but it's actually the biggest difference in the world. The fact we were all now in managerial positions with the UN made our meal that much more gratifying.

In the lobby of our hotel, we hugged, then went our separate ways. Three activists reunited in a seemingly endless battle to educate the world, forcing the most bureaucratic system in existence to advance our efforts. The pace was slow, but we were still making headway.

Two days later, at half past one in the morning, I waited for David in the hotel lobby. Piped-in music played *Miiiis-ter Jones and meeeeee...* followed on by *I learrrrrned the truth at se-ven-teen...* I sat regretting that third gin-and-tonic—the one that had earlier led me to sing some old jazz standards with the house band at the hotel bar, much to the surprise of my coworkers. Luckily David showed up in the lobby just as Janis Ian finished the last verse. He saved me from my tipsy canned-music melancholy, and we headed for the airport in a too-fast rickety old taxi.

"Hey, *mon frère, doucement.* Slowly, slowly, *s'il vous plait*," David kept repeating.

The driver ignored us. He rounded corners like a skier on a giant slalom, remarkably plopping us back on the road each time. We flew into the parking lot well before our 2:30 a.m. check-in time. Traveling in West and Central Africa is indirect at best, inconvenient at most, and impossible at worst.

David and I checked in, cleared immigration, and found a spot to sit and wait. We were both too tired to chat.

A Fragile Freedom

Monrovia

Liberia: West Africa
Population: 4.9 million
Capital: Monrovia

After changing planes in Accra, Ghana (an airport I would visit often on this trip) we arrived in Liberia around ten in the morning, sleepless but happy.

Once we emerged from Roberts International Airport, often referred to as Robertsfield, our bags were loaded into the back of a four-by-four with the telltale antenna tower common on UN transport. After being parked in the sun, even at that early hour, when we opened the doors, the four-by-four felt like an oven. We then reluctantly heaved ourselves up into the stuffy white vehicle.

Our driver, John, offered us some fresh bananas. "These are the best, from my village. Not those rrrrrotty kind in the city."

They were indeed delicious, small and firm. Their subtle sweetness was undercut with a mild, tangy afterbite. I savored the fruit as we drove the forty-five minutes over potholes, past shacks and screaming children playing on the side of the highway into the capital. If Dakar is sophistication and sleekness, Monrovia is rough-and-tumble, don't-mess-with-me madness. John deftly navigated the poorly maintained roads. We weaved in and out among the other vehicles, bicycles, motor bikes, and pedestrians. They all claimed the road at the same time with no discernible rules.

Along with Ethiopia, Liberia is one of only two modern countries in sub-Saharan Africa without roots in the European conquest. Instead, it was essentially colonized by the United States. A way to avoid freed slaves seeking a life equal to their slavemasters on US soil. A one-way passage back to Africa was offered as an alternative. By 1847, this new country had become the Republic of Liberia, with a government modeled after that of the United States. The capital, Monrovia, was named after James Monroe, who'd been a prominent supporter of colonization, along with Andrew Jackson and Abraham Lincoln, among others.

Liberia boasted being the first African nation to elect a female president, Ellen Johnson Sirleaf, who was elected in 2005 and served until 2018. But that milestone came only after decades of pain and strife, including two successive civil wars that left a quarter of a million people dead, a ruined economy, and shattered any stability Liberia had previously known. Peace was officially reached in 2003, with democratic elections following in 2005. But when I arrived five years later, the country was still recovering. Built on the backs of human suffering, and with eighty-five percent of the population below the poverty line, Liberia would have a long haul to any sort of comfort zone.

En route to the hotel, after dropping off our driver, we stopped by an ATM so I could get some local currency. David, now at the wheel, navigated red dirt roads packed with people, inching along among cars too big for their own good, all trying to avoid running anyone over. Nearly a third of the vehicles were marked in one way or another as belonging to the UN. Parking in downtown Monrovia requires surgical precision, as well as luck, but we finally squeezed in between a pair of peacekeeper trucks.

I asked, "David, why didn't just you have the driver wait for us?"

"Every time I do that, he asks to borrow money—$50 here, $100 there—and I never see it again. I can't afford to have him wait. *Really* can't!"

Cash procured, we drove along Mamba Point and pulled into a long driveway that led to a multi-storied beige stucco hotel with terracotta trim. I checked into my room—the size of a spacious studio in New York City with a view overlooking the Atlantic. I took a cold shower (by necessity, not choice) and slept for a few hours. I woke to a sunset like a golden glowing Coptic cross hovering at the horizon. Freighters dotted the skyline, trawlers in the distance, smaller fishing boats, outriggers and canoes progressively closer to shore. Scooters and dinged-up taxis tooled past on the busy two-lane below. I took another cold shower to rinse off the sweat accumulated thanks to power cuts, and decided hot water was overrated. When it's in the nineties with eighty-five percent humidity, who cares?

Later that evening, David collected me and we went for dinner at one of his favorite spots. We sat down at a heavy wooden table covered in vinyl, on white plastic lawn chairs with *God Bless You* woven into the seatbacks. I perused the menu and noticed *za'atar* on pita and *kafta, labneh,* and even *fattoush.*

I looked up. "Is this a Lebanese restaurant?"

"I guess so. Most of the restaurants here are. So are the hotels—they run everything. Very good businessmen."

"Wow, fantastic! Sunsets and eggplant. I think I like Liberia!"

"And the best part is they don't force rice on you at this place. Eeeeeesh, rice, rice and more rice. Liberians believe if you haven't had rice, you haven't eaten. I'm becoming crazy from all the rice I've swallowed here!" David grinned ruefully.

I had a hard time following the waitress's English; her accent was almost Caribbean in lilt, with distinctive pronunciations of words like "aks" and "sangwich." But at last I ordered my meal and sat back, feeling contented in this formidable, feisty, lush green country.

Liberia was in Phase 3 by UN security standards; that meant we had to be hypervigilant about following rules, and carry two-way radios. There was a midnight curfew because of what our intelligence officers deemed as "occasional multiple threats." Phase 3 is in the middle of the 1 to 6 scale, so I wasn't too concerned. When I was issued my walkie-talkie (call sign Mike Delta 9.3) I mostly left it by my bed, listening at night as it squawked military commands interrupted by static, then silence, then an intermittent blip like a digital frog. We joked that the best use of these heavy military-grade radios would be to simply hit an assailant over the head.

The best part of my briefing at the UN security office on my first work day, was when the officer in charge told me, "Don't take too-long showers —you don't want the dirty water to soak in."

This was a risk I'd never considered. I knew about brushing my teeth with bottled water, and never ordering ice, but the "not too-long shower" part just made me laugh. I'd survived much worse than questionable bath water, and have always managed to miss the mayhem. The hotel I stayed at in Kabul in 2007 was later bombed, like the restaurant where I'd dined with my colleague on that same trip. In 2002, I'd been in the line of shelling in Burundi, and in 2004, enemy tribes were headed my way in Sudan. I'd even been kept in lockdown when a coup d'état occurred— during my flight from Miami—in Bolivia in 2005. When I arrived in La Paz, I'd been greeted by a nervous driver. "*Bienvenido, señora.* I hope you will enjoy your hotel," he said once he delivered me from the airport. "Because, I'm afraid you'll not be allowed to leave. *Adios.*"

By chance, I'd stayed home from work the day of the 6.9 magnitude earthquake in San Francisco—the one where one of my colleagues died on the collapsed freeway. In 2007, the corner where I caught the subway from work in New York blew a sinkhole that swallowed entire vehicles at the peak of the afternoon commute. But I'd left early that day and missed the whole thing.

I counted myself lucky, almost bulletproof. But I also realized that you never know what will happen or when, so best not to worry about it. Life in Liberia seemed fragile, but I didn't feel threatened or worried. Certainly not about showering.

I did sense, however, the underlying pain. Liberia reminded me of Cambodia: Everyone smiley and happy on the outside, but you could sense that deep down there were still-painful scars. My trips were fly-bys. Often I barely scratched the surface of a place. But what surface I did scratch was often itchy and burning, dense with anxiety and fear.

During the week of workshops I held with coworkers in Liberia among UN staff and their loved ones, I hit wall after wall of "AIDS? Not me" and "You don't know us." The local staff was not opening up. Anything as agonizing as the AIDS pandemic could only end badly, so—already traumatized—they preferred the comfort of denial. They were surrounded by countries with high rates of prevalence, and recovering from years of strife that had frequently involved sexual violence as a weapon. Liberians needed to step up and face the reality of the pandemic. But they preferred to joke about it, to pass it off as someone else's problem. Without intending to, they insulted me over and over again with callous words and poorly-thought-out statements.

"AIDS is a disease of the weak. We are not weak," said one middle-aged man in a beige suit with short sleeves, common in tropical countries.

Am I weak? I wondered, in a moment of insecurity, looking at an assembly of colleagues, women and men alike, in vibrantly-colored outfits.

"Only bad, godless people get HIV, we all know that," said a young woman with cropped hair. "We are Christians, so we're safe. Everyone else deserves it."

They were lashing out in fear, of course, but it was hard to not take it personally. As the person warning them they needed to confront the epidemic on their own soil, I was an easy target. They knew I'd leave eventually, too, so in some ways I was expendable. They needed to release pent-up anger, so I tried to keep my guard up. But sometimes the hurtful words weaseled under my skin and stuck there for weeks.

And yet, as I listened to their glib dismissals, I thought of the pictures I'd seen of the warlord Charles Taylor's men. Soldiers dressed in ladies' lingerie and demonic masks had paraded the streets of Monrovia in far-too-recent times. They'd toted machine guns and machetes, stoned out of their brains. Just waiting for a fight to pick, a dog to kick, a skull to crack, a woman to rape and kill. If I'd survived that, I guess I'd be dismissive about HIV too.

Their anger made my work tougher, but I tried a gentle approach. During our workshops, I suggested, "It will be good for you to know all about HIV, so you can educate your children—the future leaders of Liberia. No doubt many will attend universities abroad. They must be prepared."

This spin eased their minds. They relaxed a little more into my lessons. This was a technique I'd learned long ago to capture the attention of otherwise-reluctant adults. If something might help their children, they were on board.

To balance the emotional burden of my job, I did my best to keep up with other parts of my life. I wanted to help others, but I sometimes got pulled down into remembering I was also doing this to save myself. I could get sad at these moments, especially in places where I didn't see an obvious solution. How would the world ever recover from this pandemic if I, one person, couldn't even manage to stay on an even keel about my own status? I went back to my hotel and tried to regroup.

As I write this today, the very same fears are back. How we'll all cope, long-term, with the aftermath of the COVID-19 pandemic. Most of us will survive and get through this bleak period, but how deep will our emotional wounds be? How long will we take to heal?

In the end, I'd try to push my melancholy over the seemingly-unresolvable to the back of my mind, as my Liberian colleagues did. I took a quick nap after my first day so I could get up later that night for an online chat—the best part of a virtual writing class that kept me tied to home. I was enrolled in a travel memoir class taught by

Franz Wisner, author of *Honeymoon with My Brother*, and hosted by mediabistro.com.

The power kept cutting out, though, and the rain sounded like some galactic workman moving furniture around on the next floor. I was scared by the strength of the thunder and the close proximity of the lightening zapping down around the hotel.

Remarkably, despite the storm, the WiFi was working, so I logged on. *I'm here. It's midnight in Monrovia,* I typed.

Three inches of camouflaged gecko scolded me with clicks, then slithered past my shoulder. I'd leaned my chair against the wall in search of a cool surface. My classmates were pleased I'd made it online, and Franz, the instructor, commended my enthusiasm. I got bumped off the network repeatedly, but I didn't give up. Liberia's internet highway had enough virtual potholes to rival those pocking its unfixable roads, what with two hundred inches of annual rainfall. But I persisted. I needed this virtual link to avoid getting sucked into depression.

Hearing the details of my classmates' lives in the US was a perfect diversion. Sometimes I'd get so caught up I'd forget where I was. In these moments of online chat and discussions of our writing projects, I was just another writer with an insatiable case of wanderlust, sharing adventures with like-minded souls. Although I learned a lot from the class, the camaraderie was what kept me coming back.

The next evening, I returned to the hotel after day two of our workshop. Exhausted, I headed down to the restaurant. I asked the server what was on the menu that night.

"Tonight, ma, we got *eubelewbeubelew*."

I frowned. "Pardon?"

"I say, we got *eubelewbeubelew*."

"I see." I stalled, looking around for a chalkboard with listed specials. "And what is, uh, what exactly is…that?"

"*Eubelewbeubelew*! Ev'ree'buddy know *eubelewbeubelew*. It's good, you like it. Anyway, it what we got. Yes?"

"Yes, sure, why not. I've never tried, um…that."

As it turned out, *eubelewbeubelew* was excellent—some sort of leafy greens cooked down, heavily spiced and mixed with smoked fish and roasted peanuts. Over rice, of course. Lots of rice. I have no idea what it was even now, but I did like it—she'd been absolutely right.

It reminded me of another time at Asilomar, a conference center in Monterey, California, decades before. At an absurdly early hour, the server had asked, "You are ready for your *blanfish?*"

"Say yes," whispered my colleague. "She's saying *breakfast.*"

My affirmative nod rewarded me with bacon, eggs, rye toast, and oodles of fresh fruit. I'm not always so lucky when I agree to some version of *blanfish* or *eubelewbeubelew*, but that night I was delighted.

Friday evening, after a very long and emotional week, David picked me up for a last night out before I headed to Gabon, the last leg of this trip. We drove past a well-muscled man in a tank top and Bermuda shorts walking his goat on a leash like a dog. Other strong men were out carrying, well, everything: bags of rice, suitcases, children, small refrigerators. All as effortlessly as if they were sheets of paper.

We pulled up to a beach-front restaurant with a large, loud outdoor bar. The flashing sign above promised LIVE JAZZ. Later we discovered "live jazz" translated to a guy on a synthesizer with a woman reading off a karaoke machine. Apparently, at that time, the local music scene was in a slump. Many musicians just played covers from other countries, mostly Ghana, or bad renditions of classics. In my opinion, nothing written by Bob Marley should ever—I repeat, *ever*—be played on a synthesizer with a clap track. It was akin to Mozart's "Requiem" being sung by drunken chipmunks.

The parking lot was filled with UN vehicles, Jeeps, Humvees—even a lone tank. We took a table on the sandy beach. As gentle waves lapped the shore thirty feet away, we continued our two-week-long discussion of how amazed we were to still be alive. Neither of us had managed to find true love, though I sometimes shared things about my cats, my substitutes for human affection. He talked about living in San Diego—a far cry from the slums of his native Zambia—and how the family that hosted him had a cat he'd reluctantly learned to love.

He pointed to a stray calico prowling the tables for scraps. "Like that one, but scrrrratchy-paper colored." I took that to mean the color of sand

and smiled. We exchanged stories until the tide began lapping at our feet, and it was time to go home.

The next morning, while waiting for my driver, my new self-declared friend, Richard, a thirtysomething Ghanaian also staying at the hotel, popped up. Richard always seemed to be nearby in any common space at that hotel. He insisted on getting my business card. Knowing I was leaving that day, I acquiesced. We'd chatted now and then during my stay, though I found his persistence unnerving.

He took the card, shook my hand a bit too long, then said, "I'll be touching you." With that, he left as quietly as he'd arrived.

Once in the car, I noticed a bright orange emergency vest lying on the backseat. I'd seen a variety of these on this trip. At the airport in Ghana they said *Lufthansa* or *Avianca* or even *UNMIL*—United Nations Peacekeeping Mission in Liberia—anything but the airline we were flying. My favorite was spotted outside the UN in Monrovia where a guy wore one that read *Personal Trainer*.

My driver, Kamara, announced into the radio, "One Papa onboard" as we pulled away.

"Roger that. Call from midpoint. Clear," cackled from the heavy black electronic brick.

"Roger, out."

We proceeded along UN Drive. Officially it's Tubman Boulevard—named after William Tubman, the nineteenth president of Liberia—but has been colloquially renamed since the invasion of peacekeepers. Halfway to the airport, we passed a road accident.

I saw flashing lights. Approaching sirens wailed in the distance. Stopped cars were piling up, people standing around, pointing and gesturing.

But Kamara saw the full story, the details. "A driver had too much rice wine," he told me. "He's hit a fisherman." We could see the catch of the day sprayed across the tarmac. The fisherman lay dead, the driver sat slumped forward, but alive, in his totaled car.

"I see this every week. They never learn. They drrrrrink, they drrrrrive, they die," Kamara said, shaking his head, gripping the wheel tighter as if to throttle it.

His recounting seemed like a delayed subtitle to a foreign film I couldn't quite follow. Shaken, I kept my eyes on the road ahead. We rode in silence the rest of the way, where we arrived just before the latest deluge cut loose. The computers were down, so check-in was manual for the several hundred passengers in line before me. We were an hour and a half late taking off. As the sun peeped between heavy squalls and the plane lifted off, I left that chaotic country for the last leg of my trip.

A Lovely Afternoon, Near Libreville

Libreville

Gabon: Central Africa
Population: 2.2 million
Capital: Libreville

Three flights, four stops, five countries, and twenty-six hours later, I arrived in Gabon. Even for me that was a long trip, and Libreville felt like a haven after the pandemonium of Liberia. The roads were paved. The AC worked. Hot water abounded. The croissants were the best I'd had this side of the Seine.

On Monday morning the driver called up to my room. "Madame, *je suis en bas,* I wait you."

"But we said eight thirty, *non*?" I mumbled in a sleepy haze.

"*Oui, c'est huit heure trente,*" he said.

In a flash of panic, I realized I'd never reset my watch for the new time zone. I skipped my chocolate croissant and rushed to get ready—dressing, washing my face, and brushing hair and my teeth—and headed downstairs to the white jeep with the UNAIDS logo on the doors. A stalky older man in a crisp blue uniform, he smiled as I apologized sheepishly.

"No worry, madame, *c'est l'Afrique*. No rush, no worry."

I settled into the passenger seat and tried to will myself awake.

This crowd was easier to work with, simply because their lives were generally easier than their counterparts in Liberia. At least for the people in the capital, the country enjoyed political stability, and things worked. Most citizens weren't rich, but they didn't suffer in squalor. Still, denial ran deep here, too, filling a hardened crevice deeply engraved by Gabon's religious right.

Once again, I'd be running a series of workshops to help educate staff and help them set up a local team. I was there mostly to familiarize them with the materials they'd need to run sessions for their colleagues. We'd meet with the heads of various UN agencies and lobby them to support the work. Having Salva as my contact made it all worthwhile.

It was a week I'd lived a million times in a million places—only here, the pastries were better. And the billboards were funny, although not by design. Two were for prepaid phone cards. One encouraged the reader to GAB TELCEL while another referred to B.S. GABON.

At the end of the week, I met up again with Salva to travel out of the city so I could see more than just Libreville. He picked me up early on Saturday morning and drove down to Port Môle, the fisherman's harbor. Wide, well-maintained multi-lane roads, lined with palm trees, skirted the Atlantic. We passed makeshift stalls overflowing with *fruits de mer* in the open-air market. The pungent smells of fish, saltwater, and sweat, hung heavy in the air. The chatter of the merchants and buyers negotiating in various languages melded with the clanging of boats bumping against a waterfront in need of repair.

We made our way to a tattered corner of the market, which masqueraded as a commercial dock. There we paid fifteen dollars each for a round-trip ticket to cross the estuary to the other side of the peninsula, or *"presque-ile,"* in a rusty old tugboat. There, we talked, relaxed, swam, napped and ate a quiet lunch of fresh fish at the outdoor restaurant.

Salva, a tall, slim, elegant man, was in his early fifties, and came from Burundi in the African Great Lakes region. I knew his second wife, and our social networks had overlapped again and again. When we first met,

252

in the late 1990s, he'd taken over my old job at UNAIDS. We'd met for pizza in Ferney-Voltaire in France, a neighborhood favored by ex-pats who worked in Geneva. He'd wanted to discuss the work I'd done during my tenure as NGO Liaison, and how he could build on it.

I complimented his English, which was only his third, if not fourth or fifth, after tribal languages and French. It was flawless.

"Well, I actually did my master's in the States. That's where I perfected the English and lost my accent."

"Really? Where in the States?"

"California."

"Oh, wow, I'm from California! Where did you study?"

"A small town—verrrrry hot, verrrry flat."

"Which very hot small flat town?" Now I was giggling. "I'm from one of those, too."

"Oh, Central California. Kind of a boring place, you probably don't know it."

"Come on," I encouraged. "How bad can it be? Can't be worse than where *I'm* from!"

He sighed into his Perrier. "Fresno."

I snorted. "Ha, no way! *I'm* from Fresno! I can't believe you now have my old job at UNAIDS *and* you went all the way from Bujumbura to study in the town I grew up in. What a crazy small world this is!"

We raised our glasses of mineral water. "Here's to Fresno!" he said.

I added, "And to not living there anymore!"

Relaxing on that glorious beach, catching up with an old friend, was a balm for my travel-weary soul. Finding a healthy balance was a constant struggle, but our day in the sun was a simple yet perfect way to wind up the week. The crystal-clear water and perfectly-white sand made it that much more delightful. If that day were a postcard it would read, *The weather's perfect, I wish I could stay.*

Back at my hotel, tired and relaxed from all the sun, I said goodbye to Salva. I was looking forward to an early night and a Sunday all to myself before heading back to New York on Monday, after work. Listed as a four-star hotel, the place had clearly been built in the 1970s and never touched

since. My room's décor made me giggle with the bold orange and brown stripes highlighted with green-apple accents. The switch plate around the outlet for a razor was embossed with an illustration that looked like Fred Flintstone, stubbly beard and all.

I stepped up to the mirror and saw that, despite my best efforts and SPF 40, I was sunburnt—inevitable for a pale complexion at the equator. I rinsed the saltwater from my sensitive skin in that quirky bathroom and fell into bed. Four weeks of travel had taken their toll; I quickly drifted off to sleep, and to dreams of returning to the familiarity of my bed back home.

Bed-Stuy, Do or Die

Brooklyn

After another twenty-seven hours of travel, I was back in New York, head spinning with jetlag. Eyjafjallajökull, the Icelandic volcano, had erupted. My flight home had been rerouted to avoid the ash, but we could see it from the cabin porthole as we flew over Norway toward the North Pole. A week before it erupted, I'd put down a deposit on a vacation in Iceland; a weeklong retreat. The first vacation I'd booked in seven years.

Make a plan, and God will laugh.

I reached my apartment by six-thirty that night. After flying from the equator up to the North Pole and back down again to New York, I was more than ready for bed, though, my ears wouldn't pop post-flight. The floor of my apartment dipped and rolled, as if I was on a sailboat, but I was used to this. It felt good, in a wobbly way. I'd made it. Had a great trip and got to catch up with people I respected and enjoyed. I'd seen a few proverbial lightbulbs go on and knew that at least a few of the staff had learned something.

Still, I felt really ready to move on. I'd survived the journey without any ailment. I was better, healthy again, and knew I *could* travel as I had before. But I no longer had to; there was nothing more to run away from, nothing more I needed to prove.

I loved these trips, but more than ever just wanted to be home. *Home.* A place I thought I'd never find. And maybe I still hadn't—I'm a Californian, through and through. I missed my family and had yet to warm up to the brashness of New York, but at least I was close. And that was incredibly freeing.

Held in a Body of Love

Algiers

Algeria: North Africa
Population: 43.8 million
Capital: Algiers

After a long day, my colleague Amira picked me up from the spectacular Hotel St. George, built in 1889, now known as the El-Djazair. If I was a novelist, I'd pen a book set at the St. George and title it *If These Walls Could Talk.* I'd hoped to spend my Friday night wandering the hallways of the historic hotel, admiring the remnants of Spanish Moorish architecture, and meandering through the botanical gardens that surrounded the property.

Instead, I reluctantly joined Amira for what felt like the millionth dinner with yet another colleague I barely knew. She and I had met the prior week during a regional training on the workplace I facilitated in Tunisia that summer.

Before dinner, she took me to change money inside a fruit market. When we entered, she looked at the shopkeeper, who nodded slightly toward the back of the store, behind shelves of citrus. Back there stood a makeshift (and entirely illegal) office no bigger than a phone booth. A short guy in an olive green shirt sat smoking a cigarette behind a metal grille with a slot just large enough to pass a small pizza through. The single lightbulb suspended inches above his head made him glow with an odd sort of camouflage pattern—black hair, brown skin, dull green clothing, smoke-stained beige teeth—so that he nearly blended into the wood behind him.

Despite his crooked nose and scarred face, I found myself smiling at this odd little man. Amira might have thought I was nervous, but I'd fallen into a spy-thriller fantasy. I was waiting for James Bond or Jason Bourne to show up near the bananas and whisk me away from the dangers of the Algerian black market. In fact, the banks were closed at that hour, ATMs were unreliable—so this was where everyone did their financial transactions after hours. I chose to stay in my film-noir version. It was more fun.

Once we arrived at the restaurant, El Djenina, high above the city with a view of the Mediterranean, I immediately scolded myself for wanting to isolate. The traditional North African tilework—myriad colors in intricate geometric patterns—complemented the dark wood paneling, carved with similar motifs. Other walls were inscribed with golden Arabic text. Chandeliers cast shadows onto the ceiling that looked like mandalas.

The splendor of the restaurant was matched only by the hunger-inducing aromas of their spicy cuisine. Seated next to one another at a small table along a wall-length bank of seats, covered in poufy ochre colored cushions, I perused the menu. I opted for the *chorba frik*, a crushed wheat soup in a tomato base that is eaten as a main course during Ramadan. I also decided on a side of *mhajeb*, a flatbread stuffed with tomato and onion.

As the repetitive beat of the Algerian pop known as *rai* played in the background, Amira placed our order with the waitress. When a small carafe, a single wine glass and a cola on ice arrived, I turned to her and smiled. "You're not drinking?"

"I can't." She brushed back shoulder-length brown hair.

"Are you Muslim? Somehow I thought you were Christian."

"No, I am Christian, it's not that. I just can't drink."

We'd been discussing children earlier. She and her new husband, Sami, desperately wanted to be parents. "Are you pregnant?"

She blushed. "No. Not yet, anyway. It's just, since the accident I can't. It interferes with my medication."

Amira dropped hazel eyes to the patterned the silverware as we sat in silence. Over many years as an educator, I'd learned that often the best thing to do was simply listen. For someone who needs to talk, the gift is invaluable. So I waited.

"I suffered a major head trauma," she said. "You know, from the bombing. The terrorist attack on the UN here in Algiers. In fact, I had brain damage, and now I'm prone to epileptic seizures." She took a long, deep breath. "It's dangerous—drinking, that is. Honestly, there are so many things I have to be careful about now, it's exhausting."

"I can only imagine." I nodded. Familiar, at least, with that feeling.

"I mean, just like that," she said, as her olive cheeks flushed to red. "In an instant my whole life changed. Through no fault of my own, it's forever altered, and I'll never go back to being 'normal.'"

A tingling spread across the back of my neck. What she was describing felt so familiar, so personal. But I was sure living with HIV for nearly two decades was nothing like the horror she'd survived.

Amira stared into her Coke. Then looked up at me, as if assessing how much to share. "The worst part's taking those stupid pills," she said at last. "I mean, they keep me alive, I know that, and I'm grateful. But every time I open my mouth to swallow one, I'm reminded of what happened. And I will have to do that for the rest of my life, all because of one moment in time." She paused and sipped her drink. "Each and every day a little white tablet will remind me I will never be the same. That I'm damaged and can't do a thing about it."

At this, my skin rose in goose-pimples. For her, it had been December 2007. For me, mid-May 1992 when I got diagnosed, and the Friday before Christmas 2008 when I started treatment. It seemed I knew *exactly* how she felt.

It had never occurred to me before that, through such dramatically different events, two women living on different continents, speaking different languages, coming from totally different cultures, could be facing the same daily ritual of taking life-saving medications and secretly resenting them.

I'd started mine two years before. Like her, I was grateful to have the pills, particularly when so many people in the world don't have access to proper health care. Twice a day I'd open a green and yellow plastic pillbox. Take three pills in the morning, or four at night, from their designated compartments.

"Oh, Amira." I sighed. "I know how you feel. I really do. I hate taking my pills, too. Especially this one." I showed her the big white tablet in the egg-shaped travel pillbox I keep in my purse. "It is *absolutely* disgusting. Like swallowing a stick of chalk. If I don't get it down quickly, it starts to melt and makes me want to throw up. Actually, sometimes I do. It's that nasty."

"Yuck! Mine aren't that bad, I guess." Amira squeezed her face tighter than the slice of lemon seasoning her salmon. "But it's more just *having* to take them. I mean, I know they're keeping me alive, but the randomness of what necessitates them is surreal. I feel like I'm taking them for someone I don't even know."

I smiled, encouraging her to continue, though I thought I knew what she'd say before she opened her mouth.

"I feel like I don't know what happened to the old me, the old Amira. But this other, broken woman living inside of me needs help, so I take them for her."

I nodded. "Oh, yeah. It feels otherworldly, that I'm relying on a little— or not so little—glob of chemicals to stay alive. It makes me feel helpless."

Now she was the one nodding.

"I know full well that at this point my body can't fight the HIV on its own," I said. "That pisses me off. It's like I've failed myself, even though I didn't do anything wrong. The virus is just doing what viruses do, eating away at my immune system, so I need my little pharmaceutical army to fight back. It sucks."

This was not something I was proud of, my grieving, but *it* was my reality. *It* felt really good to be honest about my lingering resentment. My eyes teared as I allowed myself a moment of release.

"*Eh oui, moi aussi,*" Amira said.

I took a deep breath. "I don't know if this will help, but there is one thing I do that makes it a tiny bit easier." I raised my glass. "As I pour water to wash down the drugs, I repeat these words: *I am held in a body of love.*"

She smiled ever so slightly, looking comforted.

"I know it's corny, but that is one thing that works for me."

I turned in my seat to face her directly. I'd never told anyone about this little ritual. "I woke up one morning, in 1996, with these words looping in my head: *You are held in a body of love.* They just…stuck. I say them whenever I need to calm my mind. I say it before I swallow my meds. I say it on the subway. Before I go to sleep. It's silly—but it helps." I realized my arms were conducting some invisible orchestra, and tried to rein my hands back into my lap.

Amira furrowed her brow. "The phrase is lovely, but it does seem kind of a…*pensée magique*. How can repeating words actually help?"

"If I see myself as broken, or as a diseased pariah," I said, "I'm not likely to care for myself, on any level. But, if I see myself as a *body of love*, that makes it feel worth the unpleasantness. It keeps me present and reminds me I love myself, warts and all."

"Hmm," Amira replied.

We sat in silence for a moment. Then she smiled. "I like it."

For me, what was done was done. I was never going to get HIV a second time. Perhaps (God forbid) I'd have some other problem in the future, but I'd never have to worry about being diagnosed with that virus again.

Amira, however, was dealing with the results of a terrorist attack that *could* (*Dieu pardonne*) occur again. It was still entirely possible. Intersections in many cities might have children selling bottles of water, or down-and-out adults offering to squeegee your windshield clean. In Algiers, cops circulated among the idling cars with metal detectors they passed beneath each vehicle before allowing it to enter the roundabout, or proceed when the light turned green.

On the way to dinner, Amira had made a detour to drive me past the bomb site, now an empty lot at the top of a hill. We'd discussed the attacks many times in the office. Despite the eeriness of this visit, I'd heard so many accounts of the bombing, and I was curious to see what remained.

"Just ten minutes after a bomb detonated near the Supreme Court in the center of town," she explained, "Another car exploded, its suicide bomber still at the wheel, on the road between two of our offices across the street from each other. On one side, UNHCR—the agency that looks after refugees—was leveled. Across the street, a building that housed six different agencies collapsed. Each bomb was loaded with a metric ton of nitroglycerine and iron nails, to increase the injuries."

Amira had worked in the collapsed section of the second building, which mainly housed the United Nations Development Programme (UNDP). Thirty-one people died that day, seventeen of them UN staff, and one hundred and seventy seven were injured—she among them. The blast had slammed her into the wall of her office and showered her with broken glass.

Now, where buildings used to stand, craters were being filled and leveled to prepare for new construction. Probably some developer would build apartments atop that broken ground.

The day of the bombings, the United Nations Security Council met in New York to condemn the perpetrators and put into motion plans to better protect the staff in Algeria. Al Qaeda in the Islamic Maghreb claimed responsibility, believing the UN to be acting as puppets for the American and French governments. After the fact, the people at headquarters decided the buildings had been too exposed, easy targets. The new offices, they believed, should be located in a more isolated area—an illogical choice, in the eyes of the local staff.

Amira's new office was in a less accessible, less populated neighborhood. Now those same staffers went to work at the terminus of a dead-end road, where they had to queue for security checks to be admitted each morning. They felt no safer, though—just trapped, and convinced it was only a matter of time before someone found a way to finish the job and blow them all to pieces.

My UNICEF colleagues in Algeria had not been directly touched by those bombings because their offices were in another part of town. But they now felt doubly at risk *because* they'd been spared—then had been moved in with the rest of the agencies at the end of that lonely street.

"The bombers were making a political statement against foreigners—not me personally, I know that—but I am the one who still suffers the consequences," Amira said bitterly.

A coworker, Meriem, had told me, "Each time I go to work, I am petrified it will happen again. That we're next."

By chance, the people who worked locally on my program, UN Cares, had been out of the office at a training session. On that most tragic day, the pandemic had actually saved their lives for a change.

In more than fourteen years with the UN, I'd never had such intimate conversations with my colleagues like the one I was having with Amira at that moment.

Around other positive people, I felt like a whiner for even bringing up the frustrations of having to take medication for the rest of my life. Some of them may have even shared my frustration. But, outwardly, they were still vocal treatment advocates. I'd sensed that if I said anything contradictory to their insistence that we should all cherish our boxes of pills, I'd be betraying the fight. So I bit my tongue. I had no right to complain when so many others around the globe had so little.

Now here I was, sitting with a woman I'd just met, discussing my deepest fears and frustrations. As I shared my feelings, Amira flushed. Tears welled up. I knew that expression. The downturned mouth about to let out a deep long sigh that says, I'm not the only one—and I'm not crazy. In my mind, I heard the words I'd been telling others for years: You are not alone.

Tonight, those words were also meant for me.

The irony was that for the first sixteen years I'd lived with HIV, the virus had been damaging my body, but I'd rarely thought about it. Yet now, since I'd started taking meds twice a day, although the virus was currently undetectable—the medical equivalent to being in remission—I thought about my illness constantly.

Every time I had to take a pill. Every time I needed to refill a prescription. Every time I booked a flight and remembered the presence of those pills in my luggage might get me blacklisted in the fifty countries that still impose travel restrictions against people like me.

"I'm so glad I got to meet you, Amira. I'm not big on support groups, but it really does help to talk, sometimes," I said. "Guess I'm still human, not the robot I pretend to be for work."

She smiled, laid her hand over mine, and gave a squeeze. "We're lucky to be alive, you and me. So many others never made it this far."

"That we are." I replied.

At that restaurant over spiced soup and excellent local red wine, I was reminded HIV could not always be the main issue. What mattered was feeling alive. And having that threatened or diminished was everyone's common ground.

Maybe this was what I'd felt in countries like Cambodia or Liberia, where so many had been so brutally murdered in recent times, but hadn't yet put a name to it. In those two countries, in particular, I'd encountered palpable resistance from trainees. The people there had faced so many threats, so much violence, and were trying desperately to hold on to the lives they'd just rebuilt. They just could not absorb the notion of another threat to their existence.

Vitality. Life. Being. These were our connectors, not the virus or the disease. The *quality* of one's life was all that mattered.

And it wasn't just Amira. In the preceding days, I'd felt this same underlying pain from nearly all the people I interacted with. It caught me off guard because Algeria—the tenth-largest country in the world, and now, since the independence of South Sudan, the largest country in Africa—has a relatively low rate. It does have one of the highest rates in North Africa, but at less than one percent, that's low compared with other African nations. I suspected few Algerians give a lot of thought to the virus.

And so, when my colleagues were engaged and attentive during my awareness trainings, I was actually surprised. When I'd previously done trainings for staff who'd endured such trauma, they often acted out like hormonal teenagers, because their pain was so close to the surface.

But sitting in that restaurant with Amira, I realized that it was exactly *because* they had endured so much pain following the bombings that they had a kind of empathy for people living with HIV. Yet, *unlike* Cambodia or Liberia, the political problems in Algeria had been going on for centuries. Everyone's accustomed to trauma.

I wonder if future generations will have similar conversations—of surviving collective trauma—about COVID-19? Grieving the millions lost. Lasting pain for those who lived but suffered serious illness or side effects of the virus. Survivors' guilt for those who remain.

There is no shame in surviving a bomb attack, whether in Algeria or anywhere else. Yet a person with HIV—regardless of where they live—is still likely to be shunned and looked down upon, if not persecuted or even murdered. I fear that battle will continue for decades to come.

As our dinner wound down, Amira made a call to her husband, speaking in a mixture of Arabic and French. Then she turned back to me with an impish grin. "Well," she said in a conspiratorial tone, "since it is the weekend, how about a midnight tour of Algiers? It's completely against UN rules to have you out after curfew, but I'm sure it's safe. And you know I don't use that word lightly!"

"Yes, please," I said. It was the first time I'd seen her really smiling.

Once we'd collected her husband—a kind man with a passion for soccer and a visible devotion to his wife—we caroused the streets for nearly two hours.

Amira insisted on paying for dinner, so I gave her some of my black market currency to top off the gas tank. We drove up above the city, which was set on a hill, much like other stunning places across the Mediterranean in Spain and France. There I could take in a panoramic view of the bay. Under the cover of night, tankers dotted the water like fallen stars, lolling about. I thought I saw the lights of land in the distance.

Heading due north, one would find Mallorca, then Barcelona, and eventually Paris. I couldn't see any of this, but my mind drew the connections to these countries so intertwined in their history. I'd never imagined Algiers would be so stunning. Since then, it's ranked in my top five, along with Nice, Cape Town, Vancouver, and San Francisco. They're all built on hills overlooking the sea. Each is green and vibrant, yet elegant with distinct architecture—the perfect mix.

As we drove past the famous Casbah, Amira's husband told me, "Merchants and villains once roamed the alleys here."

I tried to imagine such deviants and what kinds of double-dealing schemes they'd attempted, what medieval weapons they might have hidden beneath swooshing capes or ornate robes. But all I could summon in my mind was Joe Strummer from the Clash singing "Rock the Casbah."

Just as I managed to disable my inner MTV, we crossed over, and then drove below, a housing complex built into the underbelly of a six-lane overpass. There, like tribal cliff dwellings, hung structures housing countless families. It was so unexpected and clever, an amazing use of space.

Amira and Sami told me bits of history, but mostly they shared *their* Algiers. Pointing out places where friends or relatives lived. A spot where they'd taken a romantic walk or played at as a kid. This personalized tour locked that evening into a list of favorite travel memories.

Like most people, I'm influenced by stories. I tend to hear only what is offered on the surface. So I knew something about the years of political strife and the history of colonialism that left deep rifts between the French and the Algerians. And, of course, about the more recent internal conflicts in the ongoing struggle for power. These battles—some armed, some in courts and government offices—were increasing in the whole region. Algeria was not exempt. But Algiers is an absolute jewel, each facet more beautiful than the next.

The tall, shuttered, whitewashed buildings combined formal French splendor with the ornate detailing so common throughout the Arab world. Latticework carved with intricate patterns welcomed natural light but stymied voyeurs. The arched tops of shutters, rather than the French squared versions, distinguished Algiers from European capitals. The city was as majestic and refined as any I'd ever visited.

I often think back to that evening. Of standing shoulder-to-shoulder with Amira looking out through the latticed shutters of the restaurant above sprawling Algiers: a world within a world. And when I do, I repeat my mantra *I am held in a body of love.* And treasure that night, once again, and the bond she and I—and so many others—share in the fragility of life.

CHAPTER 11

my last year at UNICEF

Separation

New York

n the fall of 2011, after nearly nine years of service with UNICEF—more than fifteen since I'd joined the system as an international civil servant—I was handed official notice my job would be abolished. An uncomfortable meeting for both the director of human resources and me.

The economy was in the toilet. The US's credit standing had been lowered below AAA for the first time ever. The Fed was keeping the interest rate at an all-time low for some reason I didn't begin to understand. Politicians were pointing fingers like angry bullies in the schoolyard at who'd lost the most jobs for our fifty not-so-United States. Not a great time to be let go, to say the least.

My HR director, Christine Lloyd, who'd joined from the private sector, had likely had such conversations a million times. Yet as we sat in her sleek corner office on the 26th floor, with an unobstructed view of the Empire State Building, she seemed worried. She fidgeted with a manila folder across the glass table from me. An elegant fifty-something British blonde with blue eyes and a fabulous sense of style, she said, "Martina, I

265

certainly hope you'll be moving on to better things."

I smiled and nodded. "I hope so, too."

"What are you most proud of from your time in this position?"

I struggled to answer, scurrying to sift through my mental files: the volumes of experiences this job had afforded me. At last I settled on one from our UN System-wide Workplace Programme on HIV. "The launch of UN Cares in 2008 was my proudest moment. Certainly, one I'll always treasure."

I kept my answers short as I battled to keep my emotions in check.

She seemed pleased and sat back. "Thanks for your service to the organization, Martina. We all wish you well in whatever your future might hold."

Her expression shifted to slightly relieved when the requisite time had passed, and I could get up to leave. I felt a pang in my chest when she slid the white letter-sized envelope marked *Personal and Confidential* across the table. It contained the details outlining my separation. I squirmed in my seat, mouth dry, palms sweating, and struggled to look calm and collected.

After we shook hands, I left her office. I quietly walked through the hallway with the unopened envelope gripped tightly in one hand. Only when I reached an isolated internal stairwell did I allow myself to let out my feelings. In that dim, cold, stairwell, I punched sky with both fists, leapt up, and yelled, "Yessssssssss! I'm *free!*"

Six months prior, I'd actually been the one to propose that UNICEF abolish my post. Nobody in the UN *ever* abolishes their own post; why would they? But I really believed it was the best thing for the organization, and as a manager, I knew the money going to my salary and perks in New York would be far better spent hiring a regional coordinator based in West Africa.

And that, indeed, was exactly what was about to happen.

Most important, however, I'd done this for myself. It gave me the kick in the pants I needed to get moving toward something new. I valued my work tremendously and hoped I'd contributed to making the world a better place. But I also knew I needed to go. By taking the initiative, I was able to leave on a high note, with an astounding sense of accomplishment. It was an act of self-preservation, before I made myself ill again. Or, worse, so indifferent and burned out, I'd lose all will to pursue other things in life.

Several months after proposing the cut, I'd been told by a former human resources officer, "You are an incredibly clever woman." I'd been puzzled at the time. Now I discerned that, unbeknownst to me at the time, an abolished UN post comes with a very handsome separation package. I'd been ready to walk away with nothing but the freedom to sleep in each morning. Instead I had the bonus of a little more in my savings, and the gift of being able to take time off to regroup before directing my energy to new pursuits. December 16th, my last day, could not come soon enough.

But first, I had two more trips to make.

Not My Finest Moment

Amman

Jordan: Western Asia
Population: 10.2 million
Capital: Amman

With fewer than six weeks left on my contract, I flew to Jordan to do my last training for UN Cares. Once our interagency workplace program was launched, our agency-specific work shifted to providing global and regional support to duty stations for the whole UN.

I'd requested the chance to support the Middle East and North Africa. The most conservative of the regions we covered. This workshop was specifically for colleagues in the most difficult duty stations within this most difficult region, including Iraq, Palestine, Syria and Lebanon. Well, sure. Why make the last assignment an easy one?

Amman always felt familiar. I'd never lived there but I'd visited many times. It's hilly and the buildings are mostly white or beige. The hue of the city seems to shift throughout the day, depending on the color of the sky; a polychromatic time-lapse.

Sadly, we were unable to enjoy the cityscape as our workshop room was windowless and unremarkable. Ten or twelve tables covered in heavy white cloths were positioned around the room, each with six chairs. Metal easels with large paper flip charts and markers were set up, as was a projector. A resource table was near the front of the room where my co-facilitator, Muna, and I set out our materials. Underneath we stashed our work satchels. Muna was a Bangladeshi I'd worked with for years and in many countries. She would be taking over regional coordination once I left.

Stephen, whom I'd met in Uganda and worked with in Eritrea, came in to join our workshop. He was now fulltime with the Department of Peacekeeping Operations, stationed in Lebanon. "Princess!" He gave me a hug. "How is the Princess of Madagascar?"

"Tired," I said. "Good, but tired."

I'd spent months organizing this training and was glad it was finally happening, but also already frustrated with the reluctance of some of the participants. They were among the most stubborn I'd ever had.

"Don't let them get to you, Princess," Stephen said. "You're almost done. Then you'll never have to do this again."

"I guess…" He was right, but I was on the verge of losing my patience.

Many times over the years I'd felt offended by a local or international colleague, but I'd managed to always keep my cool.

Once, a workshop participant at a UN Cares training in Bangkok—where I'd first met Muna—asked to have lunch with me. He then proceeded to ask a lot of personal questions. I was used to that, at least as much as one can ever get used to being interrogated by strangers about one's past. But this colleague hit a raw nerve.

"So, you're married, right?" he asked.

"Was. I'm divorced now, but yes, I was married,"

"He must have been a very amazing man," he said.

"Why is that?" I thought back on how disappointing my marriage—and my husband—had actually been.

"Well, to marry *you*. I mean to marry anyone with HIV is such a brave thing."

I was seething but managed to stay composed. Perhaps I could use the interaction as a teaching moment, to help that staff member understand that being the partner of a person with HIV was not as risky as he seemed to imagine. "As long as both know their status and make informed decisions about how to protect one another, then the risk is quite low." I went on to explain that when people were on effective treatment, the amount of virus in their blood can become undetectable, indicating that the risk of transmission has been virtually eliminated.

I steered the conversation away from my marriage and onto facts that he could use in his own life. He was, to his credit, receptive to the information and genuinely seemed to appreciate the chance to talk freely.

On this day in Amman, however, I was not feeling as diplomatic. One participant was being particularly difficult. We'd been talking about the need for condoms in staff offices. I said "They can be stored in a discreet place. But in all offices affiliated with the United Nations, condoms must be available. That is nonnegotiable."

"But we can't put them in our offices," said the short woman, wearing dark slacks, a loose-fitting floral blouse and a white headscarf.

"I'm sorry, but that's not up to you to decide," I answered. "It is one of the Minimum Standards of UN Cares. We're not here to decide whether or not to have them, we're here to figure out *how* you're going to proceed."

I explained that we'd mandated putting condoms in the workspaces both to make sure they were available for those too shy to buy them, and also to break down the stigma associated with them. If people saw condoms regularly, after a while it would become easier to talk about them—and the need for safer sex to protect everyone.

"No, I will not do that," she said firmly. "Putting those things in the workplace merely encourages the illegal behavior of immoral people. Those people don't belong in our offices anyway."

I glared at her, whipped off my glasses, and rubbed my nose. "You know, when we started this workshop, I told you all that it would be the last one, because I'm leaving the UN," I said. "What I didn't tell you is why I'm leaving."

The group was now listening intently, so quietly I feared they were holding their collective breath.

"I'm leaving the UN because I can no longer listen to participants like you. There are people in this room living with HIV. *I* am one of them, and your words are insulting. Your behavior is exactly why we desperately need to fight stigma within the United Nations, so people like me will be able to visit your offices and feel welcome. Feel safe."

The room remained still, but I could distinctly hear muffled sounds of surprise. Perhaps even a few rounds of *oooooooh, no she didn't* and a finger snap or two.

I added, "Let's take a break now. Come back in fifteen minutes. Then we will separate into groups by country, and you *will* make a plan to get condoms into your offices."

The woman who'd been goading me left immediately. She stood out in the hallway, smoking cigarette after cigarette. I could never understand public health and medical professionals who smoked, but she was one.

At the end of the break, she came up to speak to me. Before she even opened her mouth, I said, "I'm sorry for my outburst. That was unprofessional."

"No, *I'm* sorry." She shook her head. "I did not mean to insult you. It's just that…my hormones are raging. I'm pregnant."

I bit my lip; this was a *doctor* who *chain-smoked* while *pregnant*.

"I was a flight attendant years ago," she continued, "so I've also done some naughty things in my past. Just because I wear the veil now doesn't mean I've always been perfect. So I understand you better than you might think."

I was speechless, unable to respond. I couldn't find the words to address someone who continued to insult me, apparently without even sensing it. "But I still think condoms don't belong in our offices," she added. "So we don't agree. But I won't stand in the way of the work, I just won't help with that part of it."

The rest of the workshop went off without a glitch, but I was shaken. I'd given so much of my life to fighting this pandemic, and *this* was how I was leaving my job?

"I shouldn't have lashed out during the training," I admitted to a few participants after we'd finished. "But I just couldn't listen to her insulting those of us in the room with HIV."

"Oh no, you absolutely should have," said one young woman with bright green eyes and a wild mane of black hair. "It was the best thing that could've happened. She's been trying to sabotage our work for ages. You did us a huge service. Said what we'd all long wanted to say, but never had the courage."

That night, I didn't go out to celebrate with friends, as I'd planned. Instead, I went up to my room, curled into the fetal position, and allowed the years of pent up frustration to release. I sobbed. I screamed into my pillow. Eventually, I slept. It felt like a cleansing.

Before leaving, Muna and I treated ourselves to two days of R&R outside Amman. At the Kempinski Hotel Ishtar, standing on cool marbled tiles, I opened my latticed shutters to watch the sunset beyond these holy lands, disputed for millennia. Jordan, Palestine, Israel, Lebanon, Syria, Iraq. Magenta to indigo to slate blue, the horizon dotted to life, matching star for star, as neighboring towns lit up for the evening.

At long last, I felt relieved of my self-imposed duty to save the world.

In the morning, I floated in a dreamlike exhaustion, buoyed by jade-green waters that would not allow me to drown.

There, suspended on the Dead Sea, I felt my soul recharging, coming back to life.

UN Plus – The UN System HIV-positive Staff Group

Nairobi, Kenya

Kate, whom I'd met decades before at my first international meeting in Mexico, was passing time before leaving for the airport. We were in the capital of Kenya for a UN Plus meeting that had just ended. She sat with me on the enormous king-sized bed of my room as we watched CNN International.

I'd miss the perks of traveling for the United Nations and, in particular, seeing friends around the world. But I was *done*. This was the last day of my last trip, and I didn't feel the slightest pang of regret. All I could think about was getting to sleep in now, on Monday mornings.

Of course, I'd miss the salary, and benefits like the six weeks paid vacation. And the diplomatic passport. But not the grinding routine of daily life in a bureaucracy. Nor would I miss the frustration of trying to find yet another new and creative way to explain the same piece of information. I'd literally been saying the same thing for nearly twenty years. Sure, I kept tweaking the script, but the content never changed. The UN joke was, "same meeting, different decade." And still, for every person we reached there were countless others around the world who still didn't know even the basics about HIV.

I was also looking forward to getting some distance from many of my fellow public health workers. If one more fool suggested that the solution to my burnout would be to change diseases, I would not be responsible for my reaction. A few weeks before, one well-meaning colleague had said, "Anyway, you don't want to work on AIDS forever, you'll get pigeonholed. You need to stay *relevant*. How about malaria? That's hot, ya know."

I couldn't just "change diseases." My work had never been just a career choice. Those years were a response to my own diagnosis. I didn't want to stay relevant. And, most definitely, there was nothing *hot* about malaria.

From time to time over the decades, however, a few individuals validated my efforts. The ones who took me aside to say, "Hey, thanks for what you're doing. I learned something today." Or "I admire your courage. It can't be easy to talk like this on a regular basis, baring your soul and all."

Them I would remember fondly. Some I'd stay in touch with thanks to social media. Some, like Kate, were in my life forever. We had a bond like that shared by troops who go to war. Nobody else will ever know or understand what happened on the battlefield; you need one another to remind yourself of what you survived. Of how fortunate you are.

A few I simply admired and felt blessed that we'd crossed paths. One of these was Sophie from Malawi. She'd been with us this week in Nairobi for the annual board meeting of UN Plus, The UN System [HIV] Positive Staff Group.

At this point, some referred to me as the Grandmother of UN Plus. Though never an active member, I'd planted the seeds in the mid-nineties that perhaps stimulated the group to grow into what it is today: a network of hundreds of HIV-positive staff around the world who support one another, personally and professionally.

They'd invited me to this meeting to share whatever last bits of wisdom I might have to impart before leaving. I tried to talk them out of it, but they insisted, and I'm glad they did. It was impressive to see how far the group had come. I felt proud to sit among them.

On the eve of our closing day, the network focal point for UNAIDS, John, organized a reception and called me up to where he was standing. On a courtyard near the pool, with cocktail tables arranged while servers passed trays of hors d'oeuvres and beverages, John took my hand. "Thank you, Martina, for what you've done to help staff living with HIV within the UN system," he said.

Mostly I felt embarrassed and relieved that I didn't have to make any remarks. Just smile and graciously accept my official gift. Pleasantly, a box of chocolates and not some sort of medal or bureaucratic certificate.

After I returned to my glass of wine and plate of cheese cubes, Sophie came to my table and took my hand. "Thank you."

"Sophie, you're welcome. But I didn't do anything."

"Oh, but you did. You just don't know it."

"If anything, I didn't do enough for staff already living with HIV. I was so focused on the rest of the personnel and their dependents."

"No, my dear. That's it exactly. You took a wide perspective with this work. You remember when you came to Malawi?"

"For the *Conversations for Change* workshop in 2006?"

Conversations for Change was a self-help guide we'd written for employees, to help them cope better with the stresses of the epidemic. It had turned out to be useful for UN staff all around the globe, and its creation was one of my proudest accomplishments.

"No. In 2002, before you joined UNICEF. You did a workshop for all UN staff."

"Sure, I remember. That was a great trip. I learned so much."

"Do you remember a woman asking a question about testing?"

"Vaguely?" I shrugged. "I mean, that was a long time ago and there were quite a few questions. Why?"

"Well, I was that woman. You told me it was better to know that you had HIV than not to know."

"Of course. But I was just doing my job," I said.

"Yes, but you were honest. And when you said you were living with HIV, I thought, 'She's so strong and healthy. She has HIV—*knows* she has HIV—and yet she's okay. I need to find out, too.'"

"But you knew already, no?"

"No. Martina, this is what I'm trying to tell you. You gave me the courage to get tested. Because of you, I found out that I do have HIV. I was afraid, but you were right. It *is* better to know than not to know. I am here today because I went for that test and got myself into proper care and treatment. I am here today for my son, because I took care of myself. I am here today because of *you*."

I hugged Sophie and whispered, "Thank you. You're wrong, though. You're here because you're the one who's strong. But thank you for letting me know that what I said helped you find the strength you already had."

Sitting with Kate in my room, on the massive bed with a half dozen pillows, late the next afternoon, I thought about Sophie and all the women with HIV I'd met around the world. How lucky I was to share a few hours with this dear friend—that we were both still alive and healthy decades later—and to know I'd made a contribution, after all. I'd always said that if even one person got tested, it would all be worth it.

I let out a deep breath, squeezed Kate's hand and changed the channel to a classic-movie station. As I did, I thought of the first thing I'd been told when I met another woman with HIV in 1992: *You are not alone.*

CHAPTER 12
COVID-19

Pandemic, Take Two: Airborne Edition

My First Floor Apartment, Brooklyn

(Part 1: Lockdown)

IV led me out into the world. COVID-19 led me—and everyone else—into a year-and-counting lockdown. Since March 12th, 2020, I've only left my neighborhood a dozen or so times (as of this writing) for in-person doctor's appointments. Beyond those jaunts, I've only walked to a pharmacy or grocery store, and only as needed.

In early March, Neal—my partner in life, my love, since 2012—flew to Florida to visit his daughter from a previous relationship, Ariel, and her son, Taylor. Once the pandemic hit, he sagely opted out of interstate travel. Consequently, I spent more than half a year on my own. Solitude doesn't bother me. I often joke that my 'quarantine adaptive gene' is strong because I'm happy to stay home and am never bored. Being isolated, in the end, was a blessing.

On April 4th, 2020, just a few short weeks into lockdown, I turned fifty-six, marking the milestone of having lived half of my life with HIV.

To honor the occasion, I used an Apple Store credit I'd been hoarding and treated myself to a pair AirPods Pro with *28 Years and Counting* engraved on the case. I'd never imagined living to be this old and felt I had earned an extravagant gift.

What I didn't know was that apparently the universe felt a more appropriate offering would be infecting me with another brand-spanking-new virus.

COVID-Positive

My First Floor Apartment, Brooklyn

(Part 2: Haven't Left Home in Two Months)

A week before my birthday, I'd begun to feel unwell, but convinced myself it was a cold. That week, I'd been to my mom-n-pop pharmacy down the street. Without forewarning, the shop had been sold to new owners. A new pharmacist was filling in and didn't yet know his way around. Preparing my prescription, which in prior visits had taken a few minutes—ten tops—took him more than an hour. It was a confined space and nobody was social distancing. Closing hour was approaching and people were getting anxious. A few even yelled out of frustration.

"How the hell could they sell and not tell us?" a tall woman spat. "I'm here for my own prescriptions, but also for my clients at the nursing home across the street. This is taking forever."

The elderly man who accompanied her, apparently a resident from the same senior care center where she worked, agreed. "This is outrageous." He sneezed, while his paper mask dangled from one ear.

"George, put your mask up and sit down. You gonna wear yourself out with that cold," the nurse told him. Her own mask was below her chin, leaving her mouth exposed.

He was right. She was seething. They were also both spraying droplets of spit. As were the other customers who'd not worn a mask, or pulled theirs down. Messaging on mask wearing in those first weeks was still unclear. I did wear one, but I was fidgeting with it. I didn't have my glasses on, so my eyes were exposed. Out of habit, I touched my face. I touched the counter. I touched my phone. I was annoyed, like the other half dozen customers in that small space, and I wasn't thinking.

In the end, I cancelled my order and asked my doctor to send my prescription to the nearest CVS, which I knew would be better able to handle it. My meds were running out and I didn't have time to request home delivery. So I rode the bus twenty minutes to reach my new pharmacy. I decided to walk back and buy a few groceries on the way. By the time I made it home, I needed to sleep for two hours. March 30th was the last time I left my house, until the end of May.

My malaise increased and on April 2nd, I finally emailed my doctor.

Hi Dr. Merrick,

Hope you're doing well in all of this craziness.

I'm checking in because I think I may have a mild case of COVID-19.

My chest has been constricted and painful, but I can still breathe fine. I don't have much of a cough, but my throat's tight and I'm always thirsty. Some fever, but nothing too high or lasting, it seems intermittent. I definitely have body aches and fatigue.

Anything else I should be doing besides staying home? Obviously, I won't go near a medical facility unless I start having serious trouble breathing.

Thank you!

Martina

My tendency to dismiss getting sick was in full force. Indeed, I've noticed that many people with chronic diseases downplay feeling unwell. For me, perhaps for others, it's a trigger. My anxiety peaks and I fear that once I fall sick, I may never recover. It's irrational, but real. I didn't have an oximeter. My thermometer, I discovered, only worked about every third try. I was shooting in the dark, functioning on gut feelings.

I'd marked the message "Medical Question: Non-Emergency" and anticipated my doctor or someone else from his clinic would respond by the next day.

Within moments, my phone rang. A nurse launched a barrage of questions. "Describe the chest pain. Start with where it hurts."

"Mostly on the left side," I said.

"Uh-huh. Is it a pressure? Do you think it could be your heart?"

"No. It's too far toward the side of my body."

"Okay, good. We can rule out a heart attack. Tell me more."

"It feels like I have claws inside my ribcage. Really sharp ones. Dipped in acid. Trying to destroy my lungs."

"I'm sorry to hear that. Definitely sounds like COVID. I'll have Dr. Merrick call as soon as possible."

He asked more questions and told me to hang in there. A combination of emails and phone calls with clinic staff continued like this every single day for nearly a month. Sensing I might not be fully grasping the severity of the situation, my doctor clarified I was one of a handful of patients on a daily call list. The ones with the most worrisome symptoms.

Since leaving UNICEF, I'd wound up as an adjunct at LaGuardia Community College, where I teach English composition and critical reading to high school students earning college credits early. With the schools suddenly shuttered, my classes had shifted online, so I taught for a few hours each day and slept the rest of the time. Blissfully, spring break arrived and I had a week and a half off.

At that point, I couldn't confirm my diagnosis with 100% certainty because it was nearly impossible to be tested without visiting a hospital. The last place I wanted to go was an emergency room crammed with the severely ill. I didn't want to expose myself further. I didn't want to get on public transportation to travel. And I certainly didn't want to add to the burden of overwhelmed health care workers just for a test. I was also getting the impression that a majority of people who were admitted to hospitals would end up in morgue freezer trucks, like the one parked on DeKalb Avenue across from the Brooklyn Hospital Center, not far from my house.

This virus made it nearly impossible for me to get out of bed on many days, and the smallest of tasks wore me out. One flight of stairs—up or down, not even both directions—felt like I'd done a thousand squats, run a marathon, and been poked with needles all at the same time.

The worst, though, was the chest pain. I've had bronchitis and I've had shingles. This was more painful than both combined. In addition to the clawing inside, it felt like a Shrek-sized monster was squeezing my chest. Tightly. It hurt more if I sat. It particularly hurt in the morning when I woke. Luckily, my then-upstairs neighbor, Charity, had been interviewing front-line health care workers. She passed on their advice, that people with COVID should avoid sleeping on their back, which seemed to impair breathing. Rather, they should sleep on their side or stomach. Charity may have saved me a one-way trip to the ER.

I also had nausea. Motion sickness on steroids. I choose to believe that whatever creature was slashing up my chest was also making sardine milkshakes for fun. The waking up to the nausea was awful, though going to sleep with it wasn't much fun either. During the day, it would sometimes abate, but not for long.

I thought I'd been spared the headaches, until I wasn't. They hit me and like a brick. I'd only ever had one migraine, but this was similar, only without photosensitivity. They seemed to come and go. Then they just stayed. And then the light-sensitivity kicked in. None of the other typical symptoms, sore throat, dry cough, fever, loss of smell or taste, seemed to impact me. My breathing was shallow, to be sure, but I never gasped for air.

I'd followed the guidelines: socially distanced, washed my hands, sanitized surfaces, and used face coverings before they were cool. But I'm imperfect, and I still got exposed and infected.

Most likely I was at higher risk because I had HIV. On the other hand, I've wondered if I managed to avoid a worse case because I already take antiretroviral medications. I don't know, nobody does. My doctor said they're designing trials to study COVID-19 in people with HIV. I

281

will gladly volunteer to be studied, as I have for more than twenty five years with WIHS, a natural history study of women living with HIV. My nephew calls me a 'living resource' which gives my survival that much more purpose. My doctor tells me I'm a pioneer yet again. All I know for certain is that I'm tired.

By early May, my doctor told me I was cleared to go outside, like actually outdoors, but I didn't. Each day I looked out the window and thought, maybe tomorrow. My amazing neighbors shopped for me. My extraordinary crew of friends, siblings and niblings checked on me, sent fruit baskets and cards, did drop-and-dash grocery runs on my behalf, leaving the goods on my doorstep. I take quarantining seriously and stayed alone inside my apartment, save for taking the trash out—just out onto the sidewalk—or checking the mail—inside the lobby of my three-unit building, for a solid two months.

Because Neal was away, I didn't have the burden of worrying about putting him at risk. Thanks to FaceTime we connected several times a day, so although I was alone physically, I was far from lonely. It may sound strange, but I'm grateful he wasn't in New York, to experience firsthand the catastrophic chaos or the incessant wailing of ambulance sirens in the city where he grew up.

And, surprisingly, (or maybe not) I felt far less alone than I did when coping with my diagnosis for HIV. We don't know much about COVID-19, but this pandemic hit like a tsunami. The numbers are staggering, but I know I am—tragically—one of millions.

With HIV, however, I felt I was on my own.

Today we're building on the experience and knowledge borne from the response to HIV and AIDS. While it is a reminder that we didn't act quickly enough in the 1980s and 1990s to that pandemic, it is, at the same time, gratifying to know that all the work done by activists and scientists, and others, has not been in vain.

By June, I felt more or less back to normal. I was finally able to get a test, but two months after infection, it was a futile effort and the results were negative. Antibody tests also came back negative, but my doctor remained convinced I'd been infected. While symptoms had mostly resolved, the headache had become persistent, and the left side of my chest still hurt.

Side Eye

My First Floor Apartment, Brooklyn

(Part 3: Yep, Still Here)

In late August, Neal returned, with his five-year-old grandson, Taylor. Since the schools were shut, his daughter couldn't work and manage remote learning as a single mom. So Taylor's been with us and along with my teaching, I'm with him each day in virtual kindergarten. I've enjoyed having them around again. Although the noise level does not help my headache, Taylor's hugs do.

By the end of summer, I was again feeling a low-grade, generalized malaise. In early October, I finally tested positive for the antibodies. I was now HIV-positive and COVID-positive. To be clear, I'd not had any testing between June and October, so perhaps I'd already developed them, but I can't be sure. As my doctor often said, "It's the wild west out there with this disease. None of us knows what will happen next."

When I resumed teaching in the fall, I soon realized I'd been shutting my left eye automatically when I read or graded papers. I figured I needed a new prescription for my glasses and dismissed it. But my head still hurt. If I so much as ran a finger lightly across my temple, pain radiated all over the left side of my head. My doctor ordered an MRI but Medicaid refused it. Twice. Eventually I had one, but it showed nothing of interest, except that I still had a brain.

In January 2021, I finally went to the eye doctor for a check-up.

"So good to see you, Martina. How have you…oh wow." Dr. Curreri abruptly stopped speaking and homed in on the files the technician had just uploaded to his computer from the various machines I'd looked into, moments before, which captured images of my eyeballs and retinas.

I'd been his patient for more than fifteen years, had friends in common, and always enjoyed chatting, catching up. He'd never spoken so curtly before.

"How's your vision been?" he said, still looking at the computer monitor.

"Uh, okay but a little weird on the left. Everything looks distorted, like I'm looking through a bottle or something. Lines of text are, I don't know, wavy? Bubbled out?"

"Yup." He shook his head.

"And if I use just my right eye, things are normal size. But if I use only the left, they're elongated, almost twice as big. Walking downstairs is a nightmare. My depth perception's all screwed up. I can't figure out how to measure equal portions when serving dinner."

"Anything else?"

"Well, I've had a headache since May. I had COVID. Maybe it's related? The pain and the eye and the virus?"

He pursed his lips. "I think you have an epiretinal membrane on your left eye. A macular pucker."

"A what?"

"A sort of . . . . growth. It's not uncommon, but yours is huge. We've actually been seeing a lot of this kind of thing post-COVID. Probably not related to your headache. But to inflammation from the virus. It hasn't been well-researched yet, but it's almost certainly linked."

"Shit."

"Yeah. Let me get my colleague in here to see this. As you know, my specialty is eye diseases. Luckily for you, his is all things retina. Hang on a sec."

As I waited, I tried to make sense of what Dr. Curreri had said.

He returned with Dr. Johnson, who smiled at me and said, "Hi, nice to mee...whoa." He turned to my doctor and said, "Man, you weren't kidding, that's huge," as he beelined for the computer screen.

After more tests and imaging, the ophthalmologists and I discussed my situation and settled on a two-step plan. First, I'd try steroid eye drops for ten days and see if that helped reduce the impairment. If that didn't work, we'd schedule an out-patient surgery to remove the membrane. If left unchecked, because of the size, it would likely pull on my retina and could result in lasting damage to my vision.

My Unexpected Journey Continues

My First Floor Apartment, Brooklyn

(Part 4: I May Never Leave Home Again)

The physical damage from COVID—damage to my eye, hyper-sensitivity on my temple, a constant headache, and persistent pain on the left side of my chest—has been more pronounced in under a year than HIV has in nearly thirty. This virus is a beast. And it's not done with me yet.

As I finish this memoir about HIV, I'm also navigating a parallel journey with COVID-19. With HIV, my life was forever changed. With COVID, the entire world has shifted. There is no going back to normal. A new normal will emerge. Eventually.

As we as a nation, and as a global community, navigate this crisis, I am reminded of the extenuating factors that surround public health. In direct correlation to the tragedy of HIV and AIDS, the issues, injustices, and rights—or lack thereof—of lesbian, gay, bisexual, transgender, queer, and non-binary people were brought to light. They'd always been there, but combating the pandemic necessitated facing these issues head on. The LGBTQ community was front and center in the US, and beyond, in fighting for the rights of those living with HIV.

Now a new reckoning is upon us. While millions huddled at home, unable to watch sports or go to the movies, we became glued to the news. On May 27th, the world watched a video of a murder, recorded on a cell phone, that immediately went viral. For nine minutes and twenty-nine seconds, Minnesota police officer Derek Chauvin calmly looked into the camera, hands in his pockets, knee firmly on George Floyd's neck as his unarmed and helpless victim struggled for breath. When he finally died, police brutality and racial injustice could no longer be swept under the rug. The pandemic made us a captive audience. We'd seen it for ourselves.

Once again, this latest pandemic has caused inordinate death rates in marginalized groups—in Black, Indigenous, and other communities of color, in low-income populations, and among our senior citizens. Health inequities were exposed. Income disparities became more glaringly obvious than ever before. Social and racial injustice was on full display. As it had been at outset of the HIV/AIDS crisis, these issues had always been there. Society at large had simply chosen to ignore them.

The massive AIDS-activist movement led to positive changes in health-care systems, accountability of researchers, and inclusion of those most directly impacted in decisionmaking processes. I am humbled to have had a tiny role.

But the work is far from over and silence is not an option. Until everyone enjoys a living wage, affordable access to quality care, education, and housing, I still have work to do. Currently, I do much of my activism through teaching our next generation how to amplify their voices through writing, speaking, and action.

With this, I close this chapter and end this book. Tomorrow I will continue fighting for racial and social justice.

What will you do?

list of abbreviations

AIDS: Acquired Immune Deficiency Syndrome

CCO: Committee of Co-Sponsoring Organizations

COVID-19: COronaVIrus Disease, 2019

DPKO: Department of Peacekeeping Operations (now the
Department of Peace Operations)

GIPA: Greater Involvement of People Living with HIV and AIDS

GNP+: Global Network of People Living with HIV

HIV: Human Immunodeficiency Virus

ICW: International Community of Women Living with HIV

ILO: International Labor Organization

NGO: Non-Governmental Organization

PCB: Programme Coordinating Board of UNAIDS

PLHIV: Person Living with HIV

STD: Sexually Transmitted Disease

UN: United Nations

UNAIDS: United Nations Joint Programme on HIV and AIDS

UNDP: United Nations Development Fund

UNESCO: United Nations Education, Scientific and Cultural
Organization

UNFPA: United Nations Population Fund

UNICEF: United Nations Emergency Children's Fund

UNMISS: United Nations Mission in the Republic of South Sudan

WHO: World Health Organization

WORLD: Women Organized to Respond to Life-Threatening Disease

acknowledgements

First and foremost, thank you to my extraordinary sisters and brothers and your partners. You never gave up on me, and continue to inspire me.

To my niblings and your respective families: being Auntie M is my greatest joy. Being Great-Auntie M is beyond comprehension, I'm so glad I'm still here for this adventure.

To my chosen family, Irma, Elaine, Trish, Jody, Pierre, Ludlow, Ed, Malene, Melya, Martina S., Janet, Maryanne, and so many others, and my bonus family, Coralie, Ariel, and Taylor, and to Neal, my love, I wouldn't be me without you.

My writing tribes. East Coast: Dyan, Leah, Wende, Theresa C., Elicia, and Sarah. Alison and Harmony. My professors and MFA cohort from Stony Brook Southampton. West Coast: Theresa P., Powell, Brenda, Rebecca, the Squaw Valley Community of Writers, Martin J. Smith, M.G. Lord, the Book Passage Travel Writers and Don George. And, in particular, thank you to Kelly Caldwell of Gotham Writers Workshop for being my greatest writing cheerleader. Thank you all for reading my pages.

To my core UN Cares colleagues, Christine, Laurie, Alan (RIP), Nick, Muna, and Dan, and all of my DPKO HIV Chiefs, I'm so proud to have worked with each of you. We made a difference. To Kim, Sinead, Maria-Clara, Niurka, and Nina, you were excellent bosses.

Team Transit Hall, Charity, and Wendy, for being my lockdown family.

Kate, Rebecca, Becky, Vanessa, River, Jo, Leigh (RIP), Fiona, Linda, Katrena, Penny, and Yolanda, for showing me how to live. Ingrid, Carolyn, and Clark (RIP), for believing I could teach our future generations.

To Lenore Hart, for singling out my manuscript as worthy and helping me bring it fully to life. To David Poyer for editing it to perfection. To Naia Poyer for making the cover and interior amazing.

And, last, to Eve for telling me I was not alone and that I am loved, as we walked the trestle in Capitola so many decades ago. You saved my soul.

Thank you all.

about the author

MARTINA CLARK holds a BA in International Relations and an MFA in Creative Writing and Literature. She worked for the United Nations system for two decades and now teaches writing, critical reading, and global politics for College Now at LaGuardia Community College/CUNY. She has been living with HIV for more than half her life—29 years and counting—and survived COVID-19 in 2020.

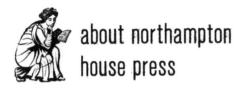

about northampton house press

Northampton House Press publishes carefully chosen fiction, poetry, and selected nonfiction. Our logo represents the Greek muse Polyhymnnia. Check out our list at www.northampton-house.com, and follow us on Facebook ("Northampton House Press"), Instagram (@nhousepress), or Twitter (@nhousepress) to discover more innovative works from brilliant new writers, for discerning readers of all ages.